Dynamite Entertainment

EDUARDO RISSO • CA

BORDERLINE

VOLUME III

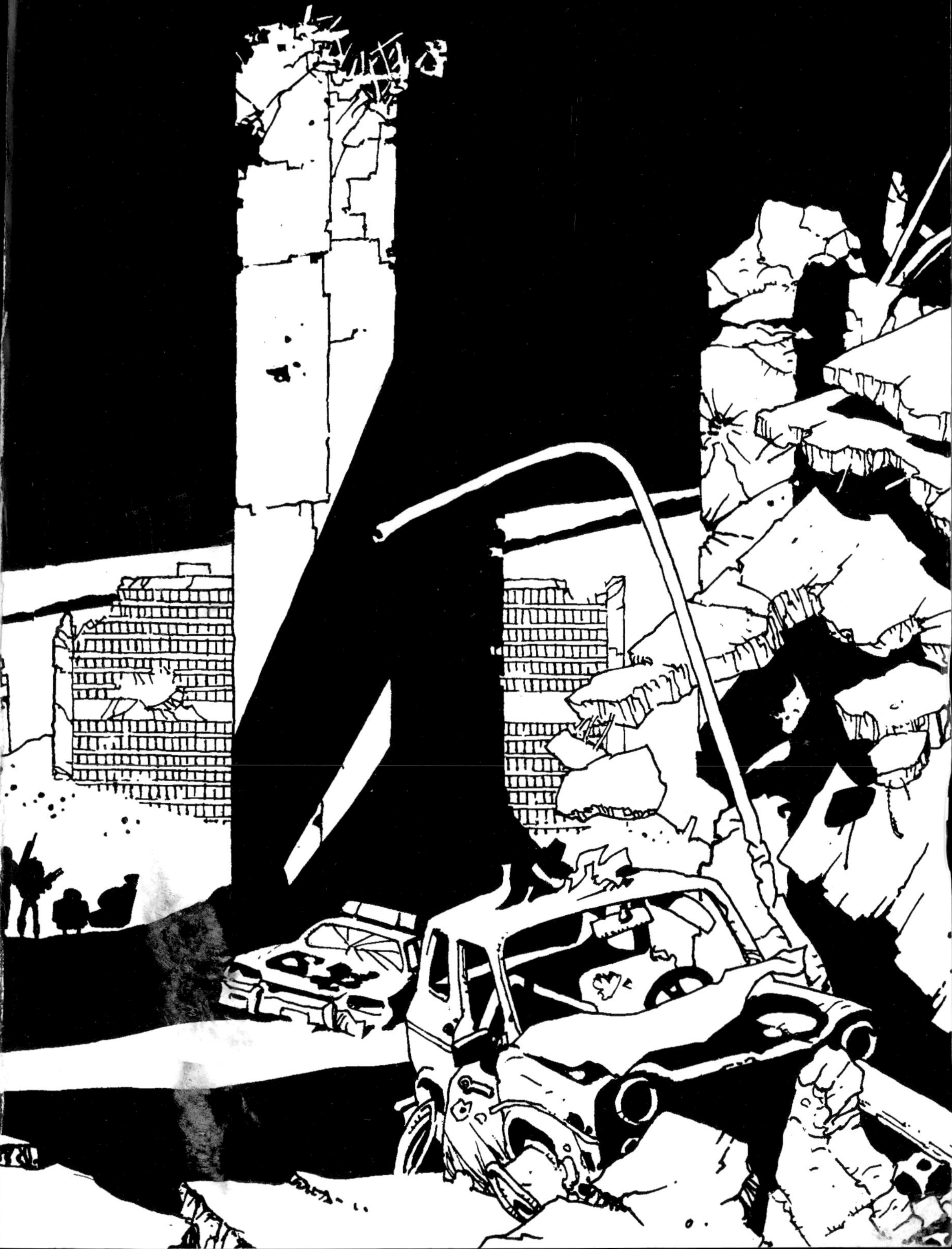

Dynamite Entertainment Presents

EDUARDO RISSO · CARLOS TRILLO

BORDERLINE ™

VOLUME III

ART AND STORY BY
EDUARDO RISSO AND CARLOS TRILLO

TRANSLATION
MARIA BARRUCCI

LETTERING
ZACH MATHENY

COLLECTION DESIGN
JASON ULLMEYER

CONTRIBUTING EDITOR
JOSEPH RYBANDT

DYNAMITE ENTERTAINMENT

NICK BARRUCCI	PRESIDENT
JUAN COLLADO	CHIEF OPERATING OFFICER
JOSEPH RYBANDT	EDITOR
JOSH JOHNSON	CREATIVE DIRECTOR
JASON ULLMEYER	GRAPHIC DESIGNER

DYNAMITE ®
ENTERTAINMENT

To find a comic shop in your area, call
the comic shop locator service toll-free
1-888-266-4226

First Printing
ISBN-10: 1-93330-522-3   ISBN-13: 978-1-93330-522-6
10 9 8 7 6 5 4 3 2 1

PREVIOUSLY, IN BORDERLINE

Set in a dystopian future, BORDERLINE tells the story of former lovers turned agents and assassins for the two ruling bodies of the remaining society. Emil works for The Commune, but before his current life, he was a junkie who sold his girlfriend Lisa to the organ harvesters on the black market. Lisa, rescued and indentured to The Council, now works for them. Their fates intertwined, the two crossed lovers are about to meet again, for the very last time...

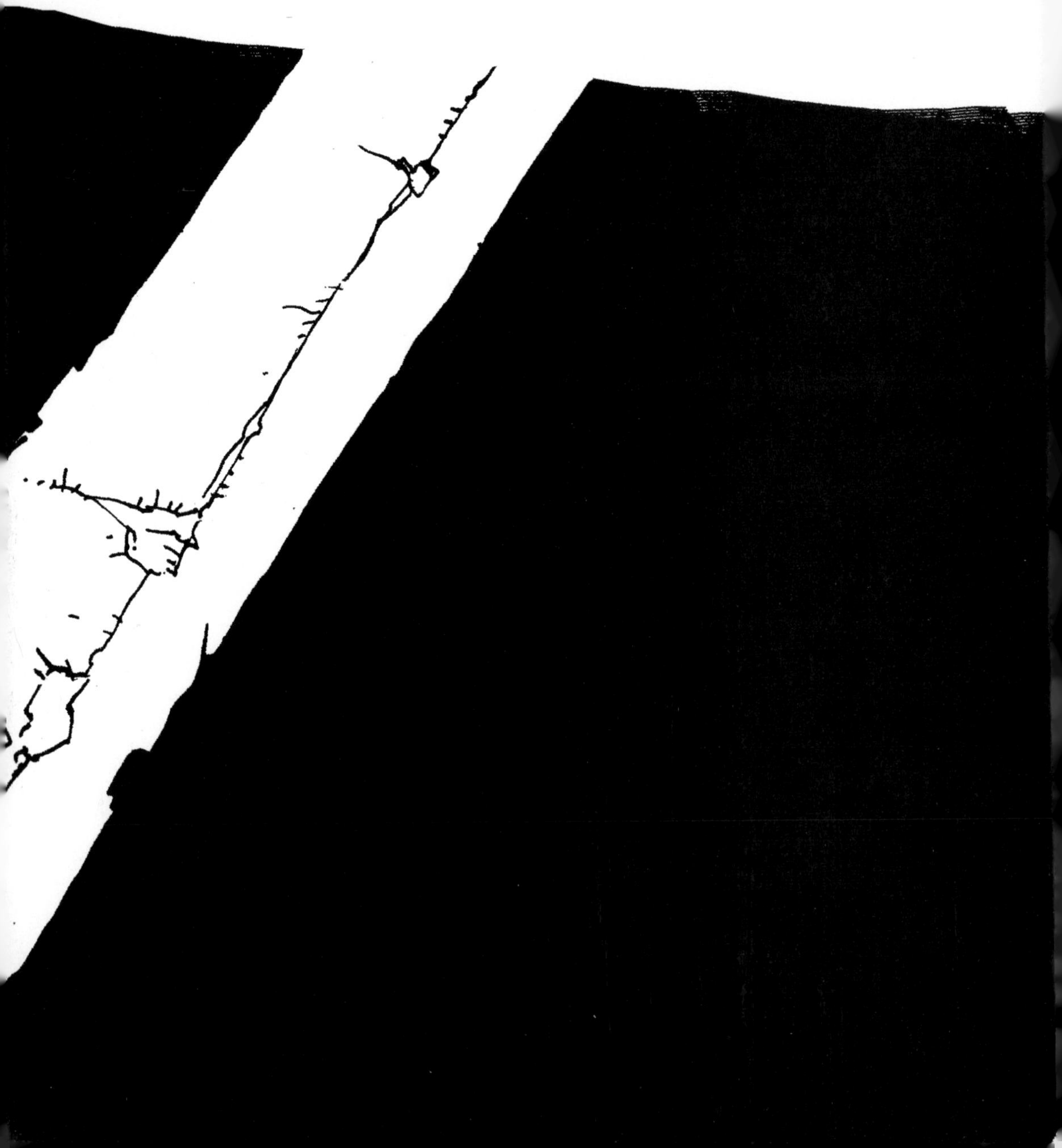

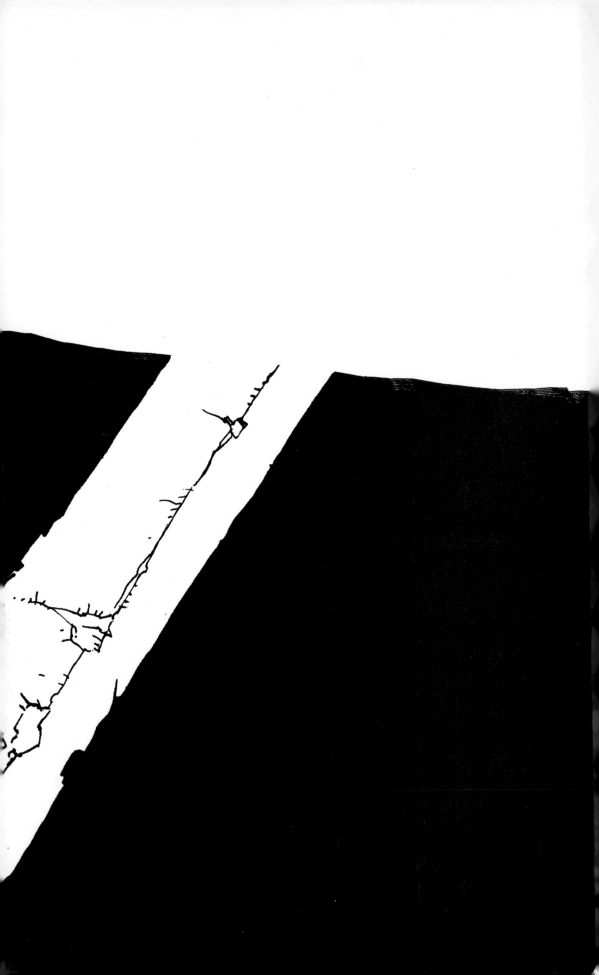

1

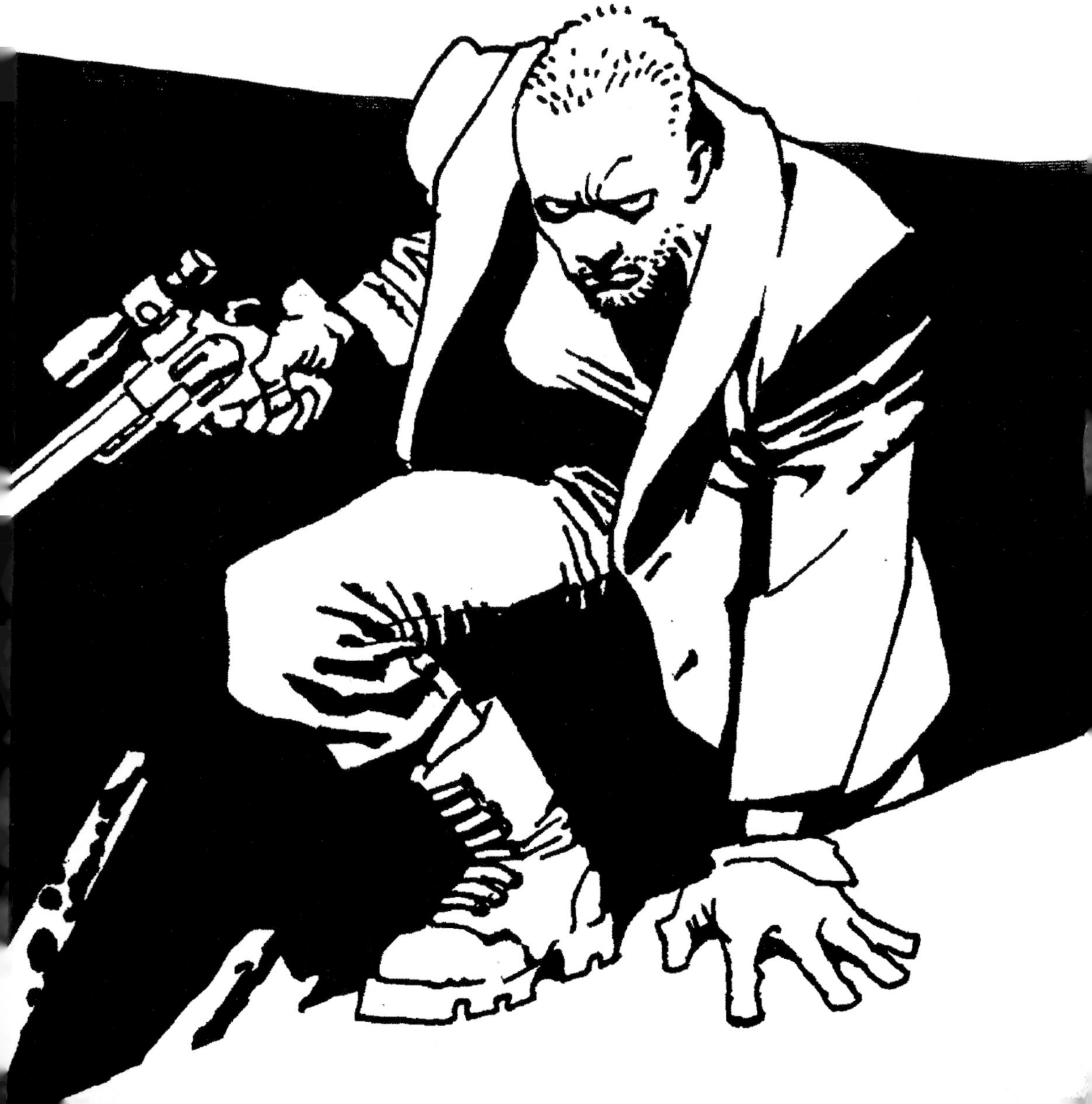

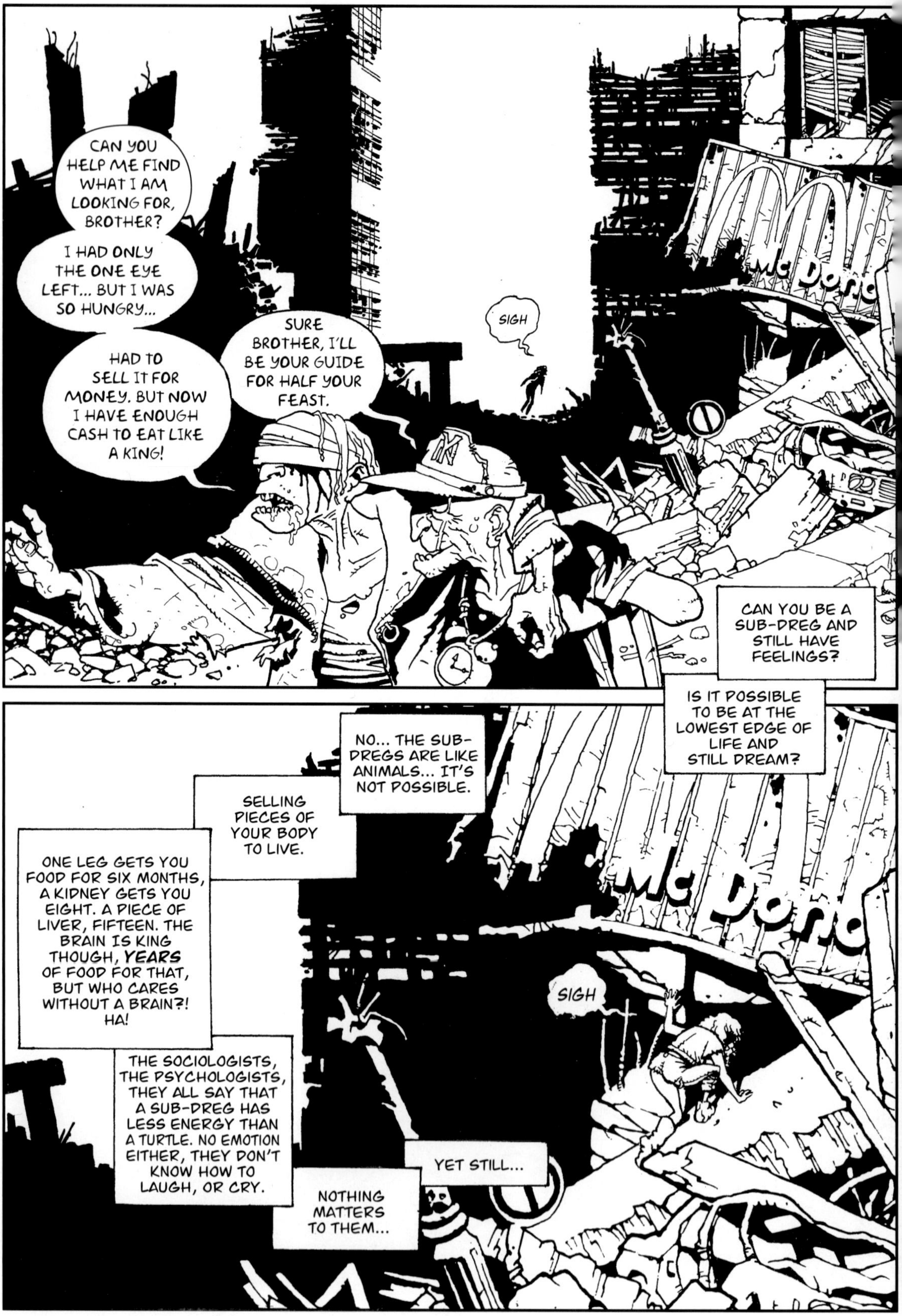
CAN YOU HELP ME FIND WHAT I AM LOOKING FOR, BROTHER?
I HAD ONLY THE ONE EYE LEFT... BUT I WAS SO HUNGRY...
HAD TO SELL IT FOR MONEY. BUT NOW I HAVE ENOUGH CASH TO EAT LIKE A KING!
SURE BROTHER, I'LL BE YOUR GUIDE FOR HALF YOUR FEAST.
SIGH
CAN YOU BE A SUB-DREG AND STILL HAVE FEELINGS?
IS IT POSSIBLE TO BE AT THE LOWEST EDGE OF LIFE AND STILL DREAM?
NO... THE SUB-DREGS ARE LIKE ANIMALS... IT'S NOT POSSIBLE.
SELLING PIECES OF YOUR BODY TO LIVE.
ONE LEG GETS YOU FOOD FOR SIX MONTHS, A KIDNEY GETS YOU EIGHT. A PIECE OF LIVER, FIFTEEN. THE BRAIN IS KING THOUGH, YEARS OF FOOD FOR THAT, BUT WHO CARES WITHOUT A BRAIN?! HA!
SIGH
THE SOCIOLOGISTS, THE PSYCHOLOGISTS, THEY ALL SAY THAT A SUB-DREG HAS LESS ENERGY THAN A TURTLE. NO EMOTION EITHER, THEY DON'T KNOW HOW TO LAUGH, OR CRY.
NOTHING MATTERS TO THEM...
YET STILL...

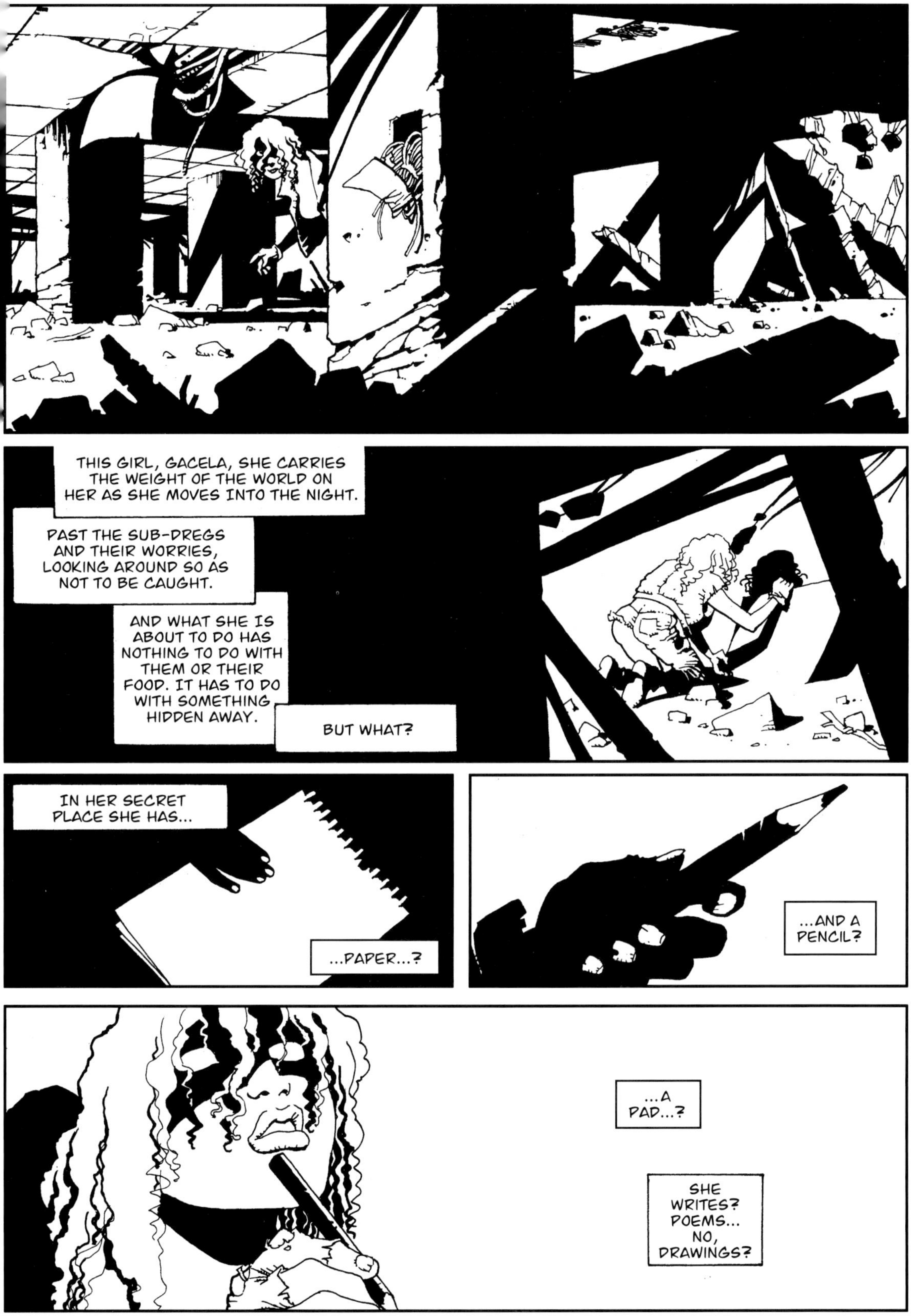
THIS GIRL, GACELA, SHE CARRIES THE WEIGHT OF THE WORLD ON HER AS SHE MOVES INTO THE NIGHT.
PAST THE SUB-DREGS AND THEIR WORRIES, LOOKING AROUND SO AS NOT TO BE CAUGHT.
AND WHAT SHE IS ABOUT TO DO HAS NOTHING TO DO WITH THEM OR THEIR FOOD. IT HAS TO DO WITH SOMETHING HIDDEN AWAY.
BUT WHAT?
IN HER SECRET PLACE SHE HAS...
...PAPER...?
...AND A PENCIL?
...A PAD...?
SHE WRITES? POEMS... NO, DRAWINGS?

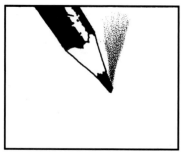

AH, YES, DRAWINGS.
... SKETCHES.

I CAN'T IMAGINE
THE WORKS OF A
SUB-DREG POET. FEH.

WHAT COULD SHE
HAVE TO SAY, LIVING
LIKE SHE DOES...

WITH
HER VACANT
EYES SHE
DRAWS...

BUT
WHAT?

AN IMPORTANT FACE TO SOME...
FOR THE CENTURIONS OF THE
ASSEMBLY, AND THE ASTRAL
DEALERS AND ALL THOSE THAT
BELIEVE THAT AFTER THIS LIFE
THERE IS ANOTHER... A HAPPY
LIFE, IN A COMFORTING AND
ETERNAL UNIVERSE.

BUT TO THIS MAN THERE ARE
ALSO THOSE WHO DON'T
SHARE THAT SAME ROSY VIEW...

THE MEMBERS OF THE COUNCIL'S
SPECIAL SQUADRON, THEY
CAN'T STAND HIM...

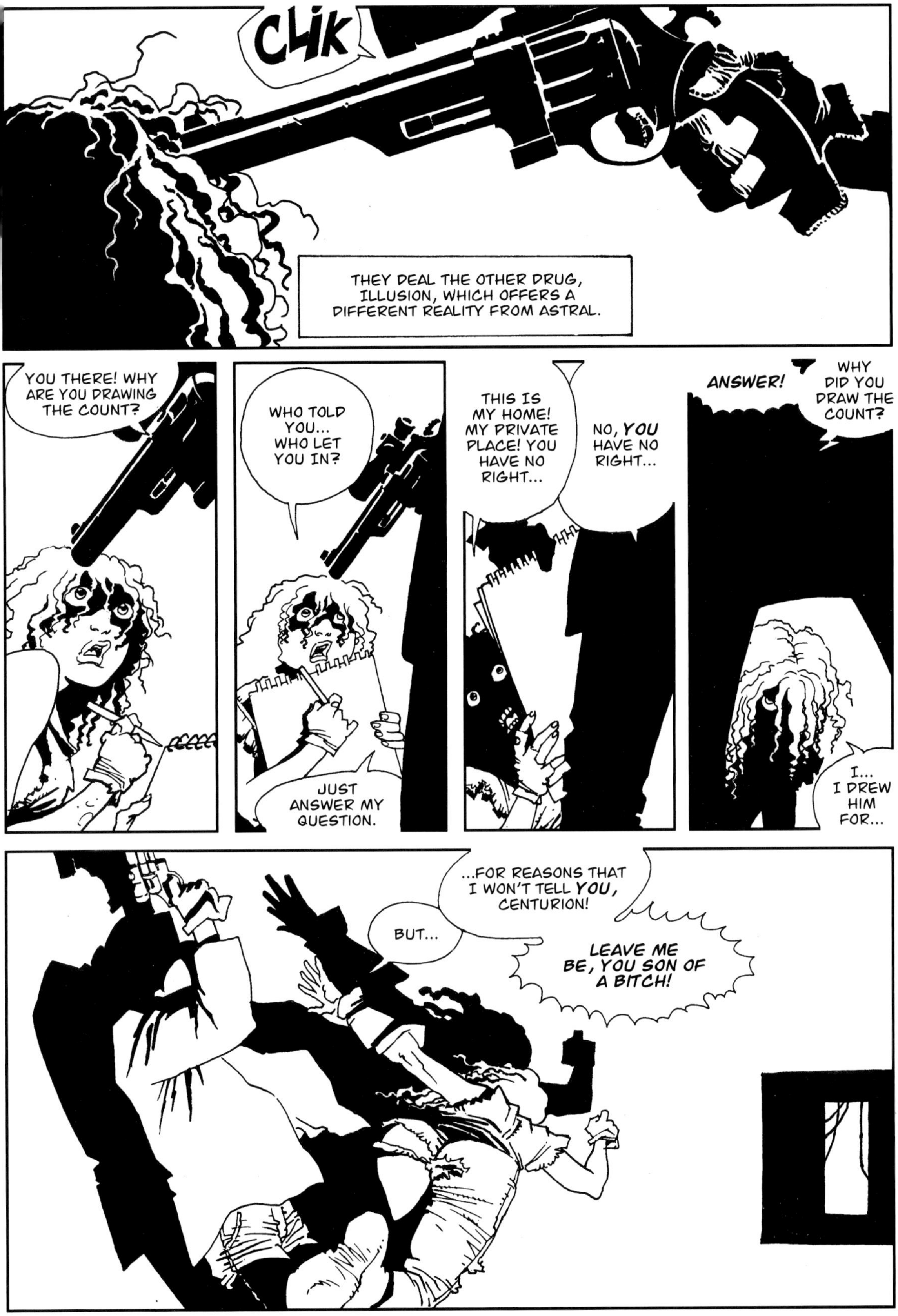
CLIK
THEY DEAL THE OTHER DRUG, ILLUSION, WHICH OFFERS A DIFFERENT REALITY FROM ASTRAL.
YOU THERE! WHY ARE YOU DRAWING THE COUNT?
WHO TOLD YOU... WHO LET YOU IN?
JUST ANSWER MY QUESTION.
THIS IS MY HOME! MY PRIVATE PLACE! YOU HAVE NO RIGHT...
NO, YOU HAVE NO RIGHT...
ANSWER!
WHY DID YOU DRAW THE COUNT?
I... I DREW HIM FOR...
...FOR REASONS THAT I WON'T TELL YOU, CENTURION!
BUT...
LEAVE ME BE, YOU SON OF A BITCH!

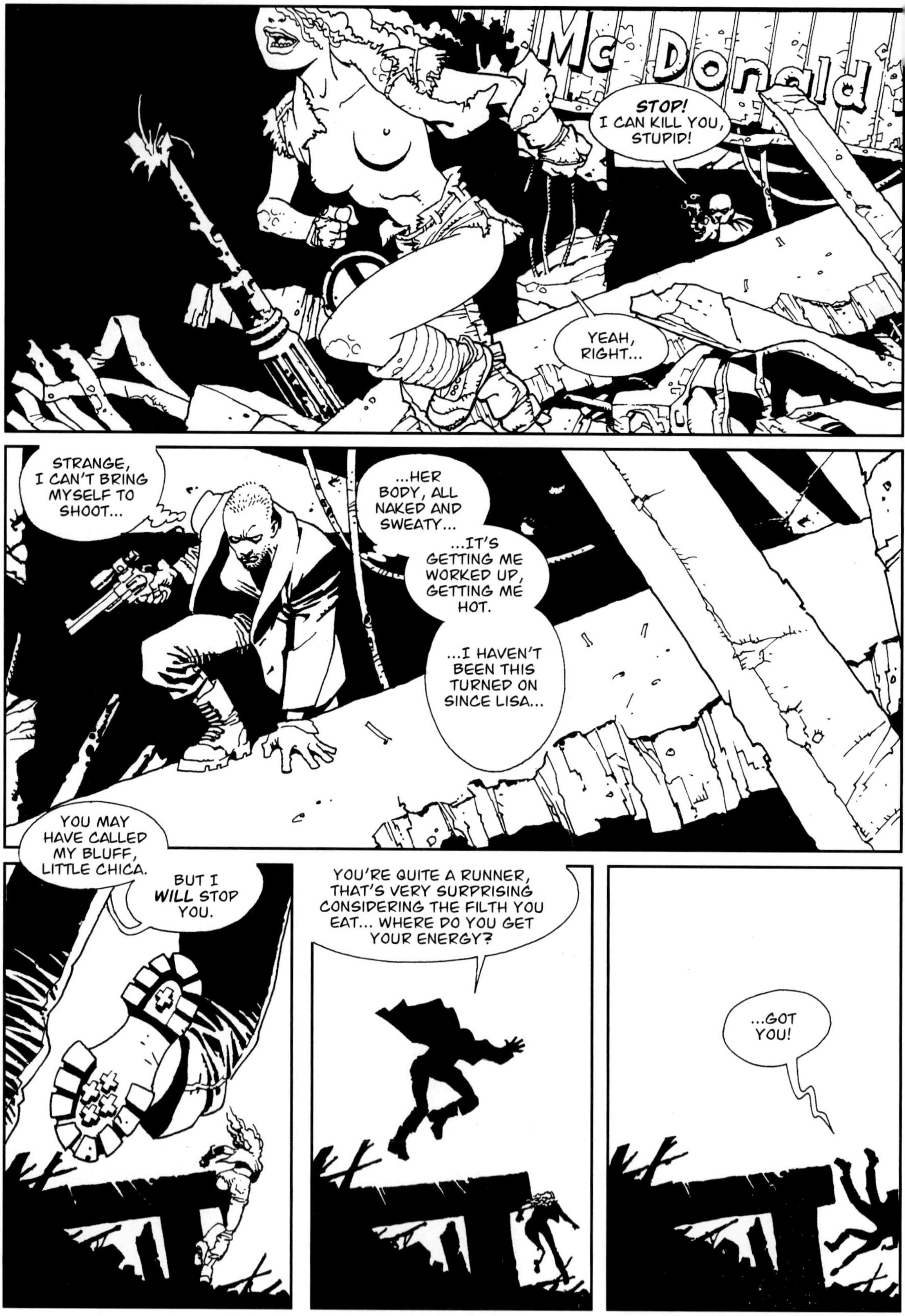
McDonald
STOP! I CAN KILL YOU, STUPID!
YEAH, RIGHT...
STRANGE, I CAN'T BRING MYSELF TO SHOOT...
...HER BODY, ALL NAKED AND SWEATY...
...IT'S GETTING ME WORKED UP, GETTING ME HOT.
...I HAVEN'T BEEN THIS TURNED ON SINCE LISA...
YOU MAY HAVE CALLED MY BLUFF, LITTLE CHICA.
BUT I **WILL** STOP YOU.
YOU'RE QUITE A RUNNER, THAT'S VERY SURPRISING CONSIDERING THE FILTH YOU EAT... WHERE DO YOU GET YOUR ENERGY?
...GOT YOU!

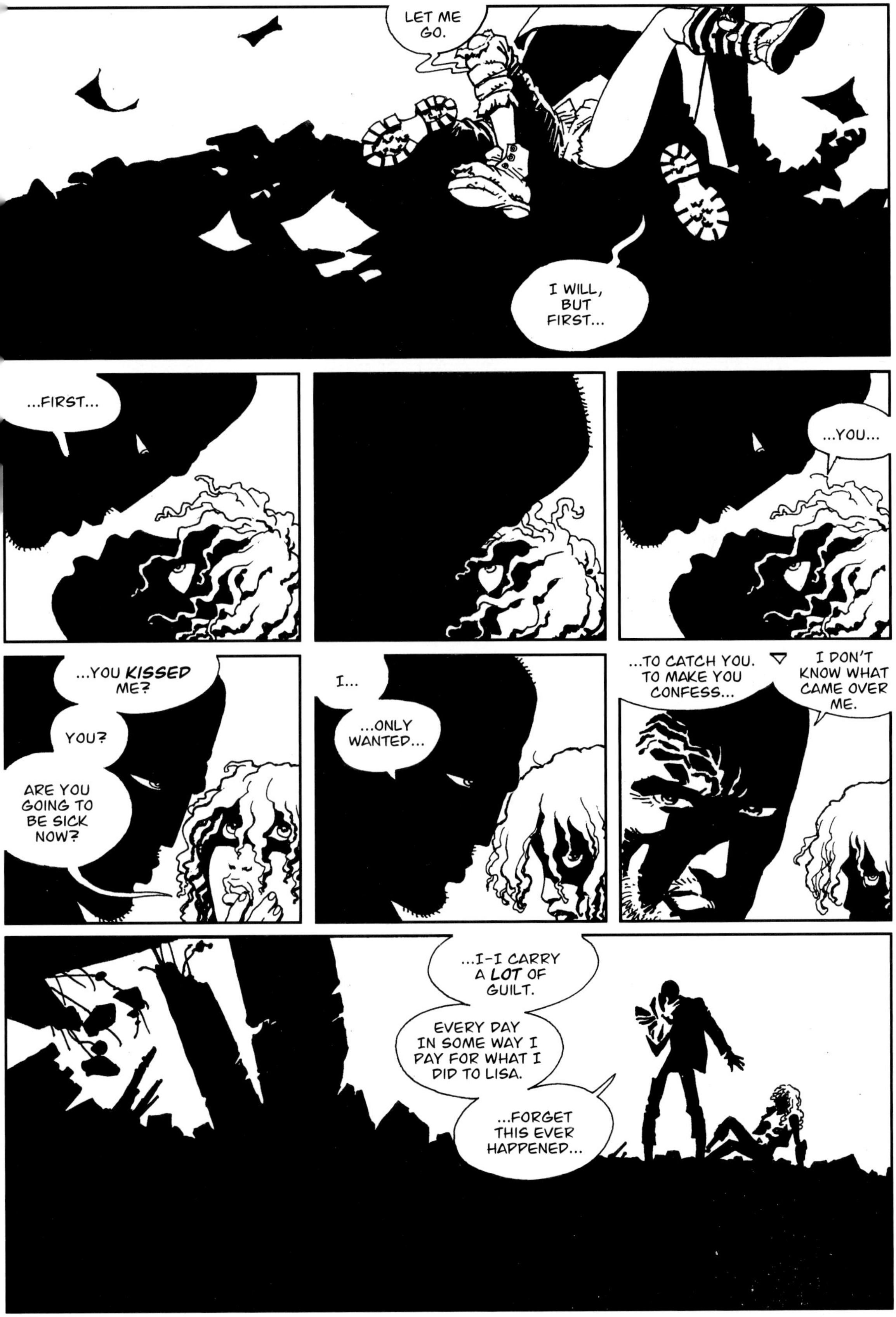
LET ME GO.
I WILL, BUT FIRST...
...FIRST...
...YOU...
...YOU KISSED ME?
YOU?
ARE YOU GOING TO BE SICK NOW?
I...
...ONLY WANTED...
...TO CATCH YOU. TO MAKE YOU CONFESS...
I DON'T KNOW WHAT CAME OVER ME.
...I-I CARRY A LOT OF GUILT.
EVERY DAY IN SOME WAY I PAY FOR WHAT I DID TO LISA.
...FORGET THIS EVER HAPPENED...

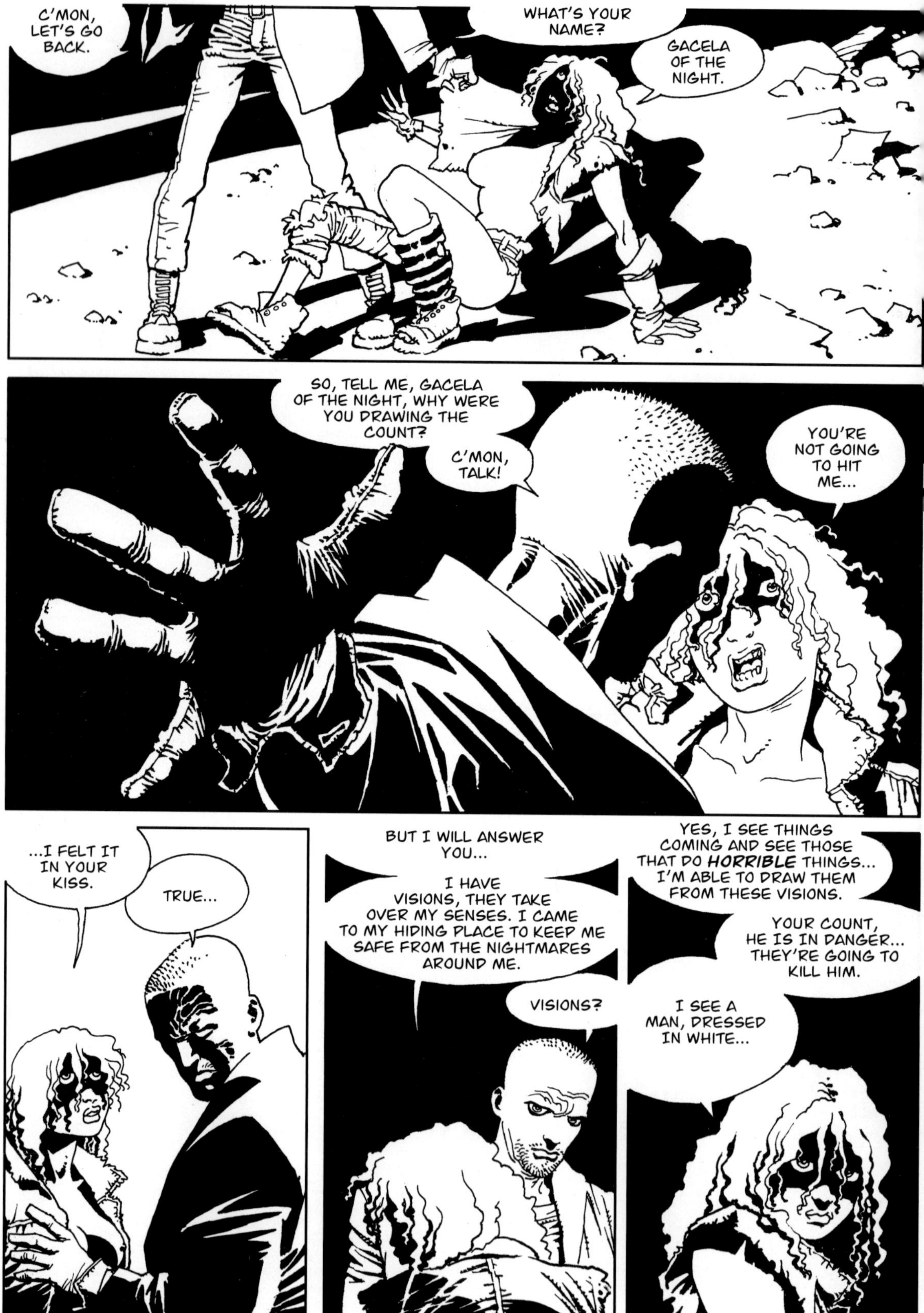
C'MON, LET'S GO BACK.
WHAT'S YOUR NAME?
GACELA OF THE NIGHT.
SO, TELL ME, GACELA OF THE NIGHT, WHY WERE YOU DRAWING THE COUNT?
C'MON, TALK!
YOU'RE NOT GOING TO HIT ME...
...I FELT IT IN YOUR KISS.
TRUE...
BUT I WILL ANSWER YOU...
I HAVE VISIONS, THEY TAKE OVER MY SENSES. I CAME TO MY HIDING PLACE TO KEEP ME SAFE FROM THE NIGHTMARES AROUND ME.
VISIONS?
YES, I SEE THINGS COMING AND SEE THOSE THAT DO HORRIBLE THINGS... I'M ABLE TO DRAW THEM FROM THESE VISIONS.
YOUR COUNT, HE IS IN DANGER... THEY'RE GOING TO KILL HIM.
I SEE A MAN, DRESSED IN WHITE...

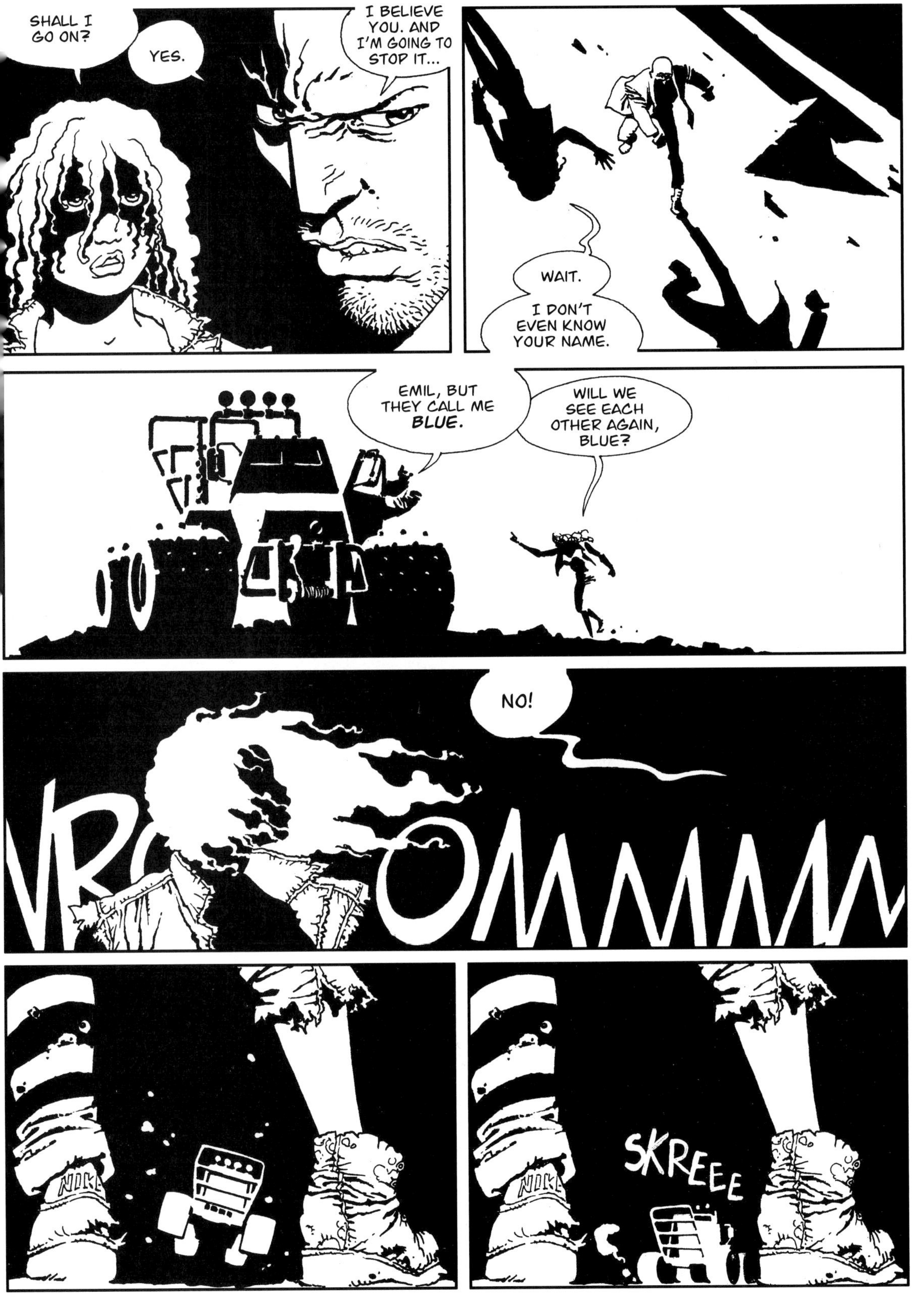
SHALL I GO ON?
YES.
I BELIEVE YOU. AND I'M GOING TO STOP IT...
WAIT.
I DON'T EVEN KNOW YOUR NAME.
EMIL, BUT THEY CALL ME **BLUE**.
WILL WE SEE EACH OTHER AGAIN, BLUE?
NO!
VROOMMMMM
NIKE
SKREEE
NIKE

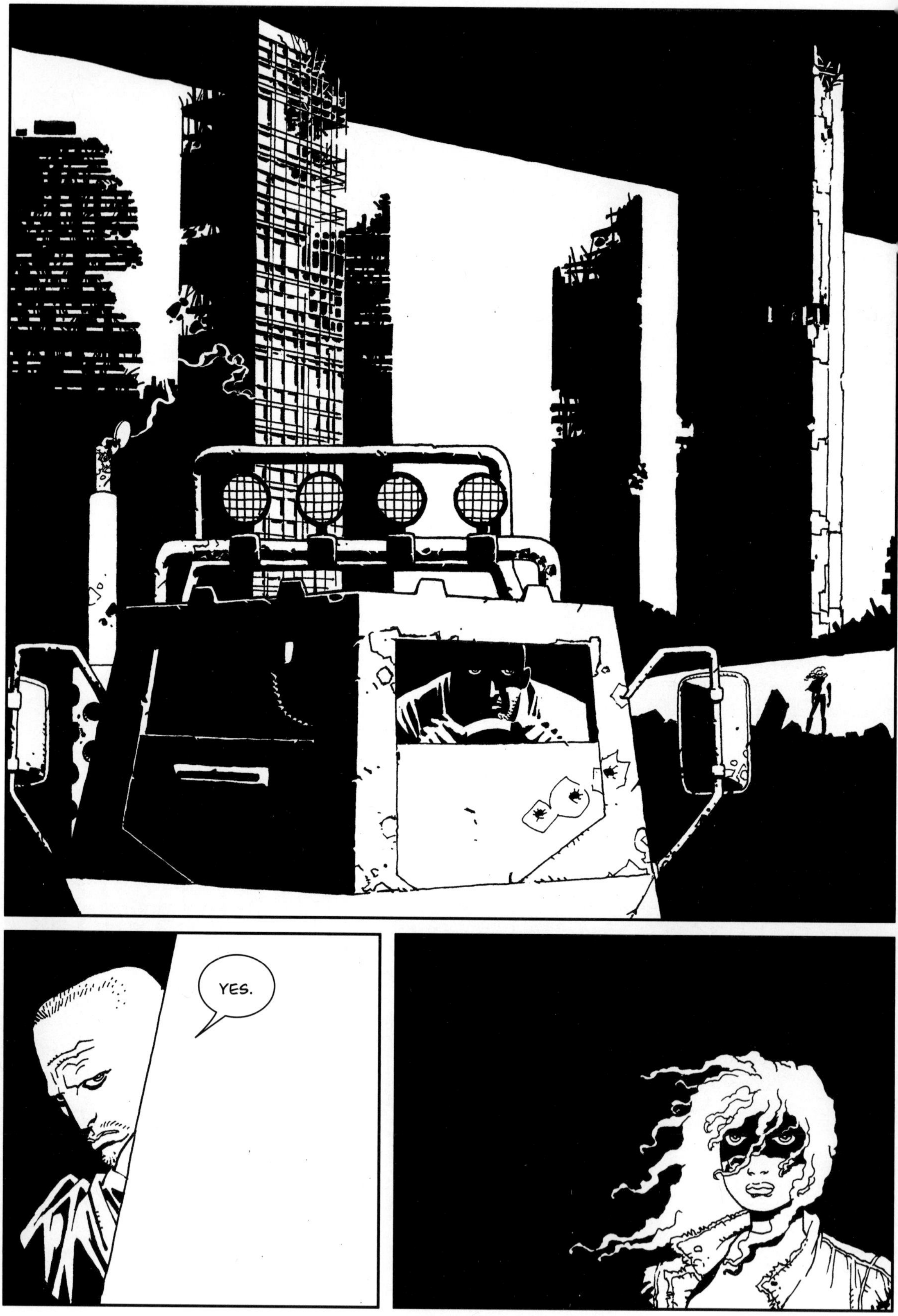
YES.

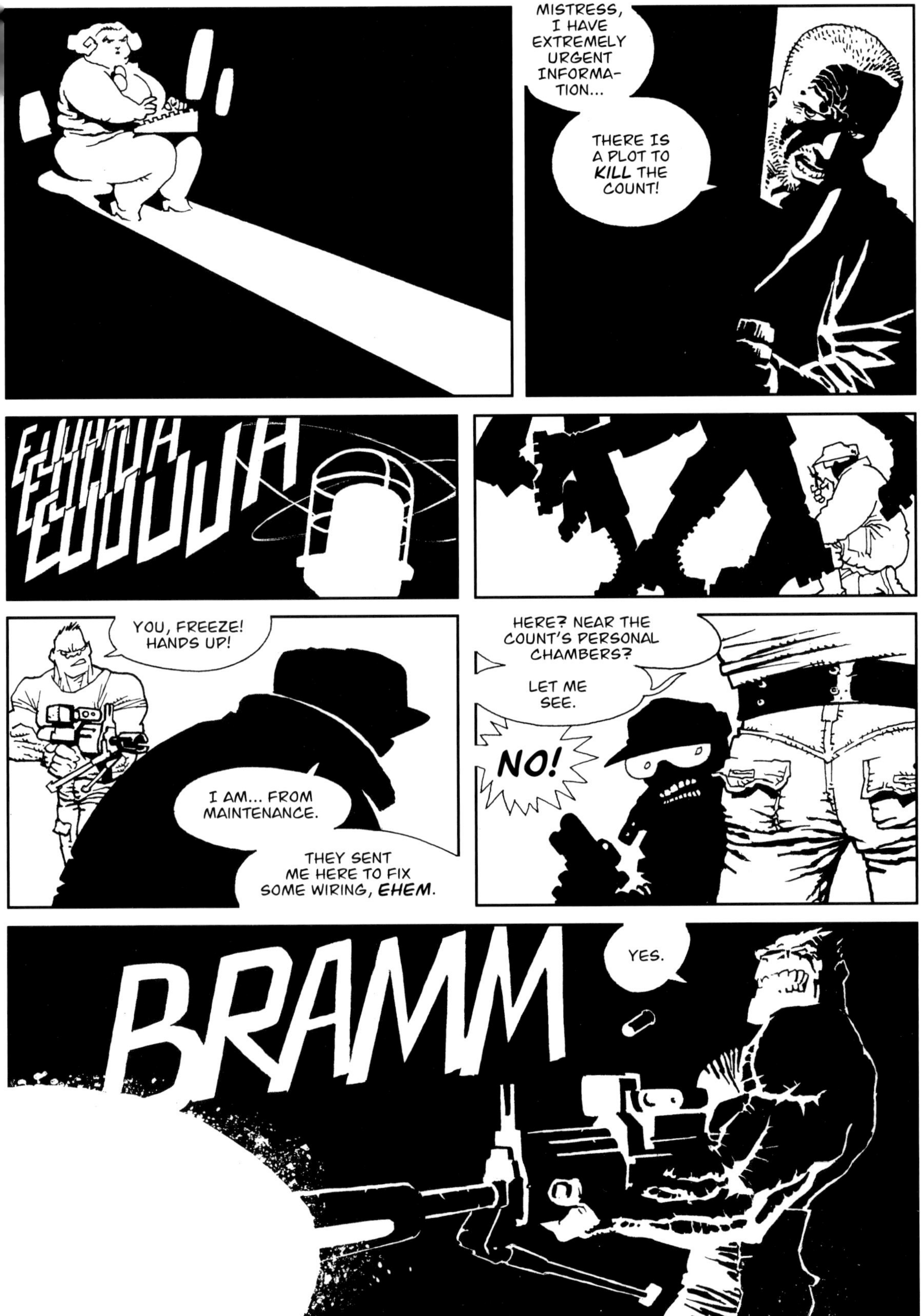
MISTRESS, I HAVE EXTREMELY URGENT INFORMA- TION...
THERE IS A PLOT TO **KILL** THE COUNT!
YOU, FREEZE! HANDS UP!
I AM... FROM MAINTENANCE.
THEY SENT ME HERE TO FIX SOME WIRING, **EHEM**.
HERE? NEAR THE COUNT'S PERSONAL CHAMBERS?
LET ME SEE.
NO!
BRAMM
YES.

HM, LOOK AT THAT.

A BOMB... A BIG ONE.

WHERE'D YOU GET YOUR INFO TEN YEAR?

ONE OF THE SUB-DREGS.

I SAW HER SKETCHING THE COUNT AND FORCED HER TO TELL ME WHY.

SHE SAID SHE HAD VISIONS AND THAT SHE SAW THE COUNT IN THOSE VISIONS.

AND IN THAT VISION, THIS GUY HERE WAS GOING TO KILL HIM.

VISIONS?

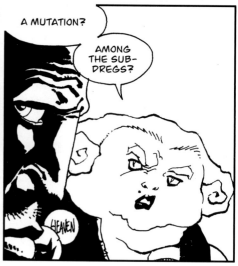

A MUTATION?

AMONG THE SUB-DREGS?

HEAVEN

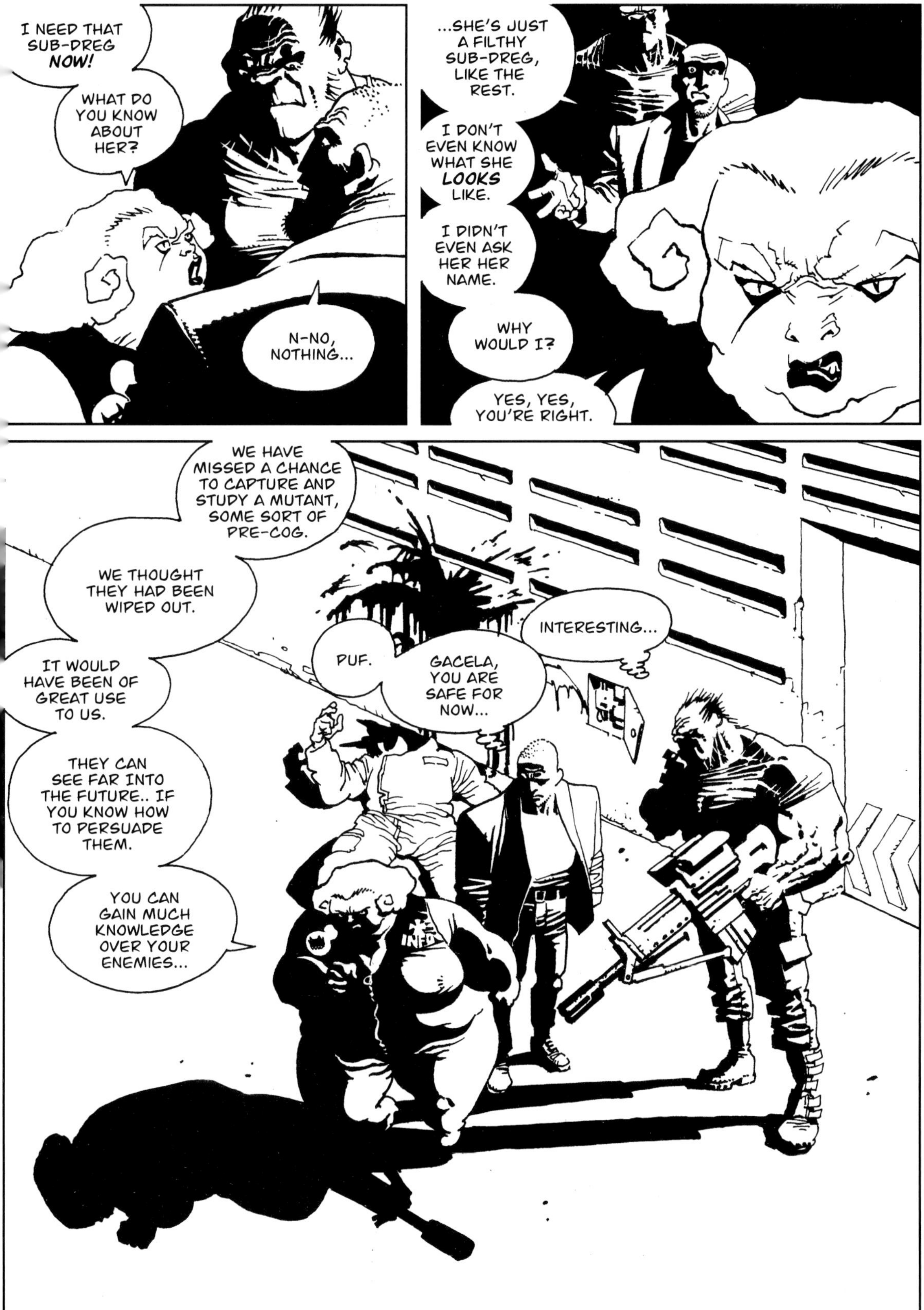
I NEED THAT SUB-DREG NOW!
WHAT DO YOU KNOW ABOUT HER?
N-NO, NOTHING...
...SHE'S JUST A FILTHY SUB-DREG, LIKE THE REST.
I DON'T EVEN KNOW WHAT SHE LOOKS LIKE.
I DIDN'T EVEN ASK HER HER NAME.
WHY WOULD I?
YES, YES, YOU'RE RIGHT.
WE HAVE MISSED A CHANCE TO CAPTURE AND STUDY A MUTANT, SOME SORT OF PRE-COG.
WE THOUGHT THEY HAD BEEN WIPED OUT.
IT WOULD HAVE BEEN OF GREAT USE TO US.
THEY CAN SEE FAR INTO THE FUTURE.. IF YOU KNOW HOW TO PERSUADE THEM.
YOU CAN GAIN MUCH KNOWLEDGE OVER YOUR ENEMIES...
INTERESTING...
PUF.
GACELA, YOU ARE SAFE FOR NOW...

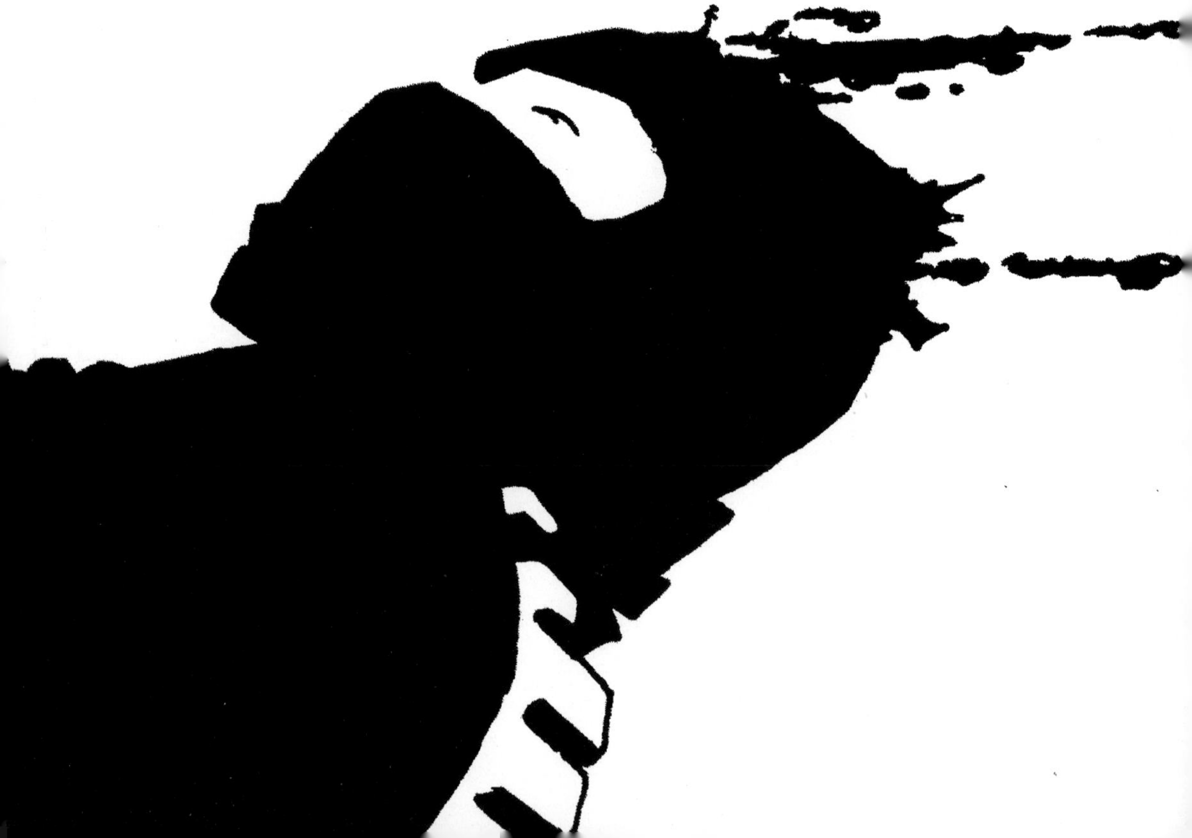

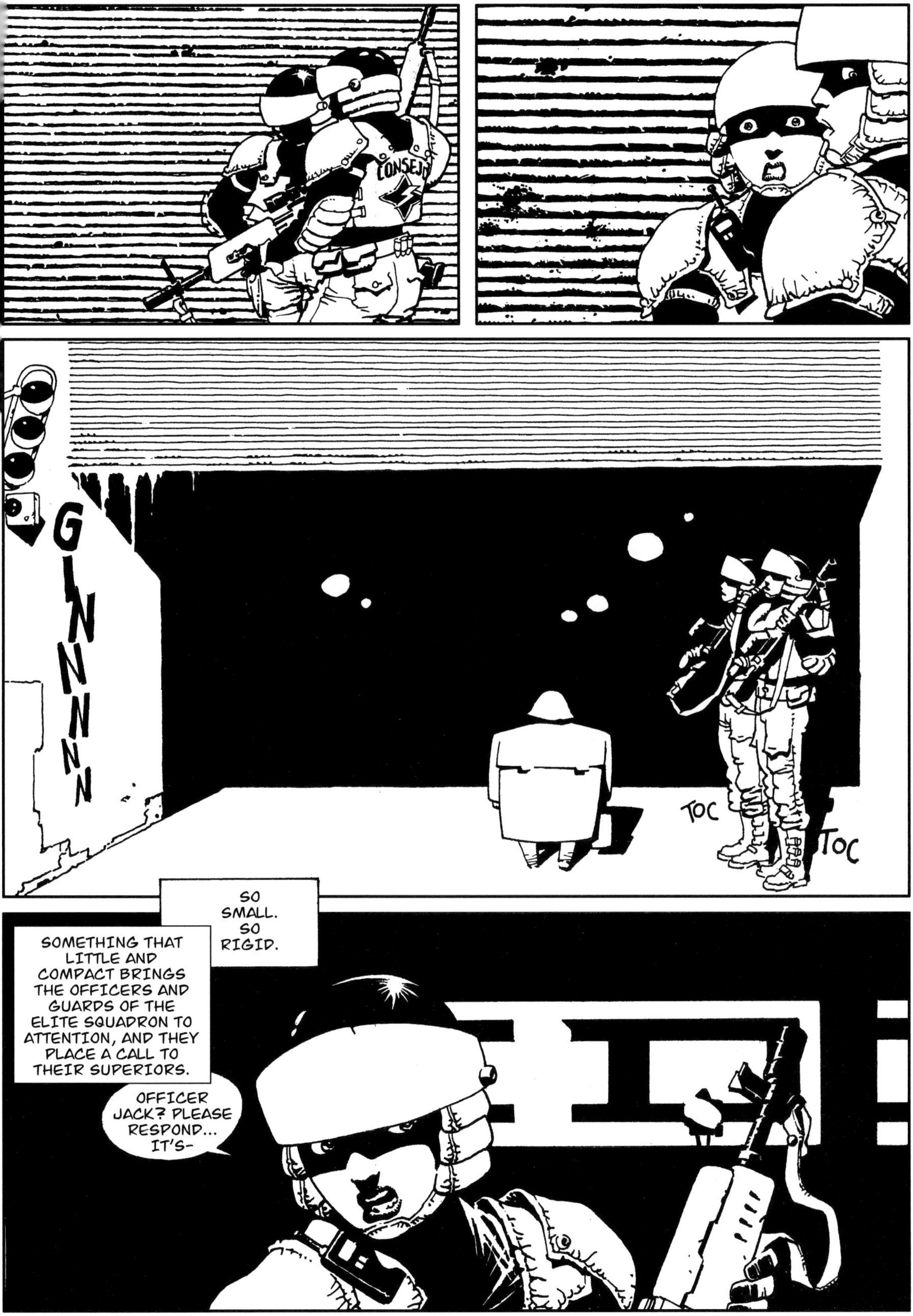
CONSEJO
GINNNNN
TOC
TOC
SO SMALL. SO RIGID.
SOMETHING THAT LITTLE AND COMPACT BRINGS THE OFFICERS AND GUARDS OF THE ELITE SQUADRON TO ATTENTION, AND THEY PLACE A CALL TO THEIR SUPERIORS.
OFFICER JACK? PLEASE RESPOND... IT'S-

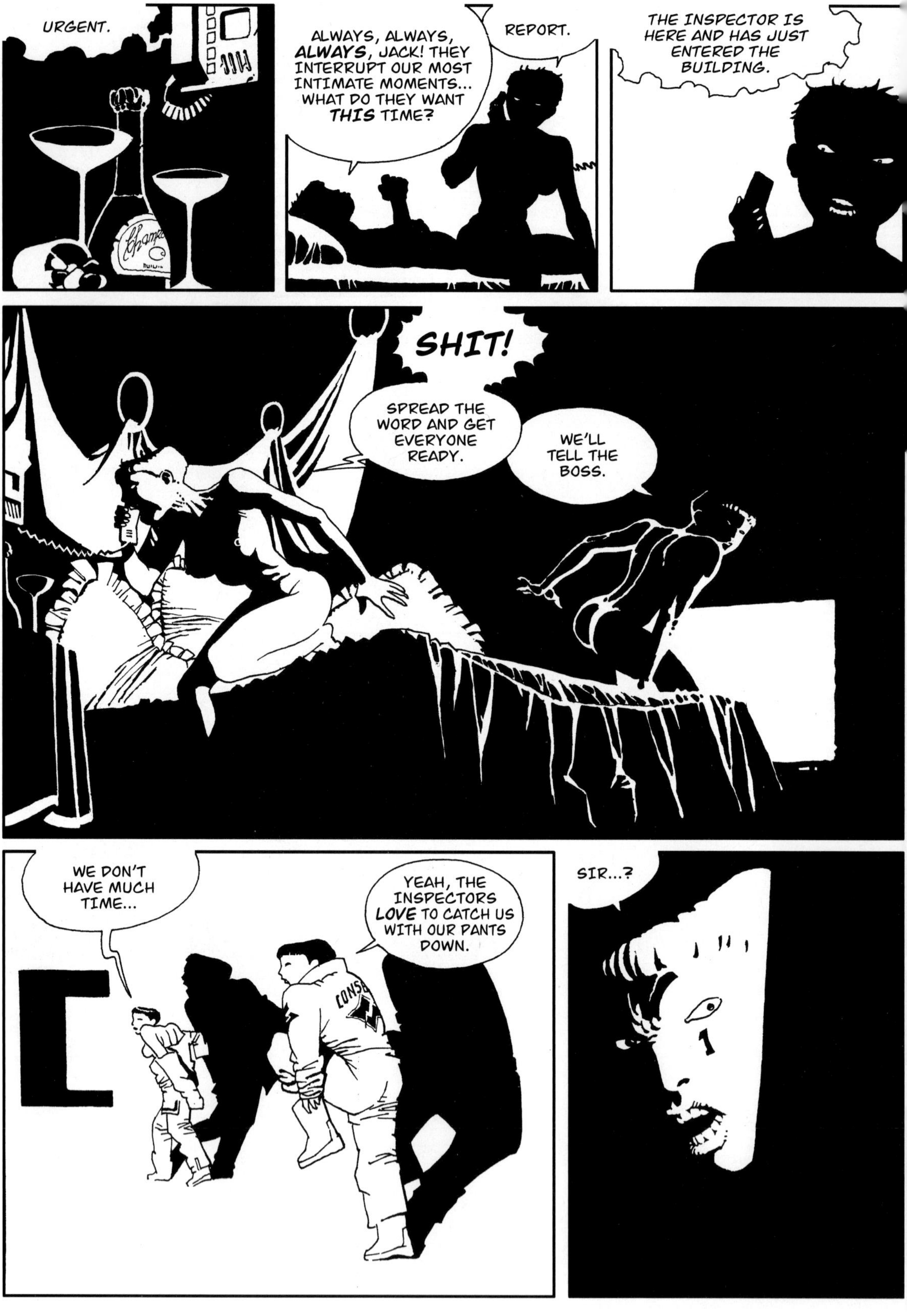
URGENT.
ALWAYS, ALWAYS, ALWAYS, JACK! THEY INTERRUPT OUR MOST INTIMATE MOMENTS... WHAT DO THEY WANT THIS TIME?
REPORT.
THE INSPECTOR IS HERE AND HAS JUST ENTERED THE BUILDING.
SHIT!
SPREAD THE WORD AND GET EVERYONE READY.
WE'LL TELL THE BOSS.
WE DON'T HAVE MUCH TIME...
YEAH, THE INSPECTORS LOVE TO CATCH US WITH OUR PANTS DOWN.
SIR...?

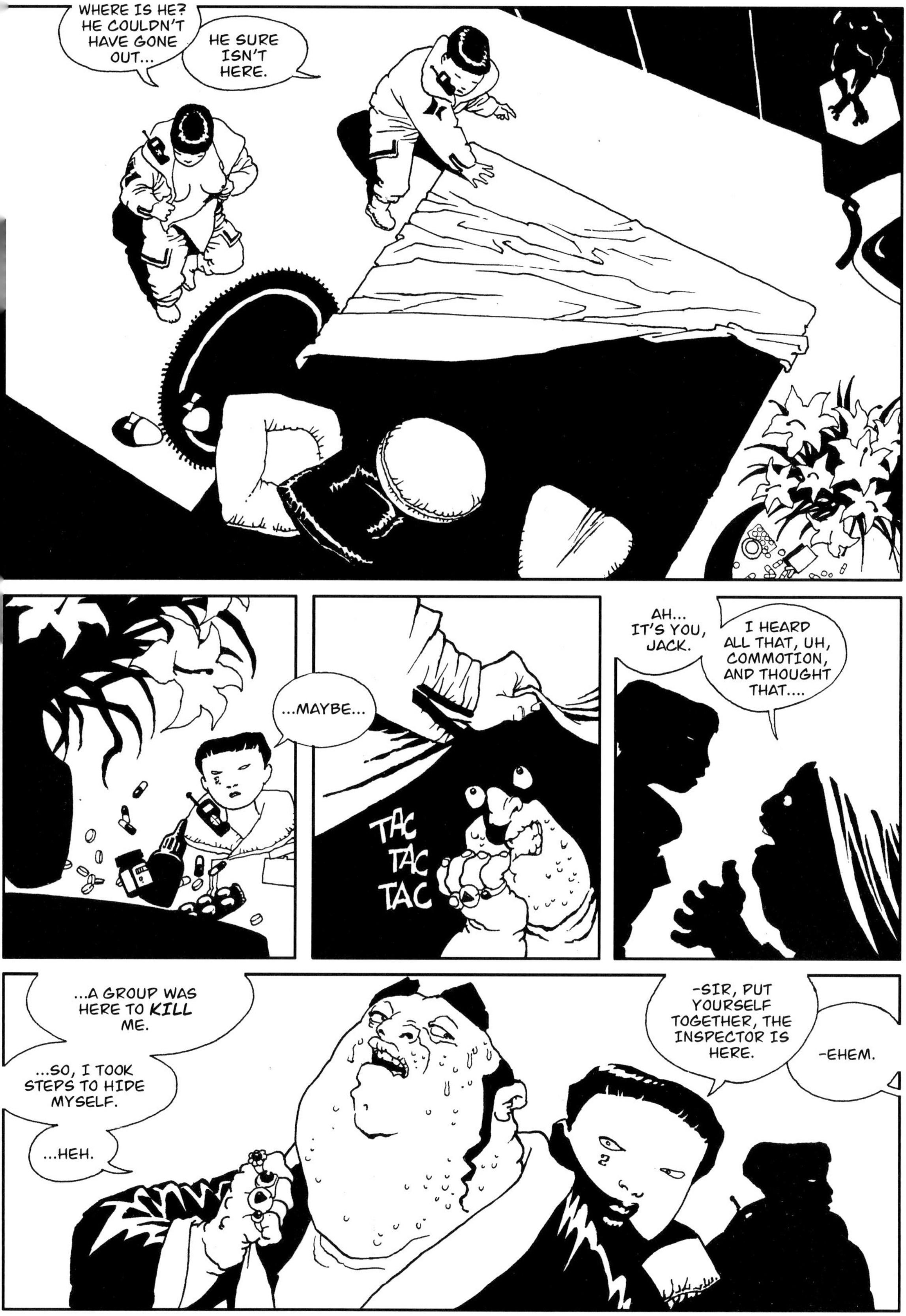

WHERE IS HE? HE COULDN'T HAVE GONE OUT...
HE SURE ISN'T HERE.
...MAYBE...
TAC TAC TAC
AH... IT'S YOU, JACK.
I HEARD ALL THAT, UH, COMMOTION, AND THOUGHT THAT....
...A GROUP WAS HERE TO **KILL** ME.
...SO, I TOOK STEPS TO HIDE MYSELF.
...HEH.
-SIR, PUT YOURSELF TOGETHER, THE INSPECTOR IS HERE.
-EHEM.

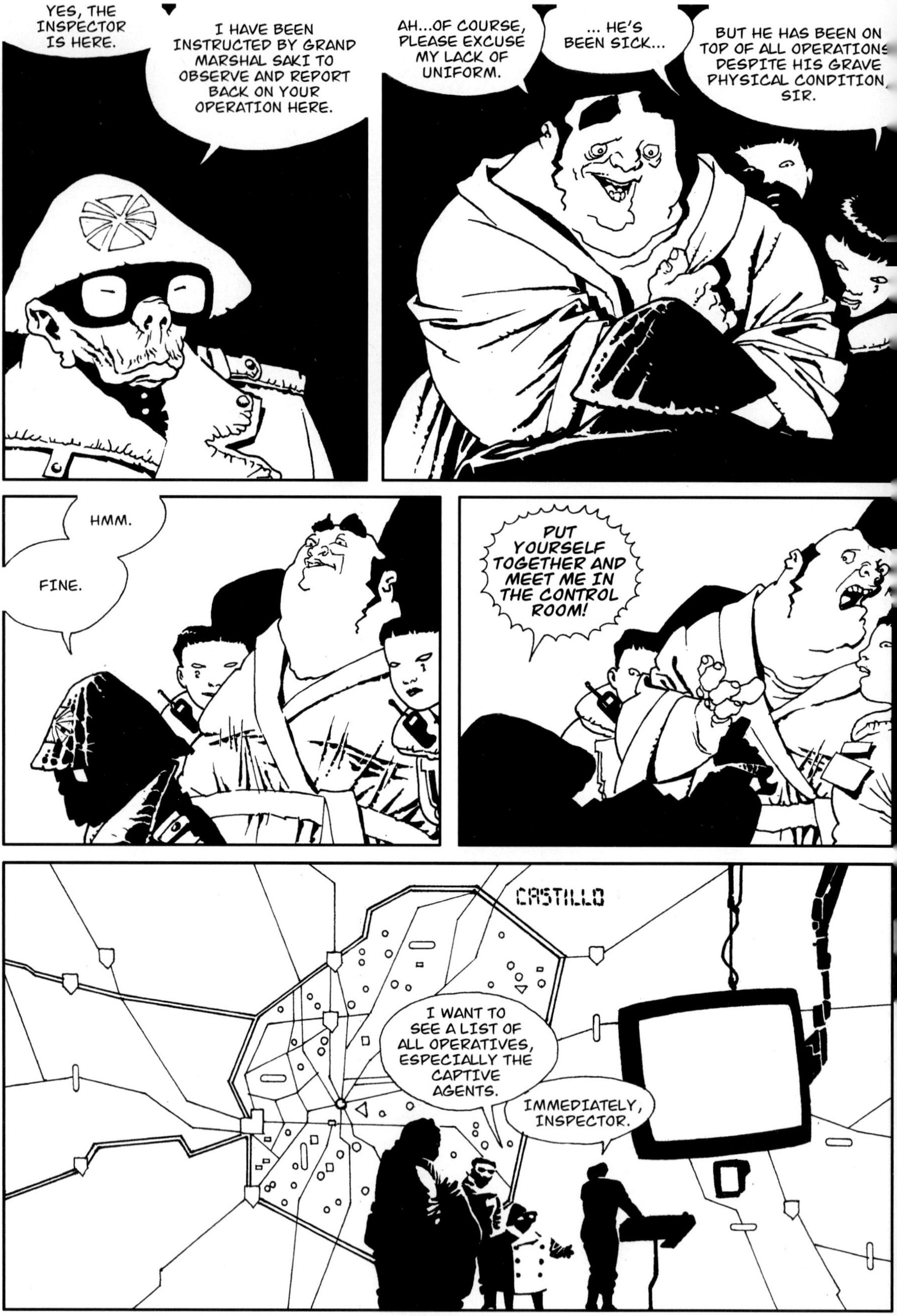
YES, THE INSPECTOR IS HERE.
I HAVE BEEN INSTRUCTED BY GRAND MARSHAL SAKI TO OBSERVE AND REPORT BACK ON YOUR OPERATION HERE.
AH...OF COURSE, PLEASE EXCUSE MY LACK OF UNIFORM.
... HE'S BEEN SICK...
BUT HE HAS BEEN ON TOP OF ALL OPERATIONS DESPITE HIS GRAVE PHYSICAL CONDITION, SIR.
HMM.
FINE.
PUT YOURSELF TOGETHER AND MEET ME IN THE CONTROL ROOM!
CASTILLO
I WANT TO SEE A LIST OF ALL OPERATIVES, ESPECIALLY THE CAPTIVE AGENTS.
IMMEDIATELY, INSPECTOR.

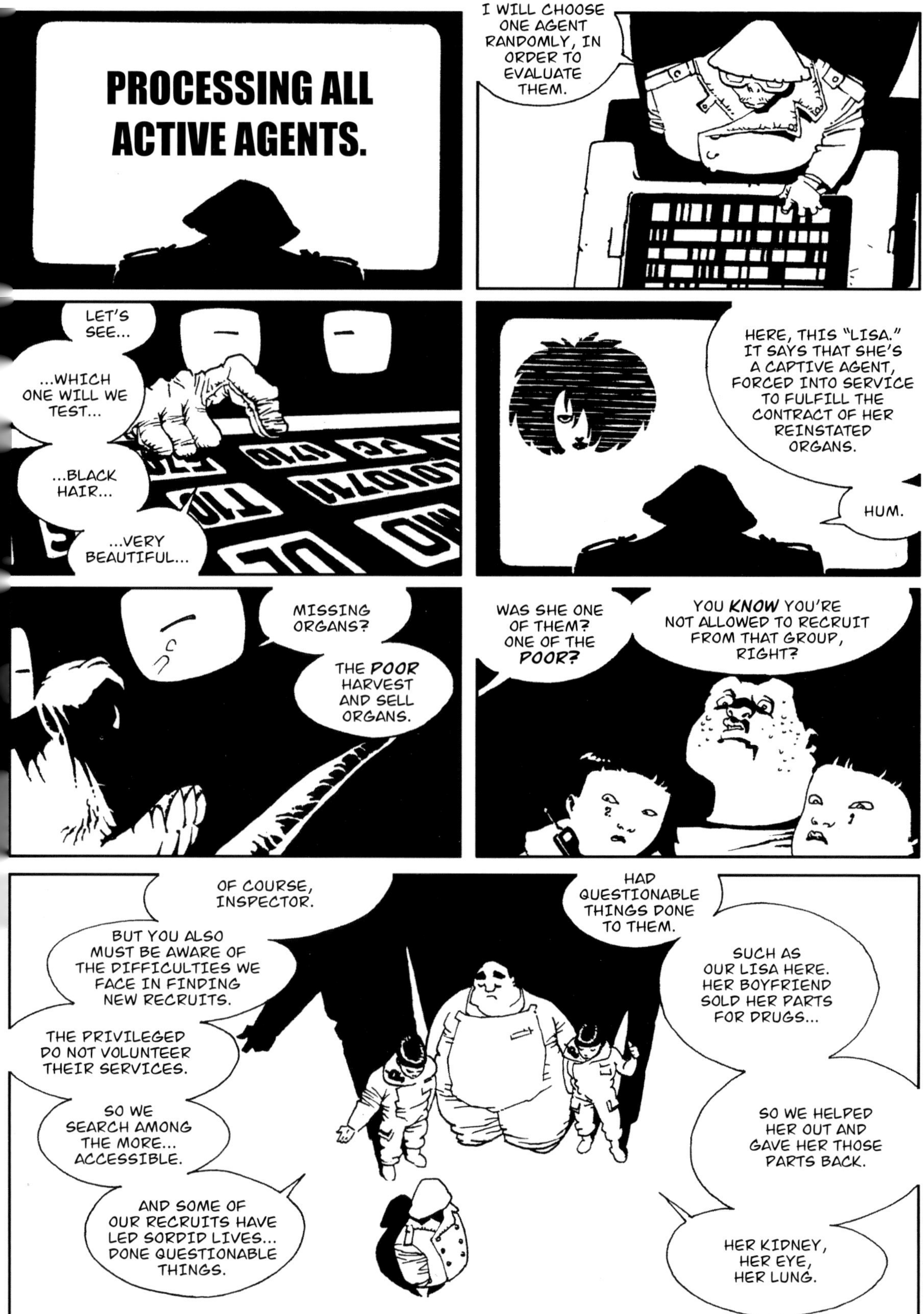
PROCESSING ALL ACTIVE AGENTS.
I WILL CHOOSE ONE AGENT RANDOMLY, IN ORDER TO EVALUATE THEM.
LET'S SEE...
...WHICH ONE WILL WE TEST...
...BLACK HAIR...
...VERY BEAUTIFUL...
HERE, THIS "LISA." IT SAYS THAT SHE'S A CAPTIVE AGENT, FORCED INTO SERVICE TO FULFILL THE CONTRACT OF HER REINSTATED ORGANS.
HUM.
MISSING ORGANS?
THE POOR HARVEST AND SELL ORGANS.
WAS SHE ONE OF THEM? ONE OF THE POOR?
YOU KNOW YOU'RE NOT ALLOWED TO RECRUIT FROM THAT GROUP, RIGHT?
OF COURSE, INSPECTOR.
BUT YOU ALSO MUST BE AWARE OF THE DIFFICULTIES WE FACE IN FINDING NEW RECRUITS.
THE PRIVILEGED DO NOT VOLUNTEER THEIR SERVICES.
SO WE SEARCH AMONG THE MORE... ACCESSIBLE.
AND SOME OF OUR RECRUITS HAVE LED SORDID LIVES... DONE QUESTIONABLE THINGS.
HAD QUESTIONABLE THINGS DONE TO THEM.
SUCH AS OUR LISA HERE. HER BOYFRIEND SOLD HER PARTS FOR DRUGS...
SO WE HELPED HER OUT AND GAVE HER THOSE PARTS BACK.
HER KIDNEY, HER EYE, HER LUNG.

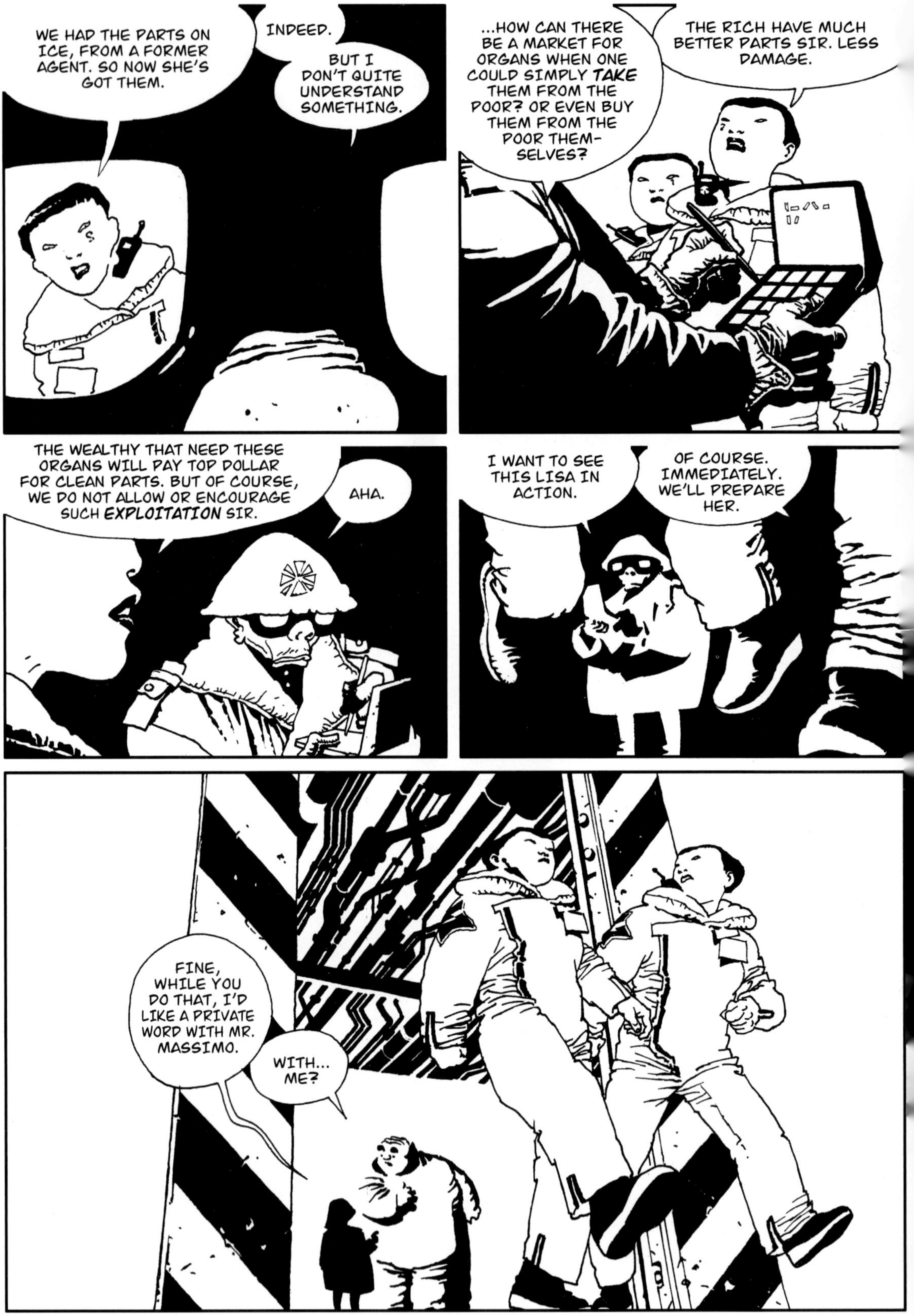
WE HAD THE PARTS ON ICE, FROM A FORMER AGENT. SO NOW SHE'S GOT THEM.
INDEED.
BUT I DON'T QUITE UNDERSTAND SOMETHING.
...HOW CAN THERE BE A MARKET FOR ORGANS WHEN ONE COULD SIMPLY TAKE THEM FROM THE POOR? OR EVEN BUY THEM FROM THE POOR THEM-SELVES?
THE RICH HAVE MUCH BETTER PARTS SIR. LESS DAMAGE.
THE WEALTHY THAT NEED THESE ORGANS WILL PAY TOP DOLLAR FOR CLEAN PARTS. BUT OF COURSE, WE DO NOT ALLOW OR ENCOURAGE SUCH EXPLOITATION SIR.
AHA.
I WANT TO SEE THIS LISA IN ACTION.
OF COURSE. IMMEDIATELY. WE'LL PREPARE HER.
FINE, WHILE YOU DO THAT, I'D LIKE A PRIVATE WORD WITH MR. MASSIMO.
WITH... ME?

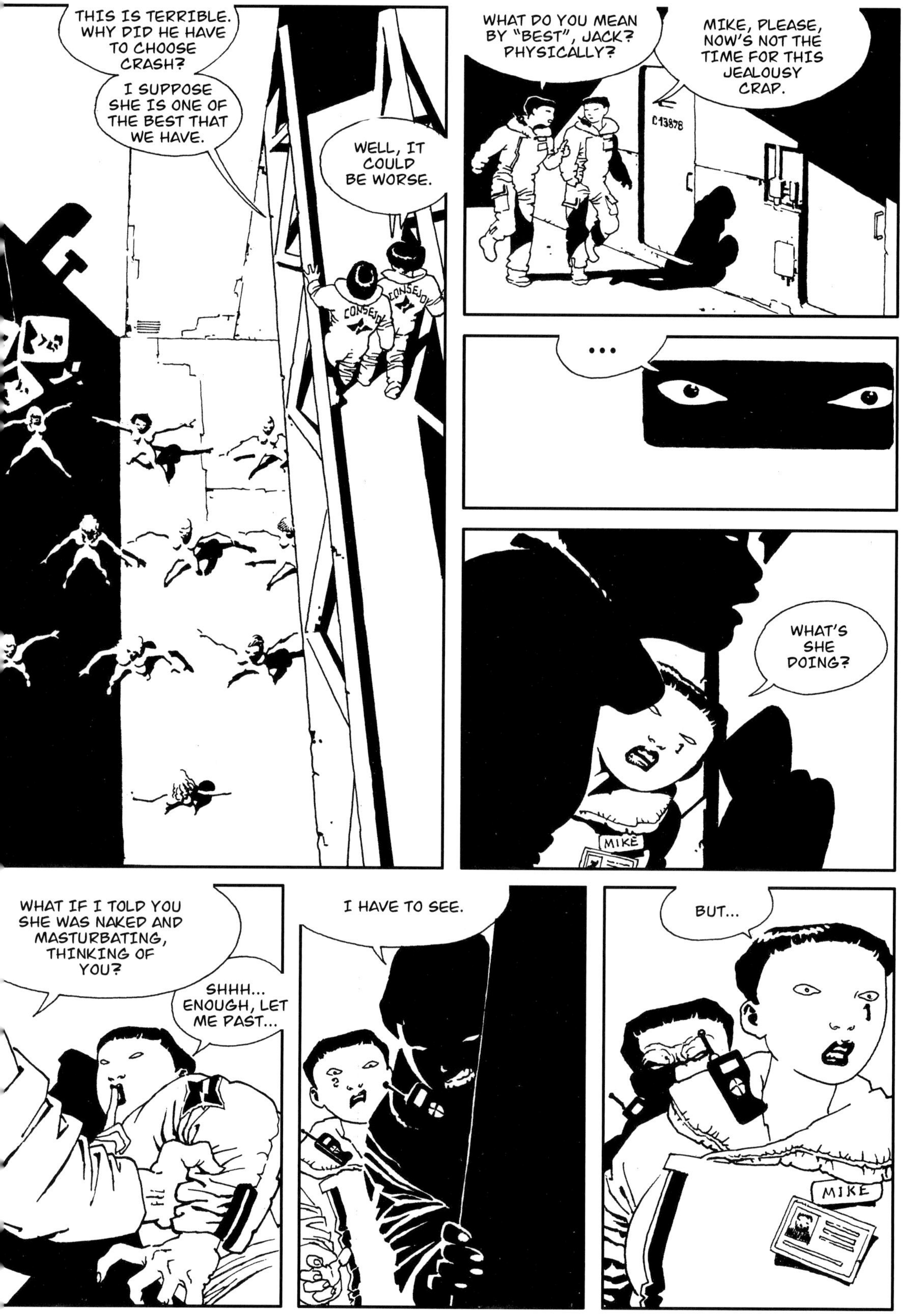
THIS IS TERRIBLE. WHY DID HE HAVE TO CHOOSE CRASH?
I SUPPOSE SHE IS ONE OF THE BEST THAT WE HAVE.
WELL, IT COULD BE WORSE.
WHAT DO YOU MEAN BY "BEST", JACK? PHYSICALLY?
MIKE, PLEASE, NOW'S NOT THE TIME FOR THIS JEALOUSY CRAP.
C13878
...
WHAT'S SHE DOING?
MIKE
WHAT IF I TOLD YOU SHE WAS NAKED AND MASTURBATING, THINKING OF YOU?
SHHH... ENOUGH, LET ME PAST...
I HAVE TO SEE.
BUT...
MIKE

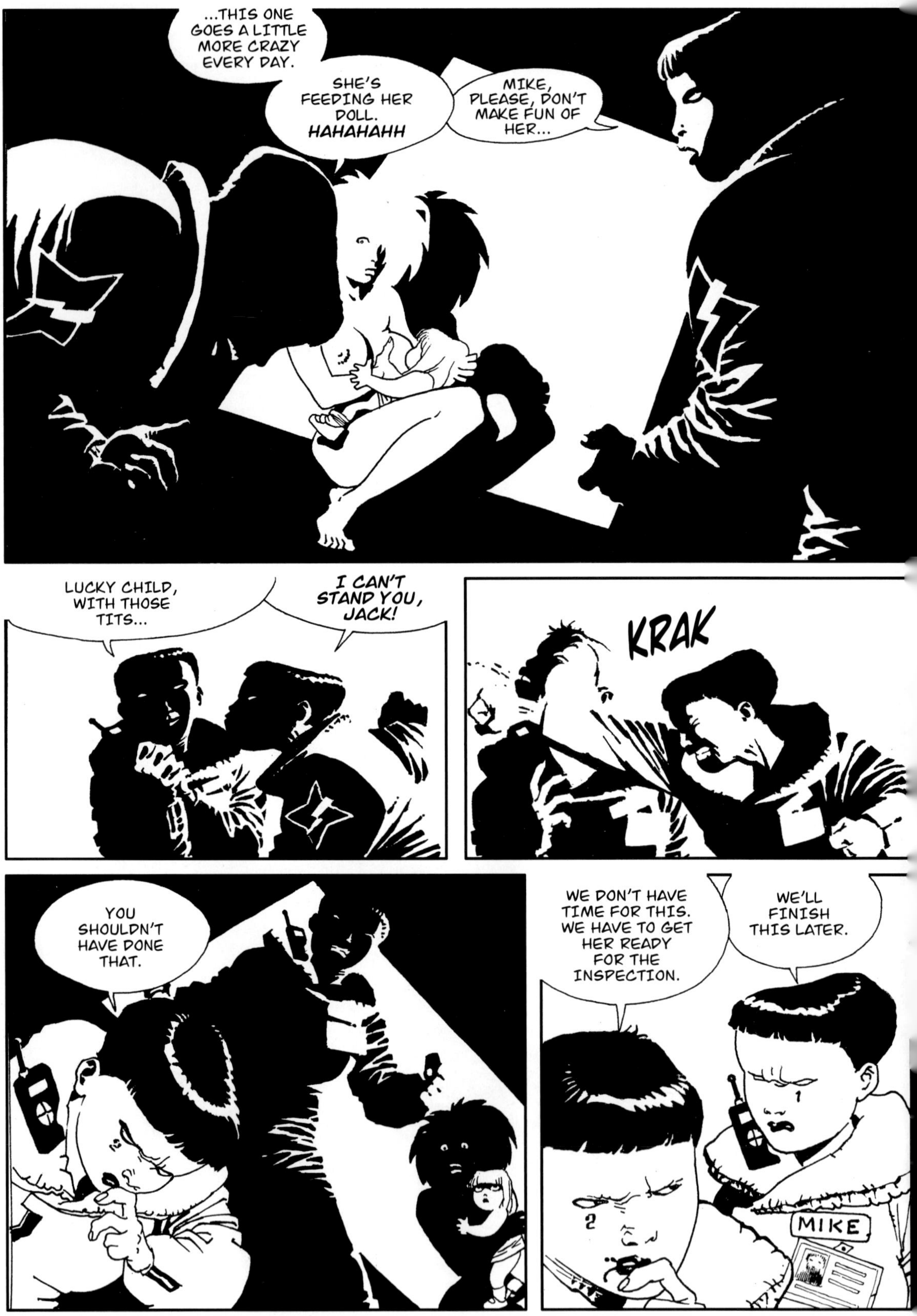
...THIS ONE GOES A LITTLE MORE CRAZY EVERY DAY.
SHE'S FEEDING HER DOLL. HAHAHAHH
MIKE, PLEASE, DON'T MAKE FUN OF HER...
LUCKY CHILD, WITH THOSE TITS...
I CAN'T STAND YOU, JACK!
KRAK
YOU SHOULDN'T HAVE DONE THAT.
WE DON'T HAVE TIME FOR THIS. WE HAVE TO GET HER READY FOR THE INSPECTION.
WE'LL FINISH THIS LATER.
MIKE

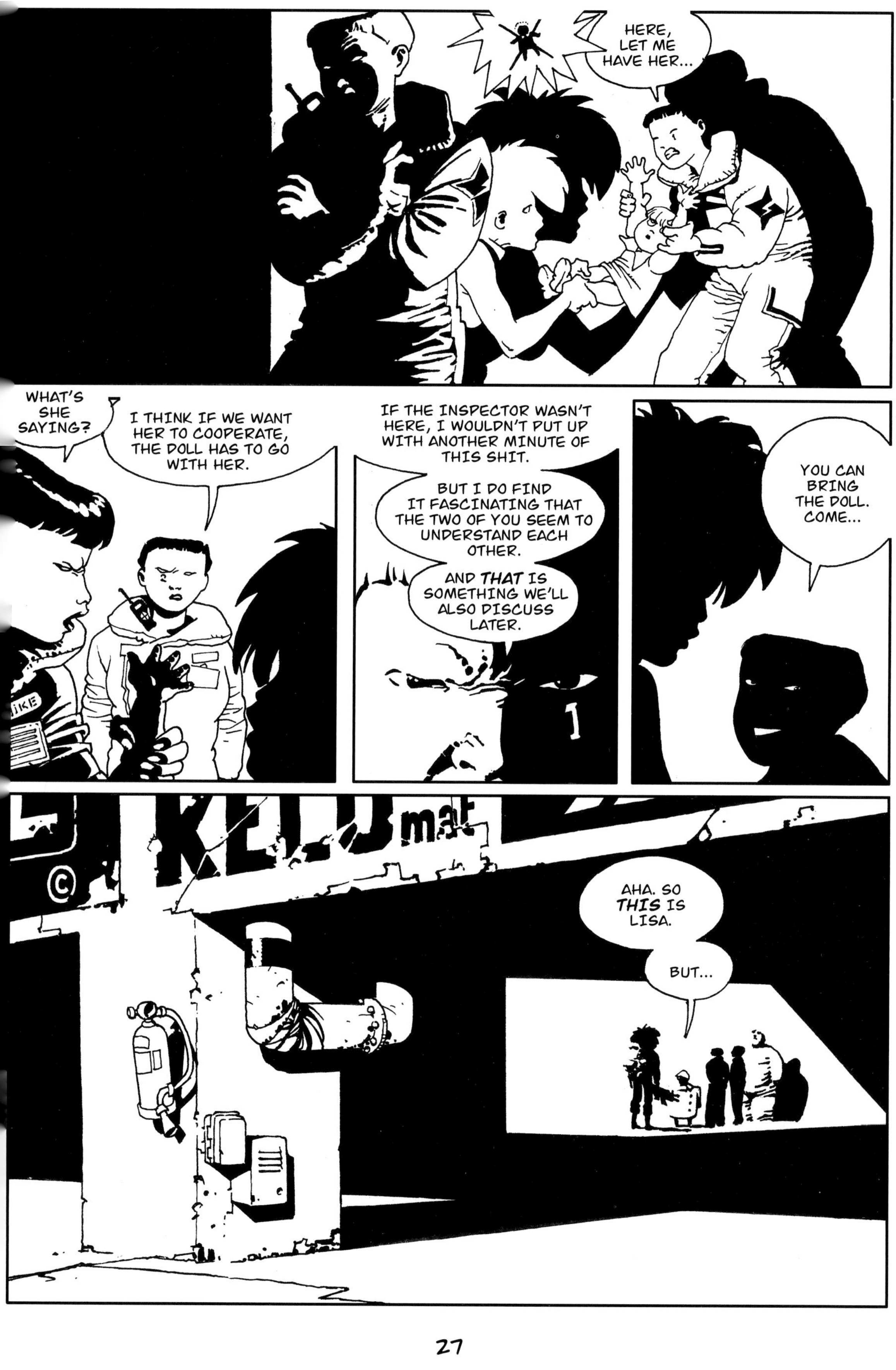
HERE, LET ME HAVE HER...
WHAT'S SHE SAYING?
I THINK IF WE WANT HER TO COOPERATE, THE DOLL HAS TO GO WITH HER.
IF THE INSPECTOR WASN'T HERE, I WOULDN'T PUT UP WITH ANOTHER MINUTE OF THIS SHIT.
BUT I DO FIND IT FASCINATING THAT THE TWO OF YOU SEEM TO UNDERSTAND EACH OTHER.
AND *THAT* IS SOMETHING WE'LL ALSO DISCUSS LATER.
YOU CAN BRING THE DOLL. COME...
mat
AHA. SO *THIS* IS LISA.
BUT...

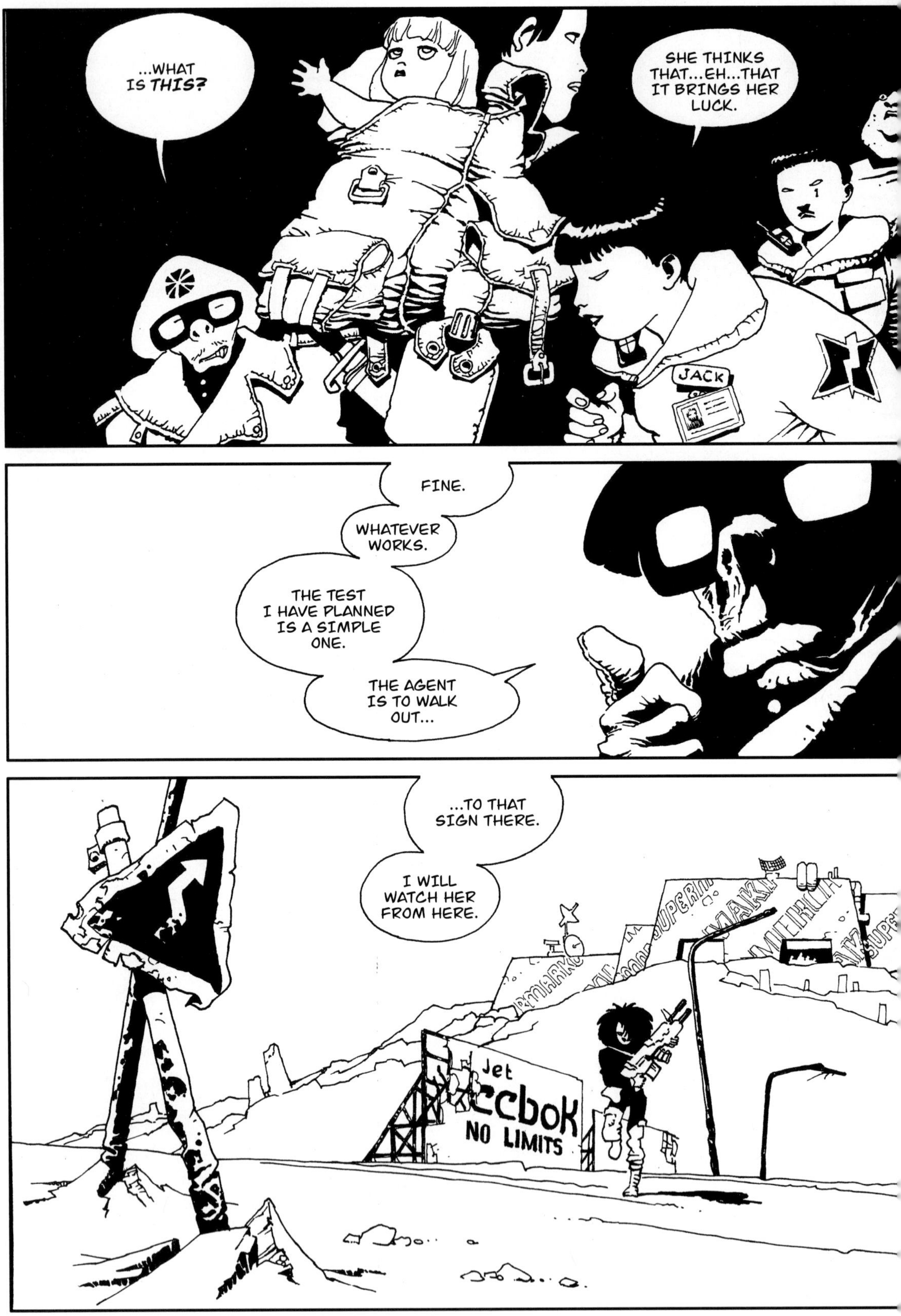
...WHAT IS THIS?
SHE THINKS THAT...EH...THAT IT BRINGS HER LUCK.
JACK
FINE.
WHATEVER WORKS.
THE TEST I HAVE PLANNED IS A SIMPLE ONE.
THE AGENT IS TO WALK OUT...
...TO THAT SIGN THERE.
I WILL WATCH HER FROM HERE.
Jet
NO LIMITS

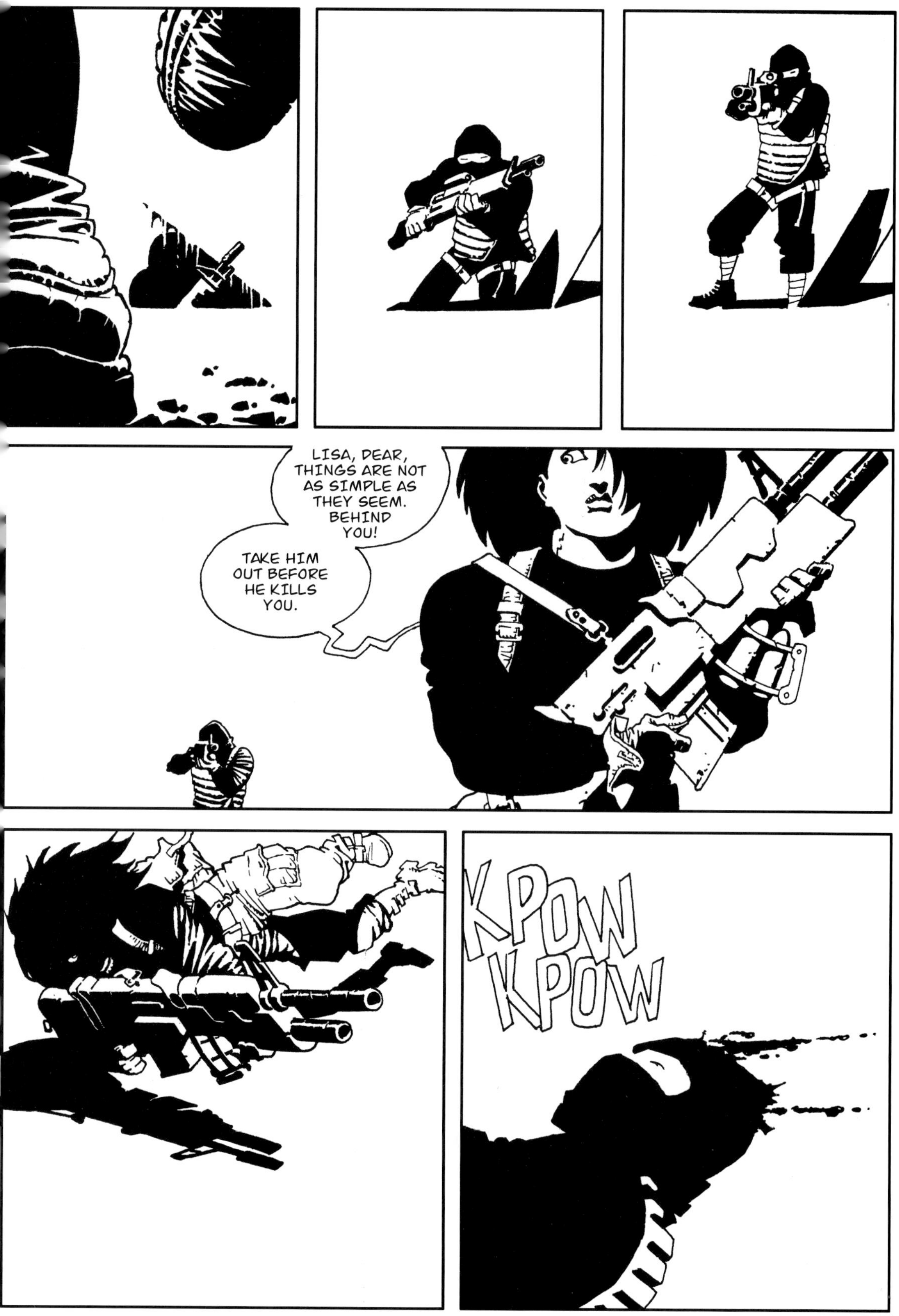
LISA, DEAR, THINGS ARE NOT AS SIMPLE AS THEY SEEM. BEHIND YOU!
TAKE HIM OUT BEFORE HE KILLS YOU.
KPOW
KPOW

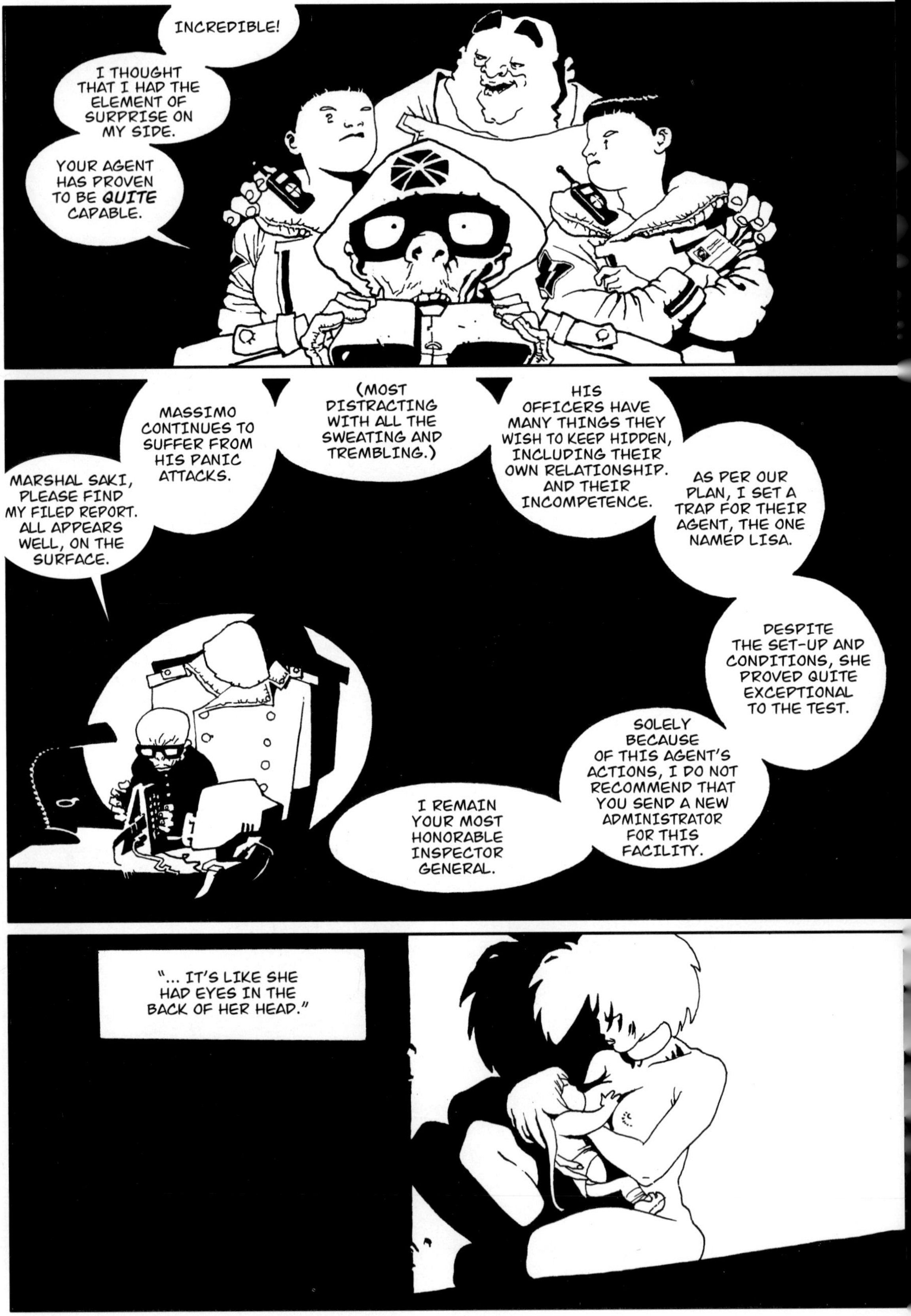

INCREDIBLE!
I THOUGHT THAT I HAD THE ELEMENT OF SURPRISE ON MY SIDE.
YOUR AGENT HAS PROVEN TO BE QUITE CAPABLE.
MARSHAL SAKI, PLEASE FIND MY FILED REPORT. ALL APPEARS WELL, ON THE SURFACE.
MASSIMO CONTINUES TO SUFFER FROM HIS PANIC ATTACKS.
(MOST DISTRACTING WITH ALL THE SWEATING AND TREMBLING.)
HIS OFFICERS HAVE MANY THINGS THEY WISH TO KEEP HIDDEN, INCLUDING THEIR OWN RELATIONSHIP. AND THEIR INCOMPETENCE.
AS PER OUR PLAN, I SET A TRAP FOR THEIR AGENT, THE ONE NAMED LISA.
DESPITE THE SET-UP AND CONDITIONS, SHE PROVED QUITE EXCEPTIONAL TO THE TEST.
SOLELY BECAUSE OF THIS AGENT'S ACTIONS, I DO NOT RECOMMEND THAT YOU SEND A NEW ADMINISTRATOR FOR THIS FACILITY.
I REMAIN YOUR MOST HONORABLE INSPECTOR GENERAL.
"... IT'S LIKE SHE HAD EYES IN THE BACK OF HER HEAD."

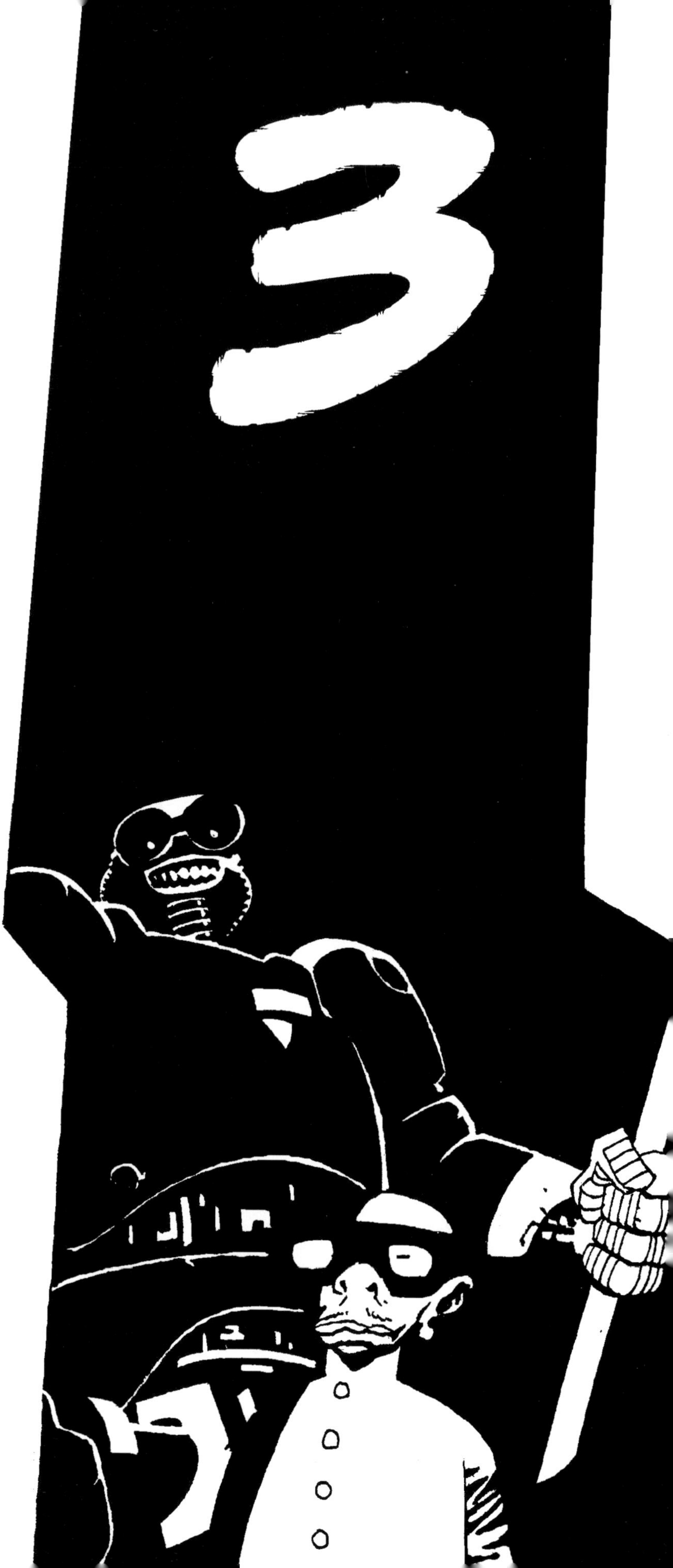
3

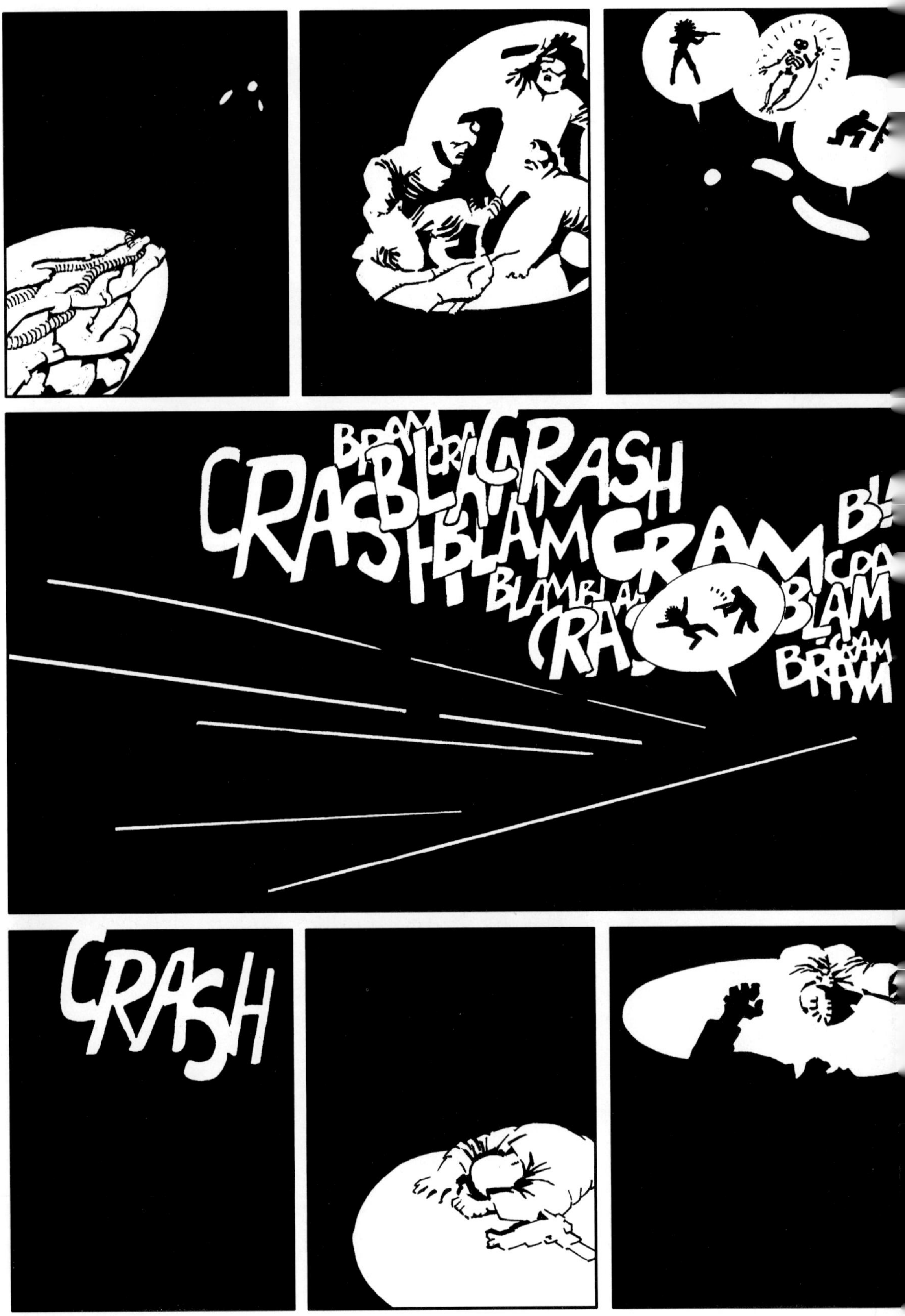
BRAM
CRASH
BLAM
CRAM
BLAM
BRAM
CRASH

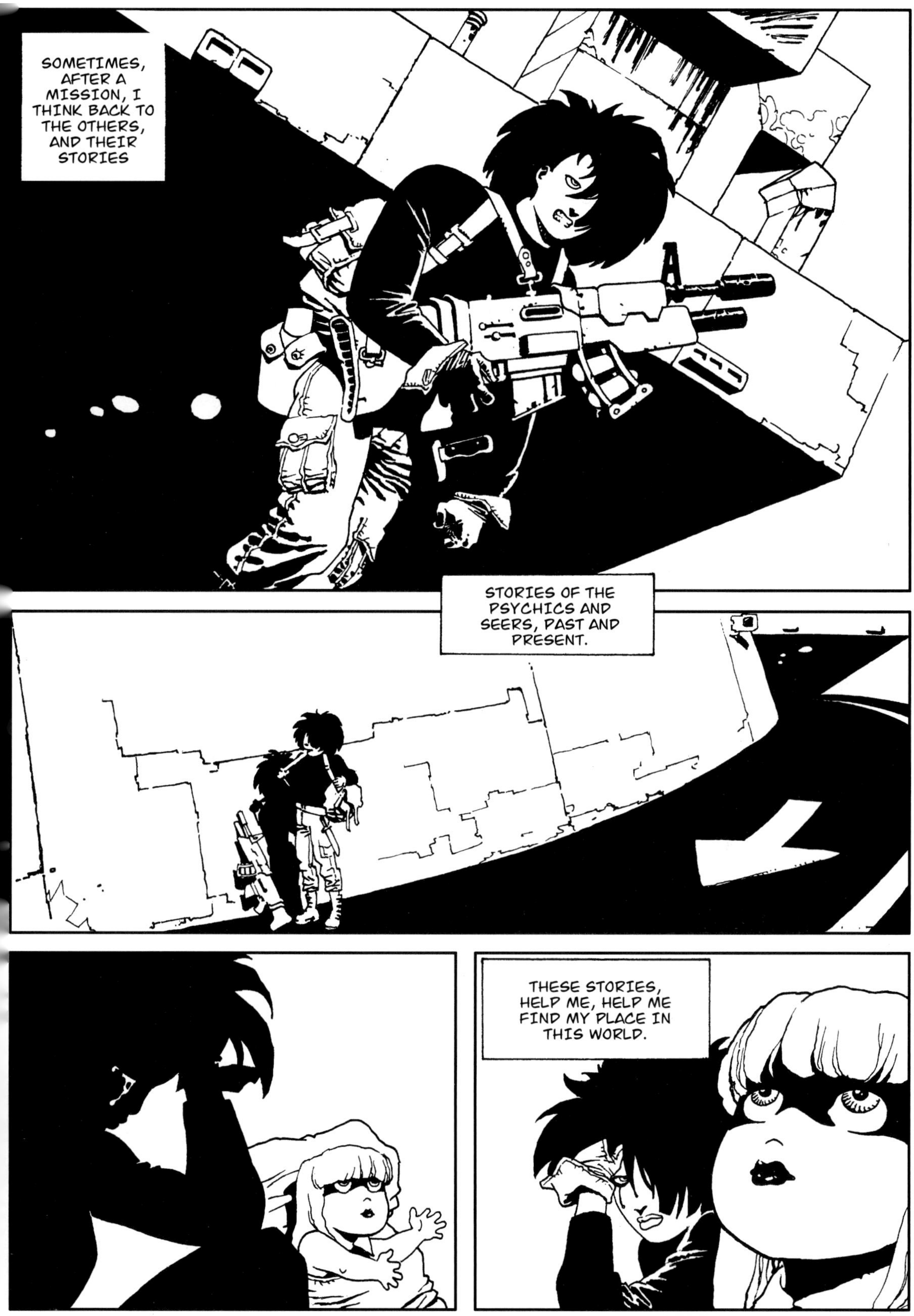
SOMETIMES, AFTER A MISSION, I THINK BACK TO THE OTHERS, AND THEIR STORIES
STORIES OF THE PSYCHICS AND SEERS, PAST AND PRESENT.
THESE STORIES, HELP ME, HELP ME FIND MY PLACE IN THIS WORLD.

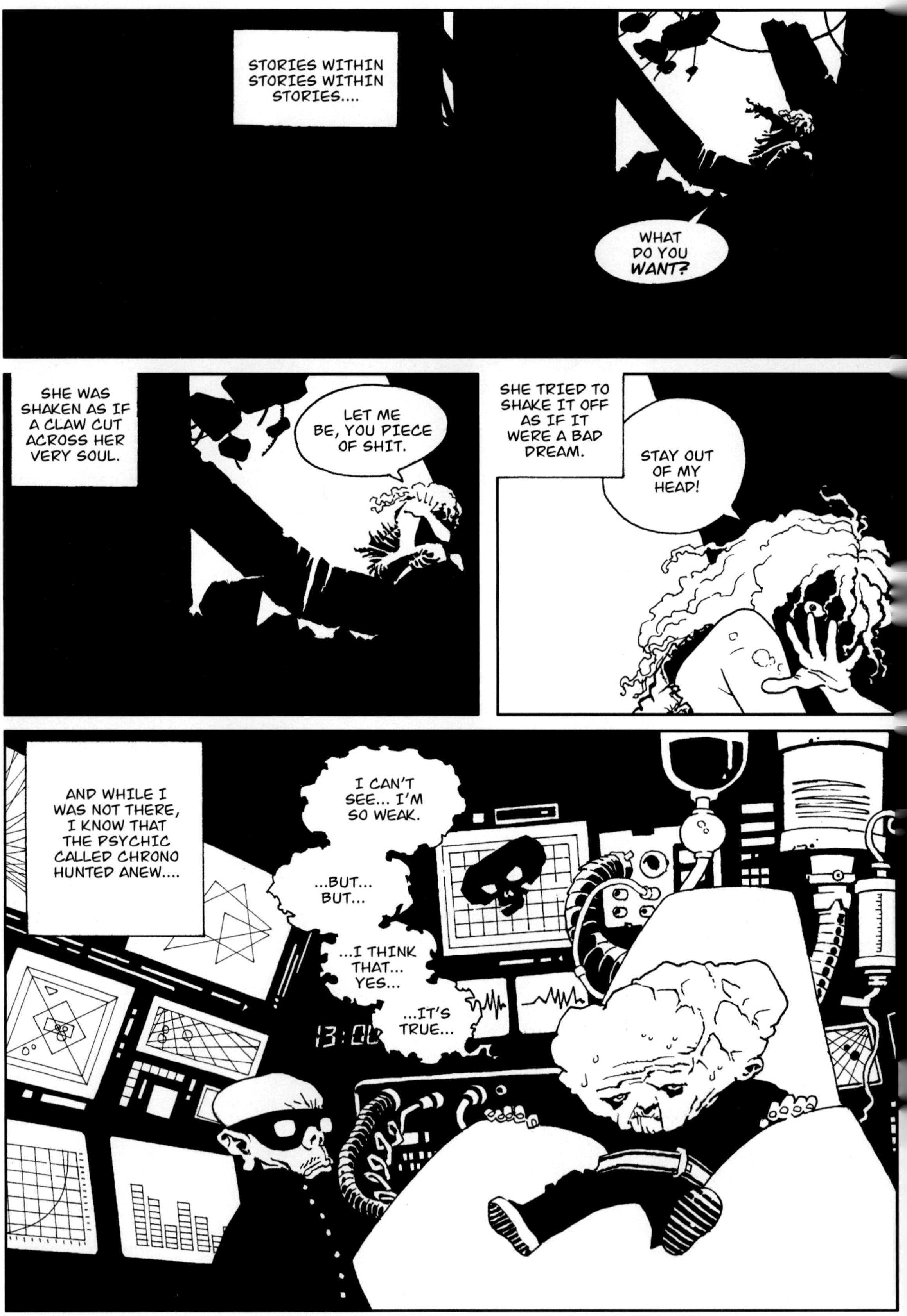
STORIES WITHIN STORIES WITHIN STORIES....
WHAT DO YOU WANT?
SHE WAS SHAKEN AS IF A CLAW CUT ACROSS HER VERY SOUL.
LET ME BE, YOU PIECE OF SHIT.
SHE TRIED TO SHAKE IT OFF AS IF IT WERE A BAD DREAM.
STAY OUT OF MY HEAD!
AND WHILE I WAS NOT THERE, I KNOW THAT THE PSYCHIC CALLED CHRONO HUNTED ANEW....
I CAN'T SEE... I'M SO WEAK.
...BUT... BUT...
...I THINK THAT... YES...
...IT'S TRUE...
13:00

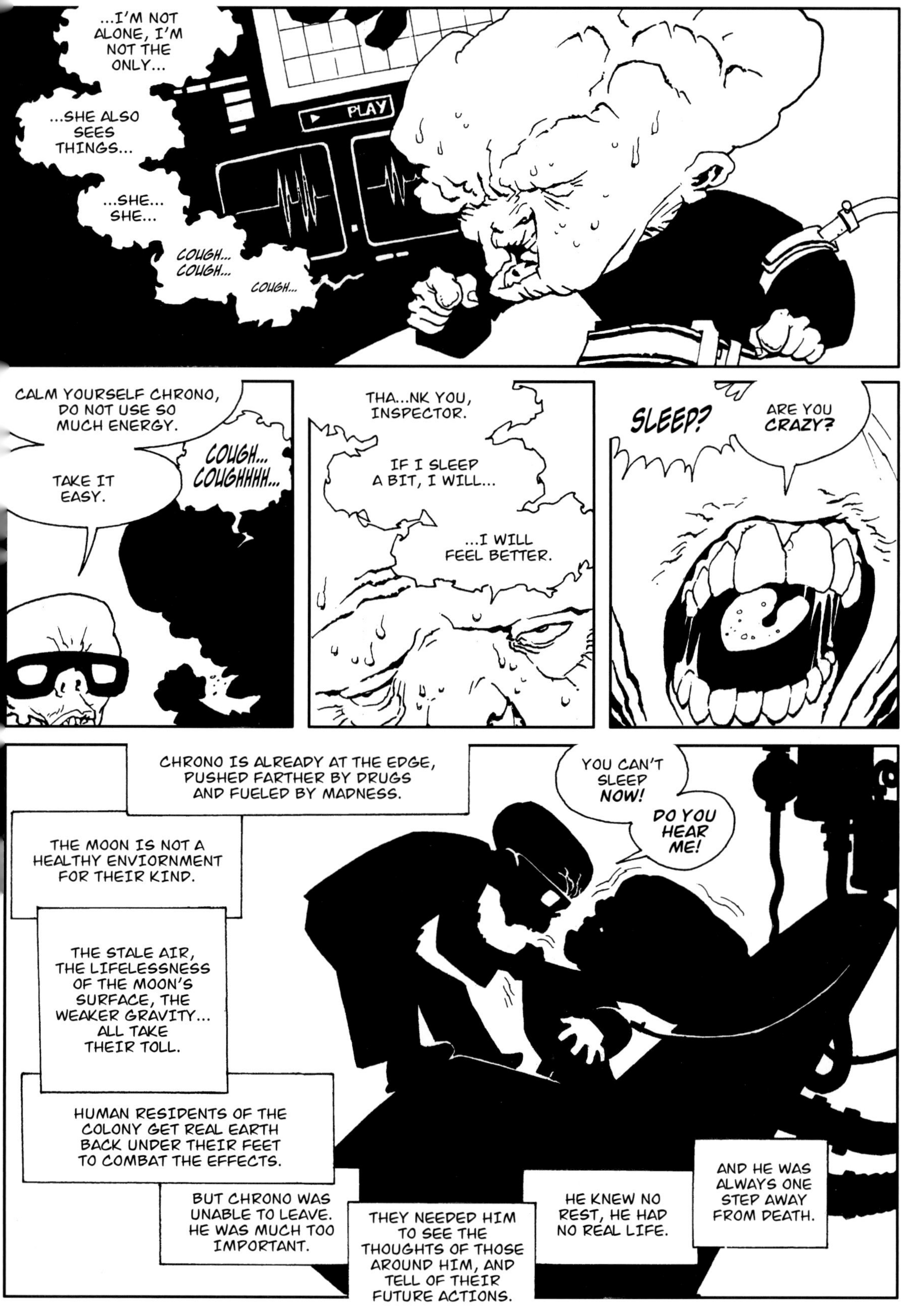
...I'M NOT ALONE, I'M NOT THE ONLY...
...SHE ALSO SEES THINGS...
...SHE... SHE...
COUGH... COUGH...
COUGH...
PLAY
CALM YOURSELF CHRONO, DO NOT USE SO MUCH ENERGY.
TAKE IT EASY.
COUGH... COUGHHHH...
THA...NK YOU, INSPECTOR.
IF I SLEEP A BIT, I WILL...
...I WILL FEEL BETTER.
SLEEP?
ARE YOU CRAZY?
CHRONO IS ALREADY AT THE EDGE, PUSHED FARTHER BY DRUGS AND FUELED BY MADNESS.
YOU CAN'T SLEEP NOW!
DO YOU HEAR ME!
THE MOON IS NOT A HEALTHY ENVIORNMENT FOR THEIR KIND.
THE STALE AIR, THE LIFELESSNESS OF THE MOON'S SURFACE, THE WEAKER GRAVITY... ALL TAKE THEIR TOLL.
HUMAN RESIDENTS OF THE COLONY GET REAL EARTH BACK UNDER THEIR FEET TO COMBAT THE EFFECTS.
BUT CHRONO WAS UNABLE TO LEAVE. HE WAS MUCH TOO IMPORTANT.
THEY NEEDED HIM TO SEE THE THOUGHTS OF THOSE AROUND HIM, AND TELL OF THEIR FUTURE ACTIONS.
HE KNEW NO REST, HE HAD NO REAL LIFE.
AND HE WAS ALWAYS ONE STEP AWAY FROM DEATH.

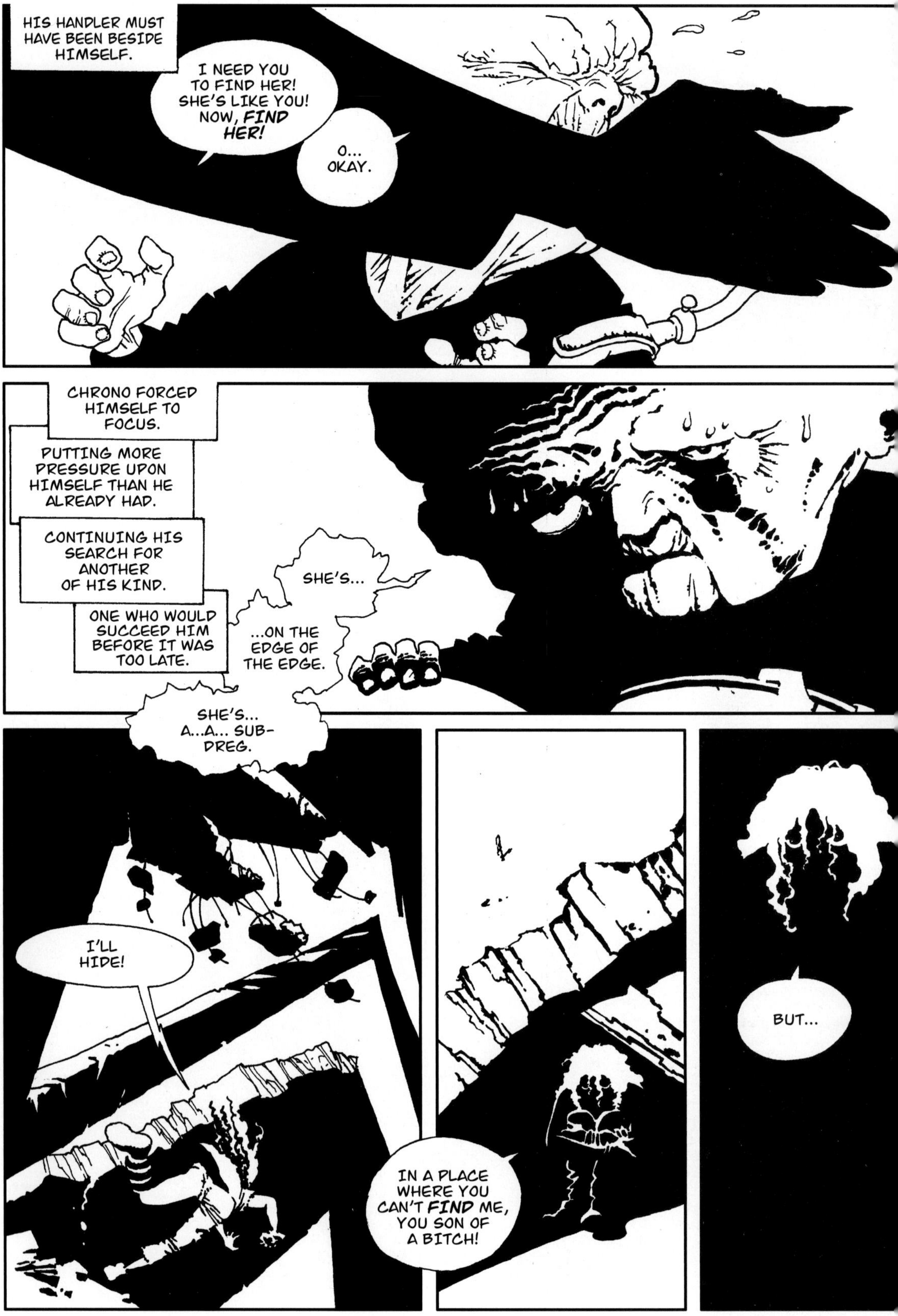

HIS HANDLER MUST HAVE BEEN BESIDE HIMSELF.
I NEED YOU TO FIND HER! SHE'S LIKE YOU! NOW, FIND HER!
O... OKAY.
CHRONO FORCED HIMSELF TO FOCUS.
PUTTING MORE PRESSURE UPON HIMSELF THAN HE ALREADY HAD.
CONTINUING HIS SEARCH FOR ANOTHER OF HIS KIND.
ONE WHO WOULD SUCCEED HIM BEFORE IT WAS TOO LATE.
SHE'S...
...ON THE EDGE OF THE EDGE.
SHE'S... A...A... SUB-DREG.
I'LL HIDE!
IN A PLACE WHERE YOU CAN'T FIND ME, YOU SON OF A BITCH!
BUT...

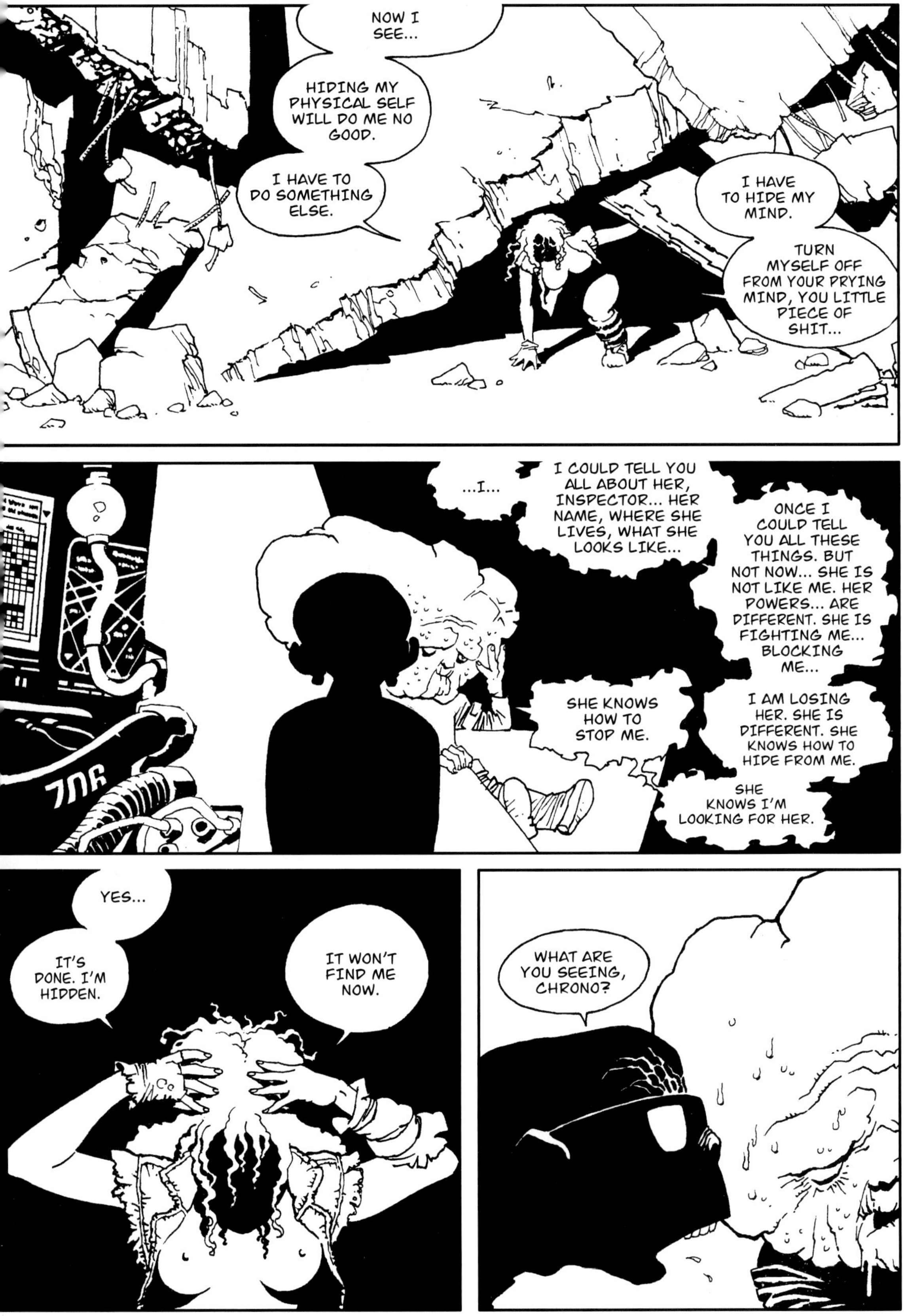
NOW I SEE...
HIDING MY PHYSICAL SELF WILL DO ME NO GOOD.
I HAVE TO DO SOMETHING ELSE.
I HAVE TO HIDE MY MIND.
TURN MYSELF OFF FROM YOUR PRYING MIND, YOU LITTLE PIECE OF SHIT...
...I...
I COULD TELL YOU ALL ABOUT HER, INSPECTOR... HER NAME, WHERE SHE LIVES, WHAT SHE LOOKS LIKE...
ONCE I COULD TELL YOU ALL THESE THINGS. BUT NOT NOW... SHE IS NOT LIKE ME. HER POWERS... ARE DIFFERENT. SHE IS FIGHTING ME... BLOCKING ME...
SHE KNOWS HOW TO STOP ME.
I AM LOSING HER. SHE IS DIFFERENT. SHE KNOWS HOW TO HIDE FROM ME.
SHE KNOWS I'M LOOKING FOR HER.
706
YES...
IT'S DONE. I'M HIDDEN.
IT WON'T FIND ME NOW.
WHAT ARE YOU SEEING, CHRONO?

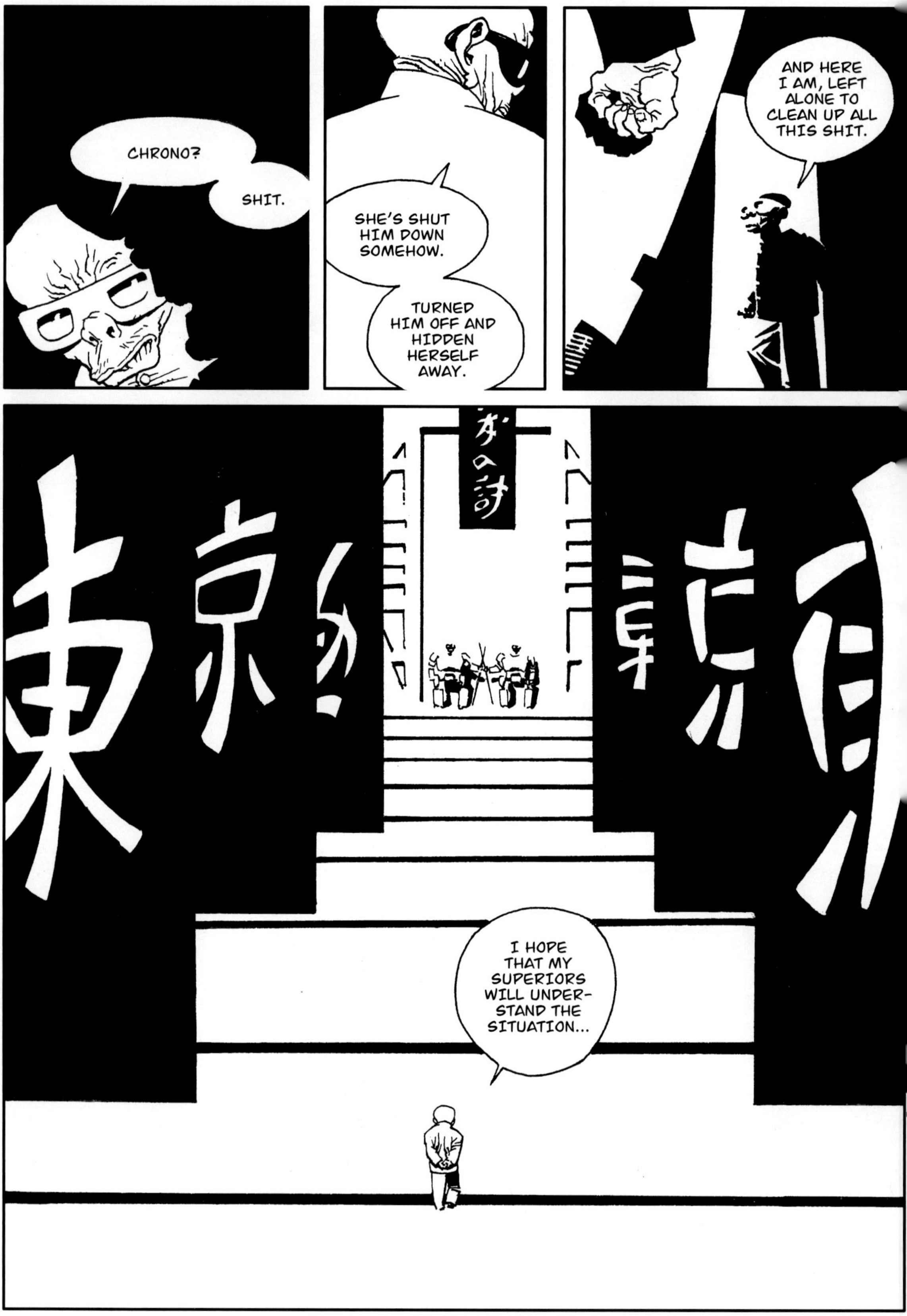
CHRONO?
SHIT.
SHE'S SHUT HIM DOWN SOMEHOW.
TURNED HIM OFF AND HIDDEN HERSELF AWAY.
AND HERE I AM, LEFT ALONE TO CLEAN UP ALL THIS SHIT.
I HOPE THAT MY SUPERIORS WILL UNDER-STAND THE SITUATION...

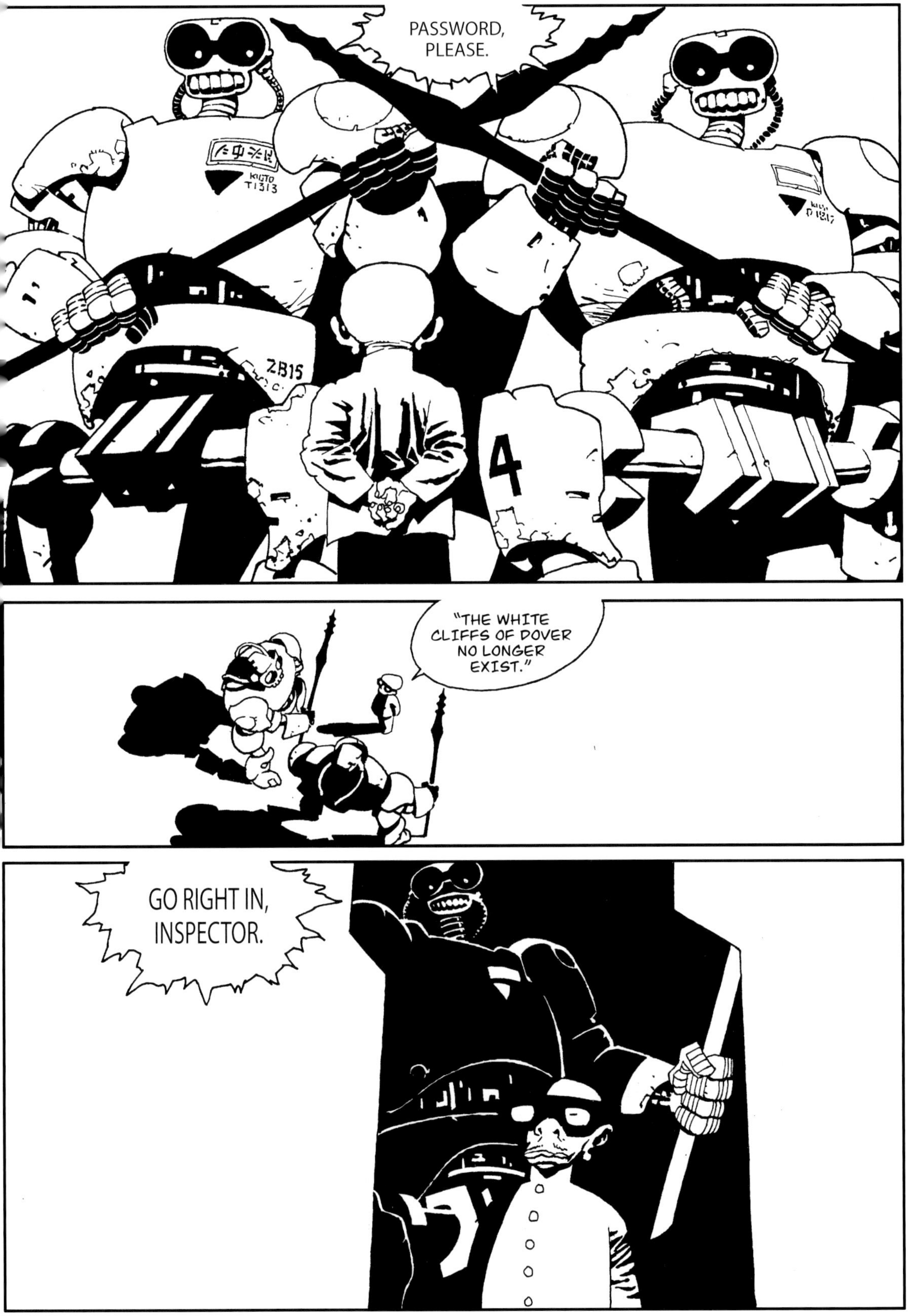
PASSWORD, PLEASE.
"THE WHITE CLIFFS OF DOVER NO LONGER EXIST."
GO RIGHT IN, INSPECTOR.

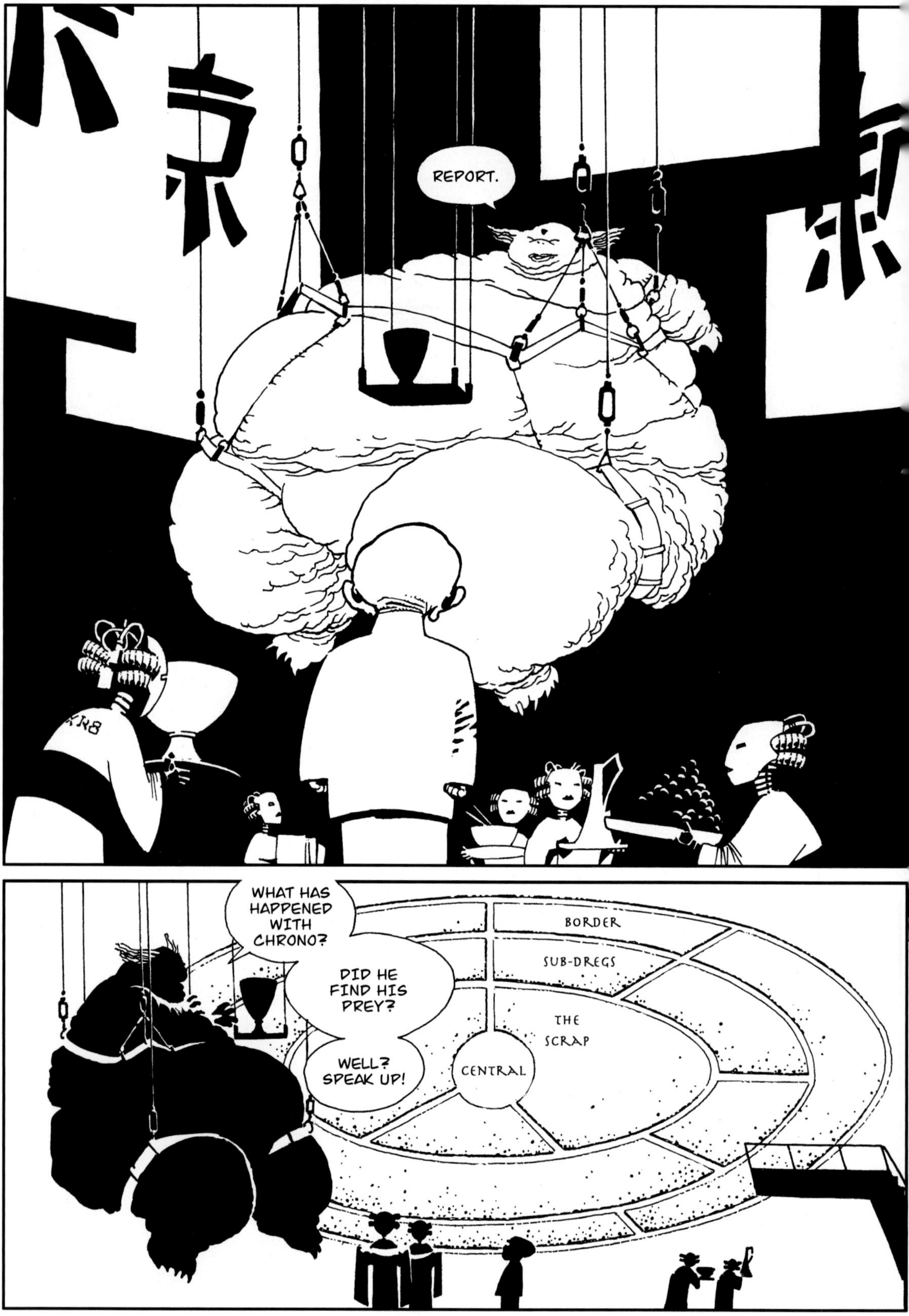
REPORT.
WHAT HAS HAPPENED WITH CHRONO?
DID HE FIND HIS PREY?
WELL? SPEAK UP!
BORDER
SUB-DREGS
THE SCRAP
CENTRAL

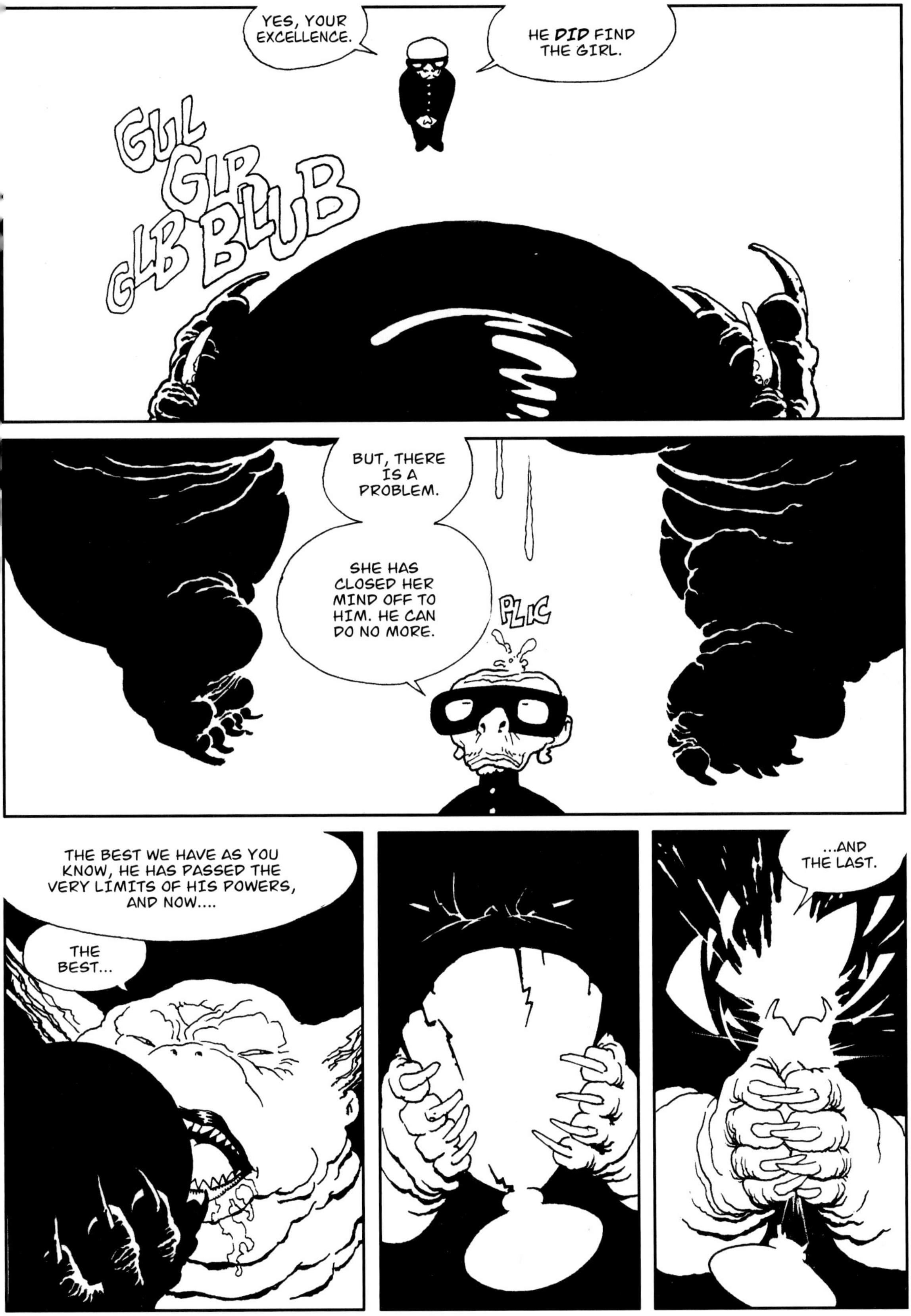
YES, YOUR EXCELLENCE.
HE *DID* FIND THE GIRL.
GUL GLR GLB BLUB
BUT, THERE IS A PROBLEM.
SHE HAS CLOSED HER MIND OFF TO HIM. HE CAN DO NO MORE.
PLIC
THE BEST WE HAVE AS YOU KNOW, HE HAS PASSED THE VERY LIMITS OF HIS POWERS, AND NOW....
THE BEST...
...AND THE LAST.

IN ORDER TO KEEP OUR HOLD, TO KEEP OUR POWER, HE IS ESSENTIAL TO US.

BUT EVERY TIME HE SERVES OUR WILL, HE SLIPS FARTHER AWAY.

AND THIS OTHER... WOMAN YOU SAY.

GOOD, GOOD, GOOD, GOOD.

WE NEED HER.

...

BRING HER TO ME INSPECTOR.

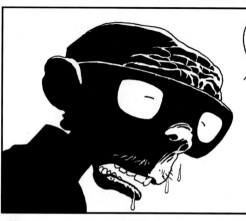

SIR, AS I'VE BEEN *TRYING* TO SAY...

SLURP.

SPIT IT OUT, INSPECTOR!

SHE'S BLOCKED CHRONO'S POWER, HIS SIGHT.

HE WAS ONLY IN CONTACT FOR A FEW MINUTES.

HE KNOWS THAT SHE LIVES WITH THE SUB-DREGS.

SHE HERSELF IS A SUB-DREG.

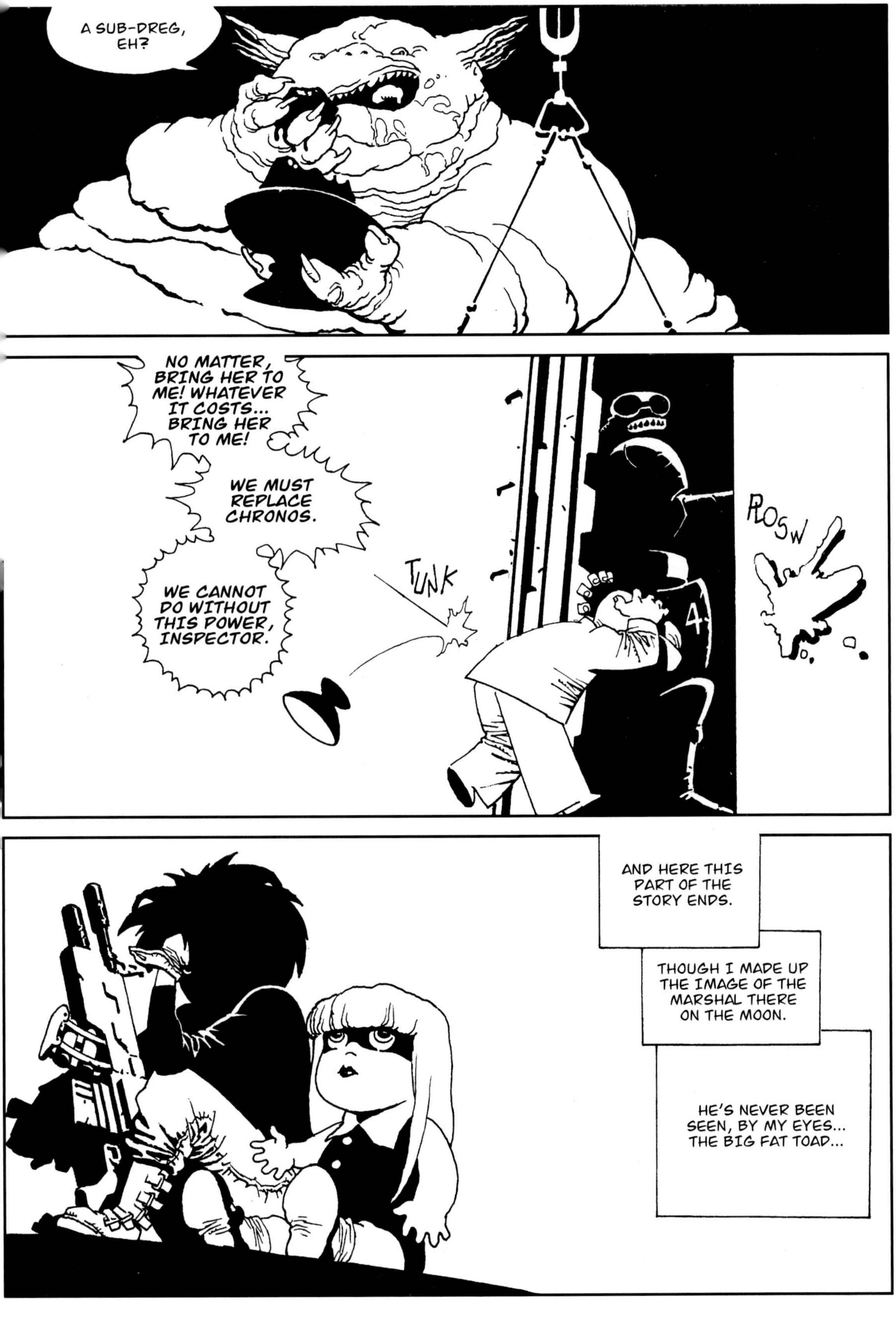
A SUB-DREG, EH?
NO MATTER, BRING HER TO ME! WHATEVER IT COSTS... BRING HER TO ME!
WE MUST REPLACE CHRONOS.
WE CANNOT DO WITHOUT THIS POWER, INSPECTOR.
TUNK
FLOSW
AND HERE THIS PART OF THE STORY ENDS.
THOUGH I MADE UP THE IMAGE OF THE MARSHAL THERE ON THE MOON.
HE'S NEVER BEEN SEEN, BY MY EYES... THE BIG FAT TOAD...

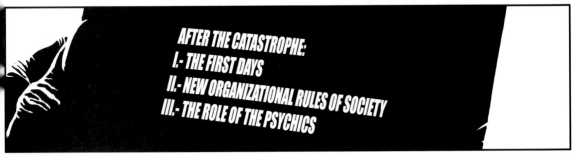

AFTER THE CATASTROPHE:
I.- THE FIRST DAYS
II.- NEW ORGANIZATIONAL RULES OF SOCIETY
III.- THE ROLE OF THE PSYCHICS

YES, LET'S WATCH IT AGAIN.

AND PAY ATTENTION, YOU TWO.

FOR YOURSELVES, AND FOR ME, **PLEASE** PAY ATTENTION.

YOU KNOW THAT I HAVE BEEN A LITTLE DISTRACTED, LATELY.

YES, BOSS.

KLIK

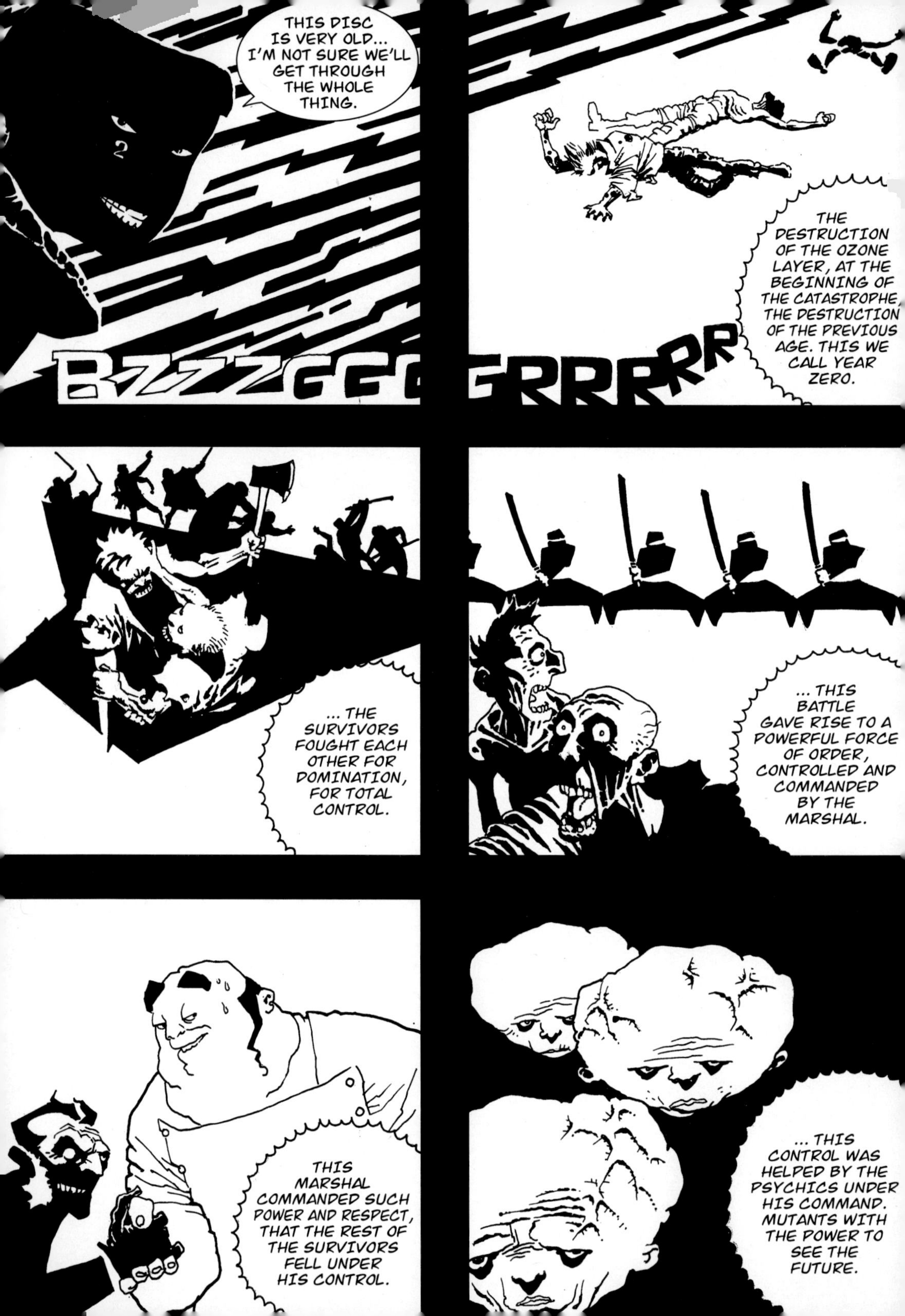
THIS DISC IS VERY OLD... I'M NOT SURE WE'LL GET THROUGH THE WHOLE THING.
BZZZGGGGRRRRR
THE DESTRUCTION OF THE OZONE LAYER, AT THE BEGINNING OF THE CATASTROPHE THE DESTRUCTION OF THE PREVIOUS AGE. THIS WE CALL YEAR ZERO.
... THE SURVIVORS FOUGHT EACH OTHER FOR DOMINATION, FOR TOTAL CONTROL.
... THIS BATTLE GAVE RISE TO A POWERFUL FORCE OF ORDER, CONTROLLED AND COMMANDED BY THE MARSHAL.
THIS MARSHAL COMMANDED SUCH POWER AND RESPECT, THAT THE REST OF THE SURVIVORS FELL UNDER HIS CONTROL.
... THIS CONTROL WAS HELPED BY THE PSYCHICS UNDER HIS COMMAND. MUTANTS WITH THE POWER TO SEE THE FUTURE.

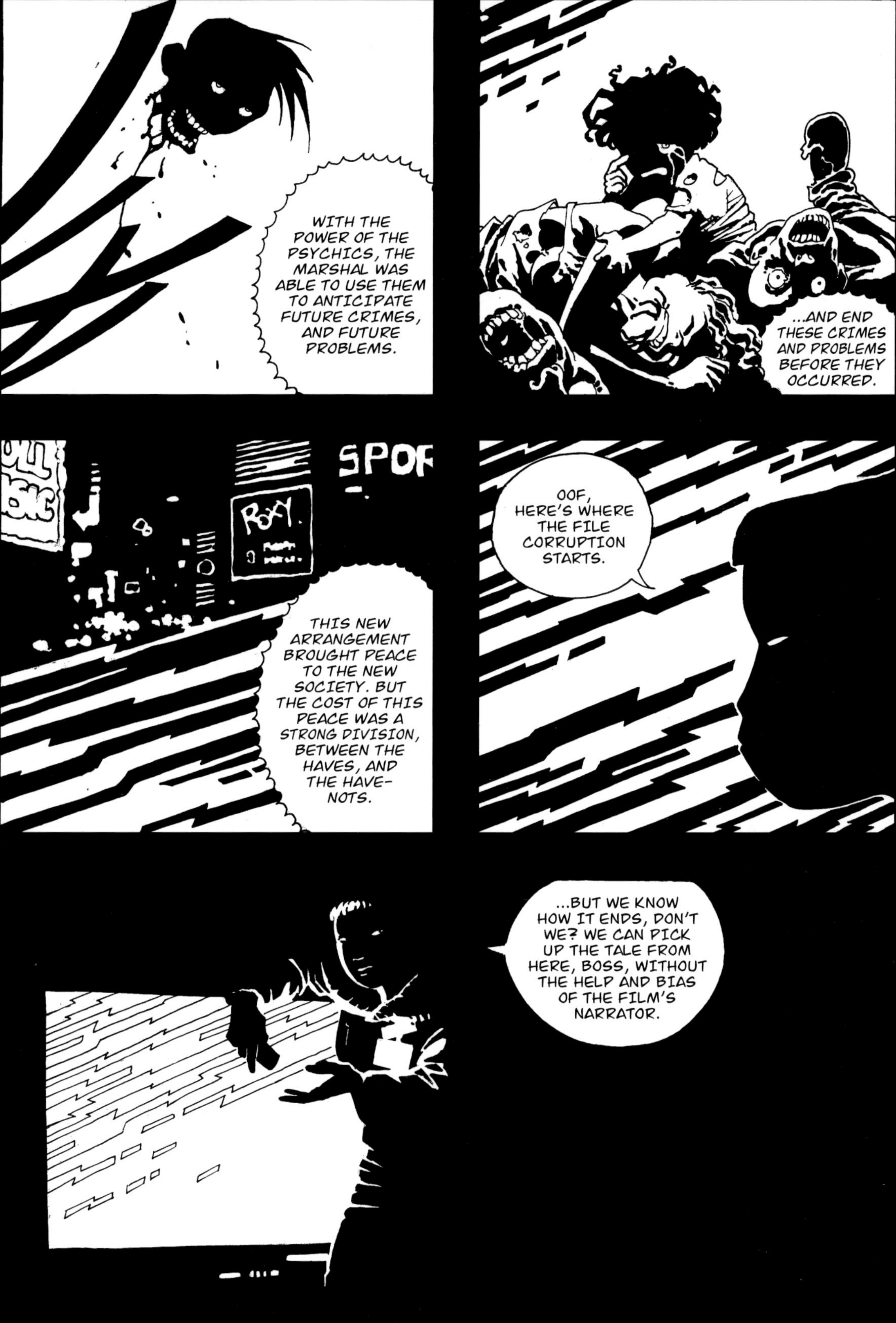
WITH THE POWER OF THE PSYCHICS, THE MARSHAL WAS ABLE TO USE THEM TO ANTICIPATE FUTURE CRIMES, AND FUTURE PROBLEMS.
...AND END THESE CRIMES AND PROBLEMS BEFORE THEY OCCURRED.
SPOR
ROXY
THIS NEW ARRANGEMENT BROUGHT PEACE TO THE NEW SOCIETY. BUT THE COST OF THIS PEACE WAS A STRONG DIVISION, BETWEEN THE HAVES, AND THE HAVE-NOTS.
OOF, HERE'S WHERE THE FILE CORRUPTION STARTS.
...BUT WE KNOW HOW IT ENDS, DON'T WE? WE CAN PICK UP THE TALE FROM HERE, BOSS, WITHOUT THE HELP AND BIAS OF THE FILM'S NARRATOR.

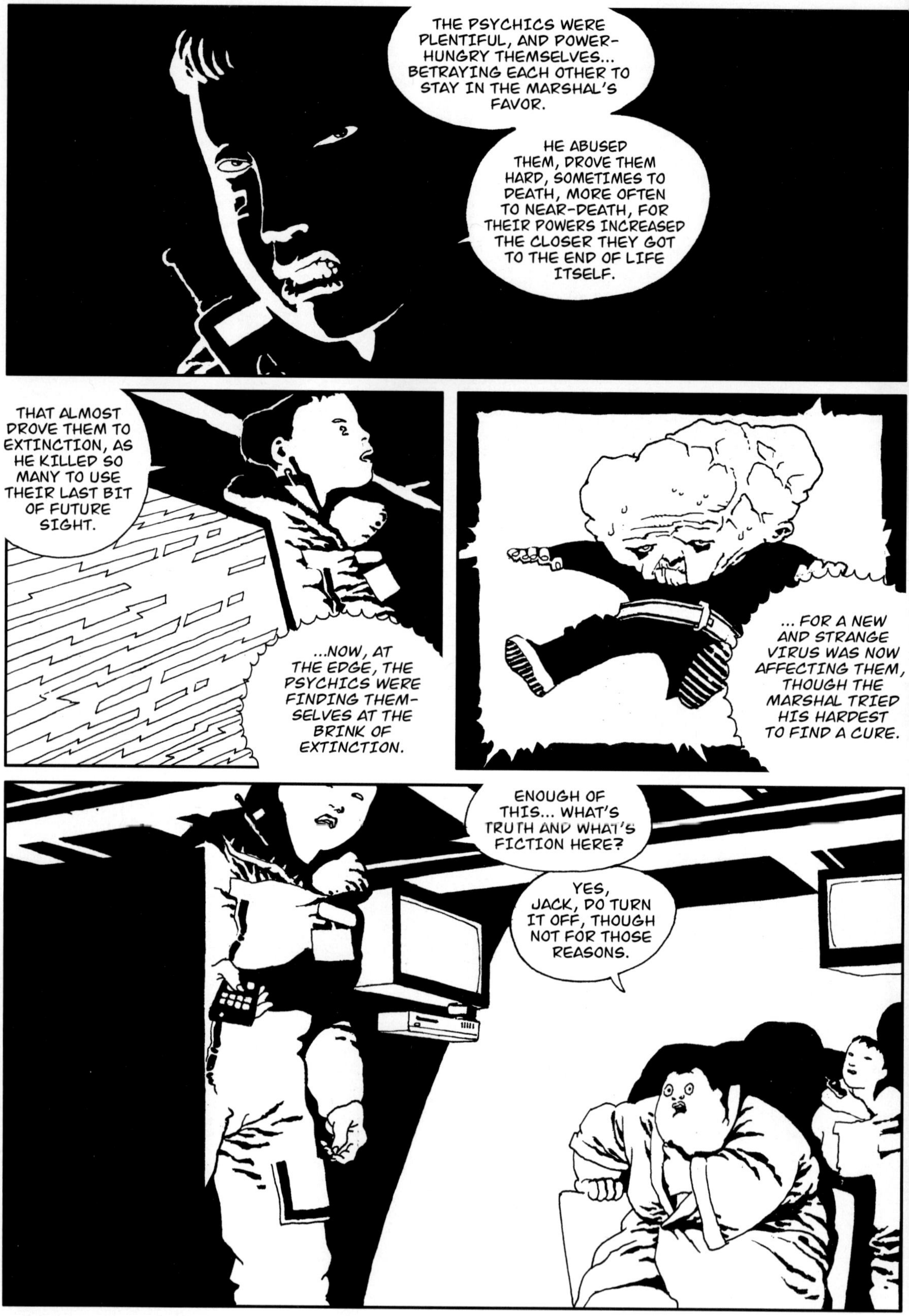
THE PSYCHICS WERE PLENTIFUL, AND POWER-HUNGRY THEMSELVES... BETRAYING EACH OTHER TO STAY IN THE MARSHAL'S FAVOR.
HE ABUSED THEM, DROVE THEM HARD, SOMETIMES TO DEATH, MORE OFTEN TO NEAR-DEATH, FOR THEIR POWERS INCREASED THE CLOSER THEY GOT TO THE END OF LIFE ITSELF.
THAT ALMOST DROVE THEM TO EXTINCTION, AS HE KILLED SO MANY TO USE THEIR LAST BIT OF FUTURE SIGHT.
...NOW, AT THE EDGE, THE PSYCHICS WERE FINDING THEMSELVES AT THE BRINK OF EXTINCTION.
... FOR A NEW AND STRANGE VIRUS WAS NOW AFFECTING THEM, THOUGH THE MARSHAL TRIED HIS HARDEST TO FIND A CURE.
ENOUGH OF THIS... WHAT'S TRUTH AND WHAT'S FICTION HERE?
YES, JACK, DO TURN IT OFF, THOUGH NOT FOR THOSE REASONS.

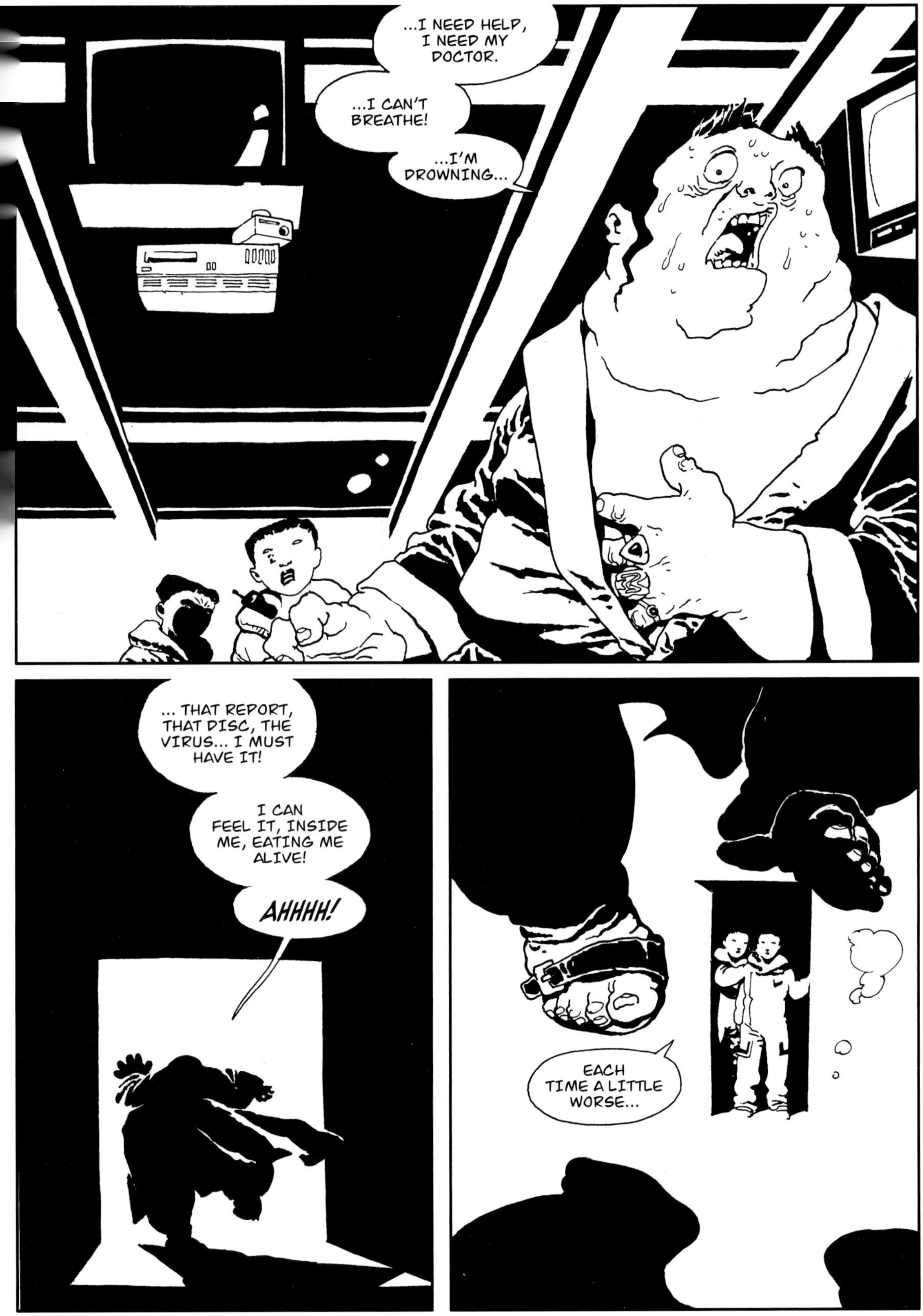

...I NEED HELP, I NEED MY DOCTOR.
...I CAN'T BREATHE!
...I'M DROWNING...
... THAT REPORT, THAT DISC, THE VIRUS... I MUST HAVE IT!
I CAN FEEL IT, INSIDE ME, EATING ME ALIVE!
AHHHH!
EACH TIME A LITTLE WORSE...

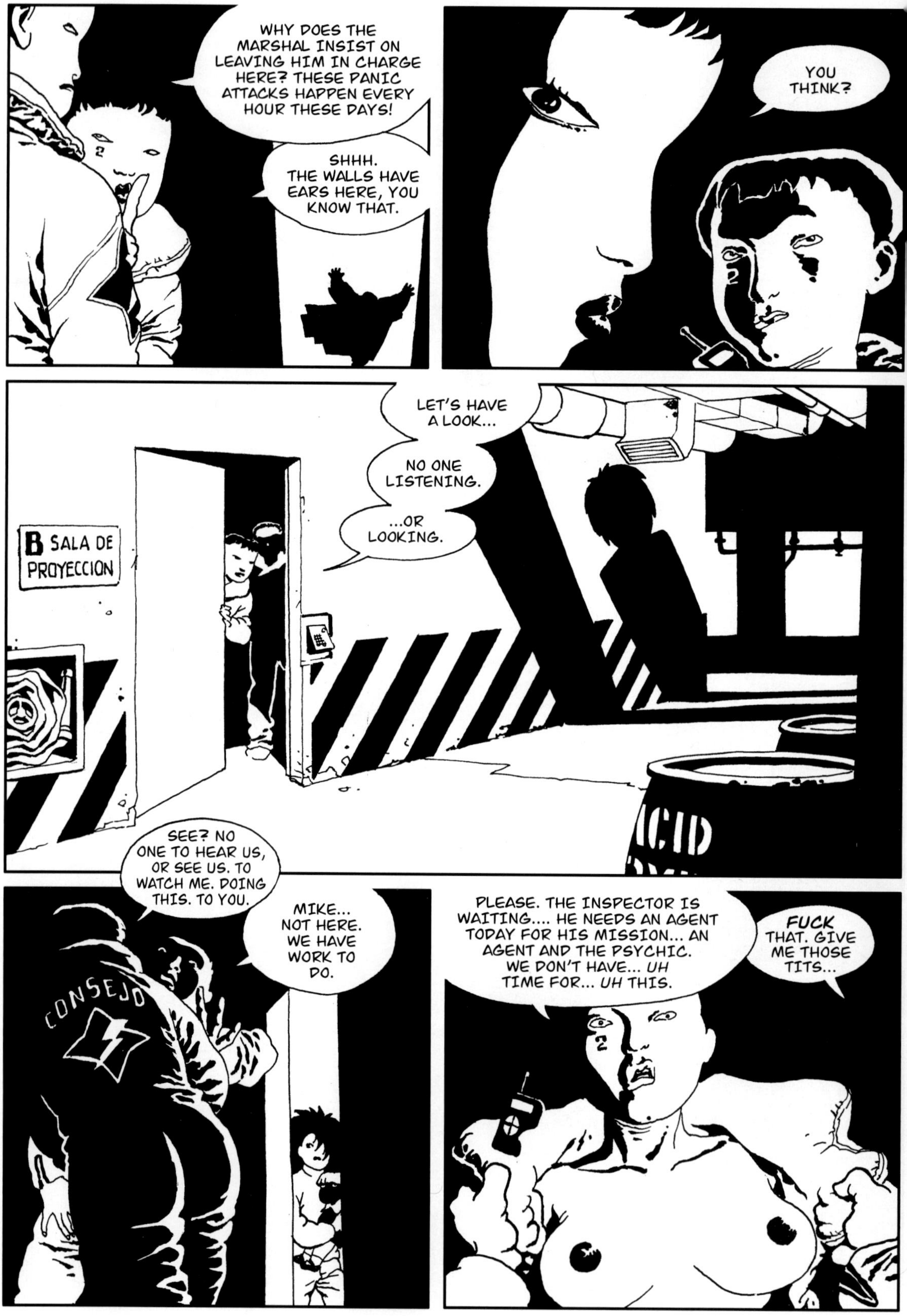
WHY DOES THE MARSHAL INSIST ON LEAVING HIM IN CHARGE HERE? THESE PANIC ATTACKS HAPPEN EVERY HOUR THESE DAYS!
SHHH. THE WALLS HAVE EARS HERE, YOU KNOW THAT.
YOU THINK?
LET'S HAVE A LOOK...
NO ONE LISTENING.
...OR LOOKING.
B SALA DE PROYECCION
ACID
SEE? NO ONE TO HEAR US, OR SEE US. TO WATCH ME. DOING THIS. TO YOU.
MIKE... NOT HERE. WE HAVE WORK TO DO.
CONSEJO
PLEASE. THE INSPECTOR IS WAITING.... HE NEEDS AN AGENT TODAY FOR HIS MISSION... AN AGENT AND THE PSYCHIC. WE DON'T HAVE... UH TIME FOR... UH THIS.
FUCK THAT. GIVE ME THOSE TITS...

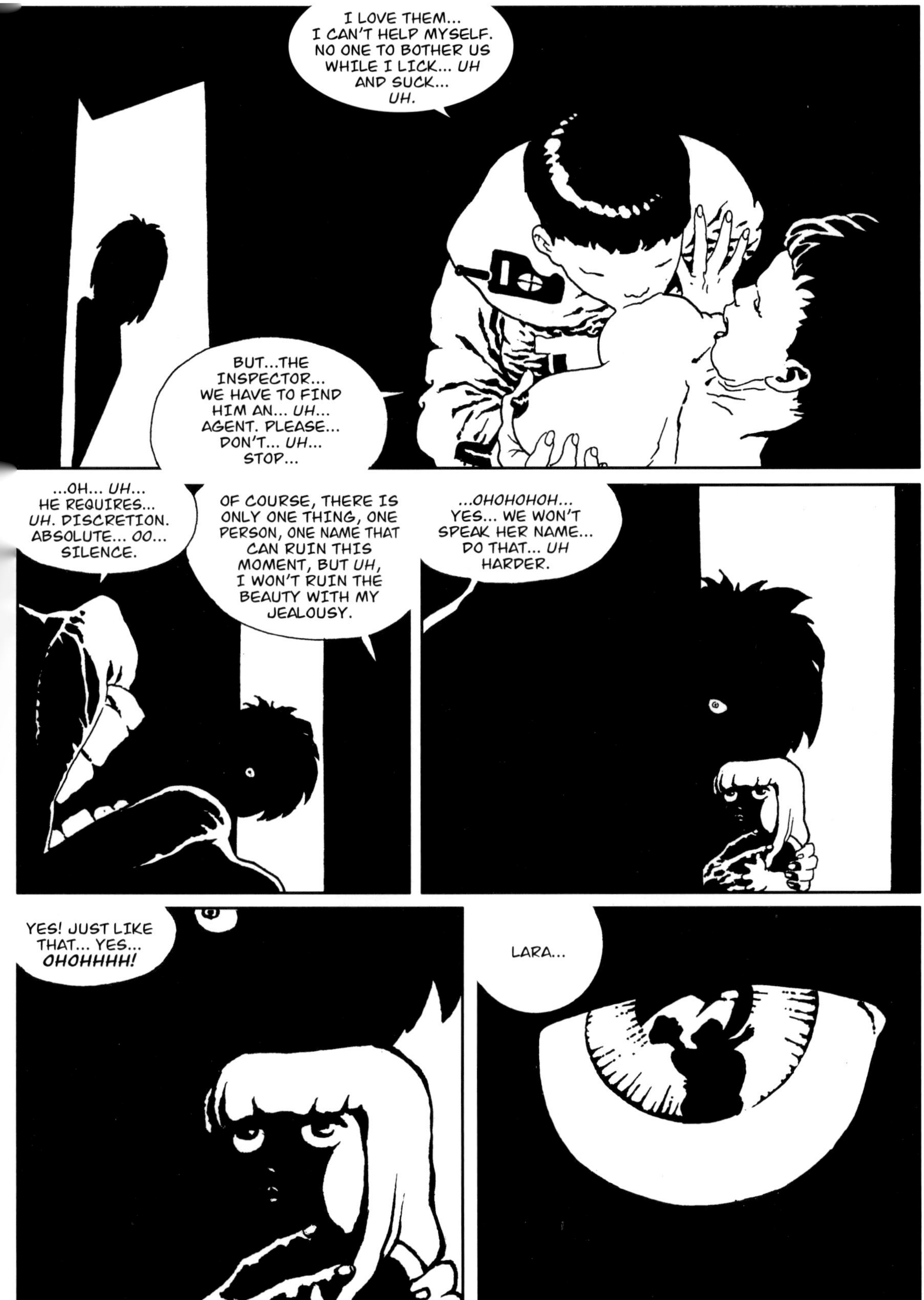
I LOVE THEM... I CAN'T HELP MYSELF. NO ONE TO BOTHER US WHILE I LICK... *UH* AND SUCK... *UH.*
BUT...THE INSPECTOR... WE HAVE TO FIND HIM AN... *UH*... AGENT. PLEASE... DON'T... *UH*... STOP...
...OH... *UH*... HE REQUIRES... *UH.* DISCRETION. ABSOLUTE... *OO*... SILENCE.
OF COURSE, THERE IS ONLY ONE THING, ONE PERSON, ONE NAME THAT CAN RUIN THIS MOMENT, BUT *UH*, I WON'T RUIN THE BEAUTY WITH MY JEALOUSY.
...*OHOHOHOH*... YES... WE WON'T SPEAK HER NAME... DO THAT... *UH* HARDER.
YES! JUST LIKE THAT... YES... ***OHOHHHH!***
LARA...

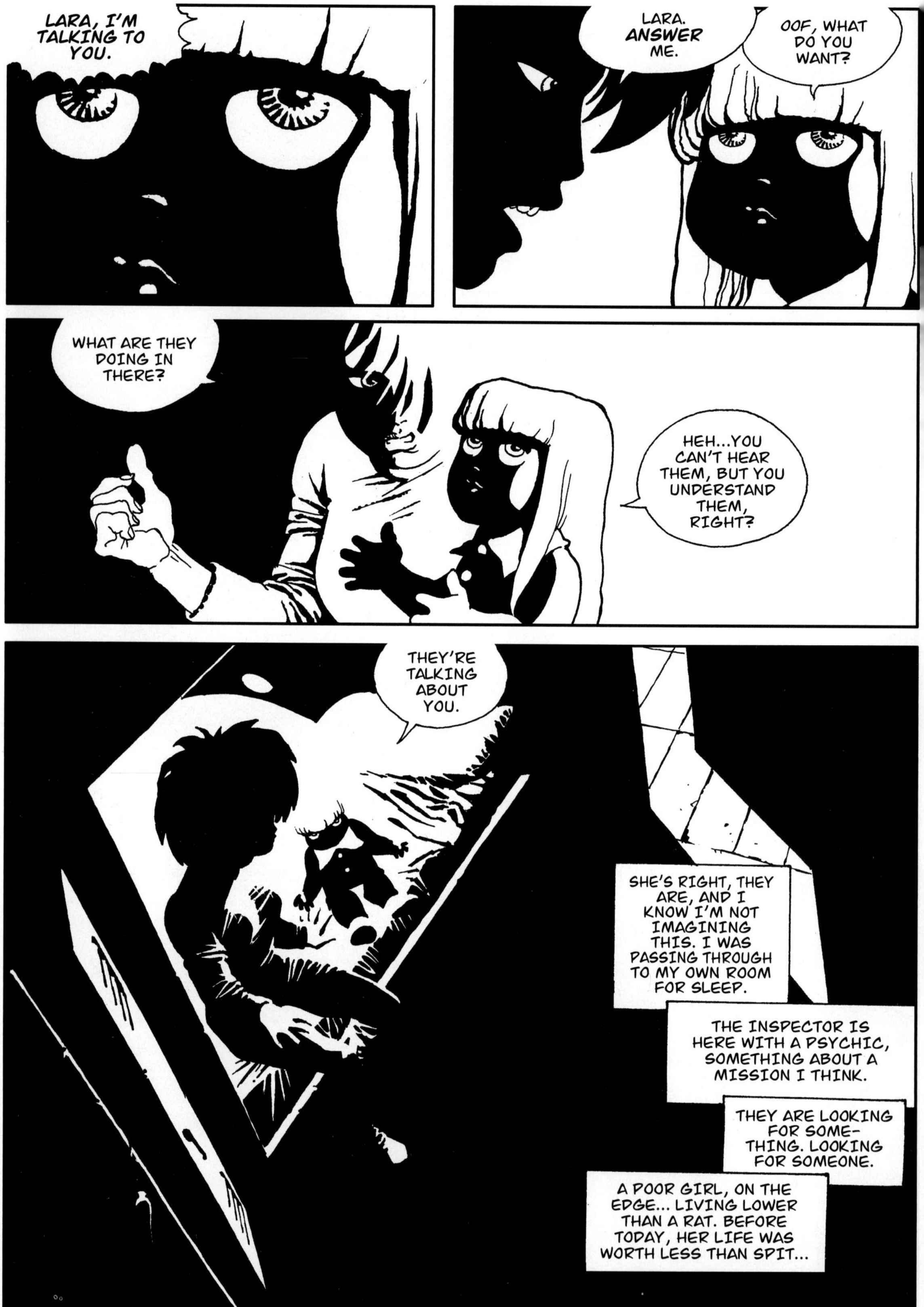
LARA, I'M TALKING TO YOU.
LARA. ANSWER ME.
OOF, WHAT DO YOU WANT?
WHAT ARE THEY DOING IN THERE?
HEH...YOU CAN'T HEAR THEM, BUT YOU UNDERSTAND THEM, RIGHT?
THEY'RE TALKING ABOUT YOU.
SHE'S RIGHT, THEY ARE, AND I KNOW I'M NOT IMAGINING THIS. I WAS PASSING THROUGH TO MY OWN ROOM FOR SLEEP.
THE INSPECTOR IS HERE WITH A PSYCHIC, SOMETHING ABOUT A MISSION I THINK.
THEY ARE LOOKING FOR SOME-THING. LOOKING FOR SOMEONE.
A POOR GIRL, ON THE EDGE... LIVING LOWER THAN A RAT. BEFORE TODAY, HER LIFE WAS WORTH LESS THAN SPIT...

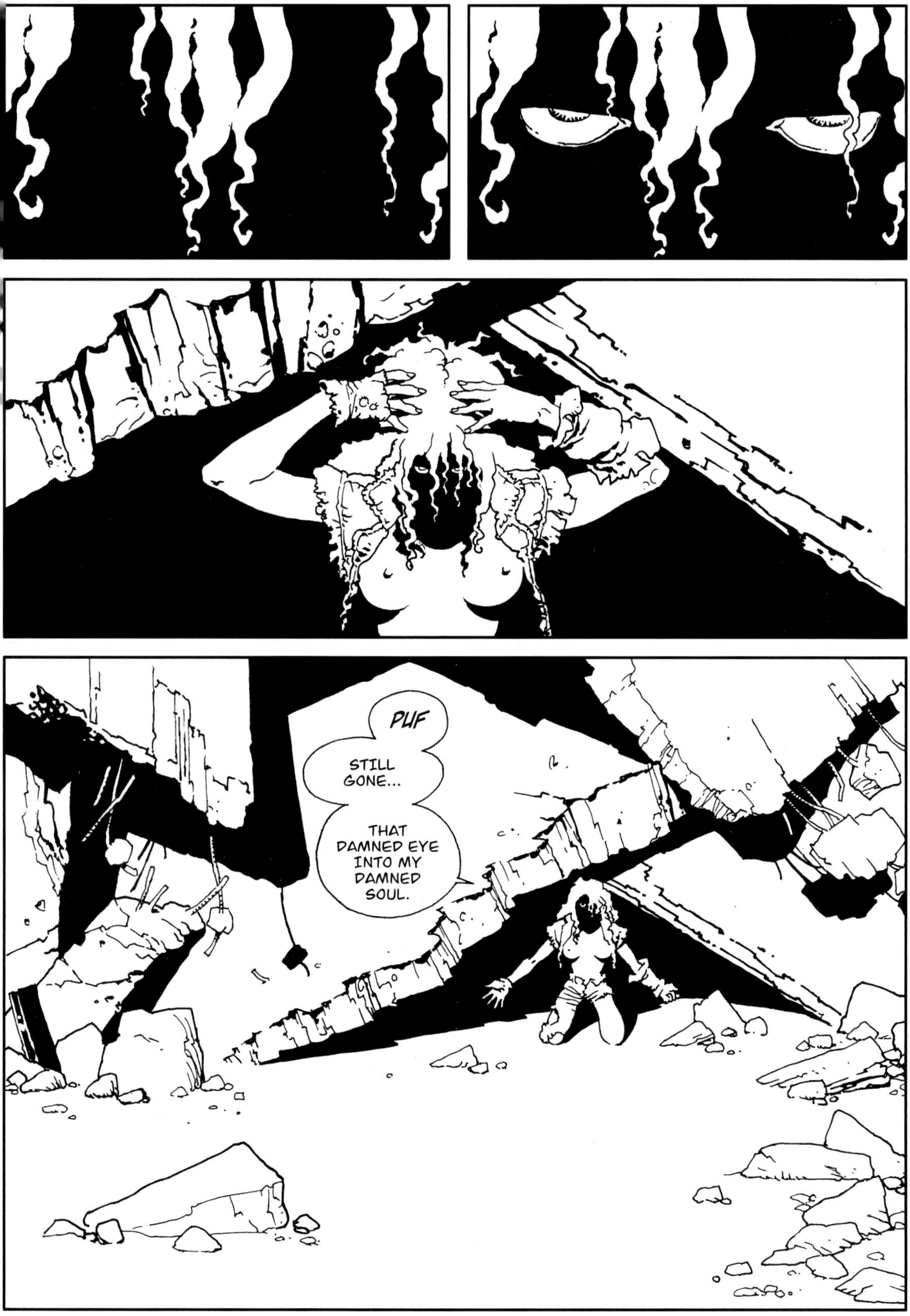
PUF
STILL GONE...
THAT DAMNED EYE INTO MY DAMNED SOUL.

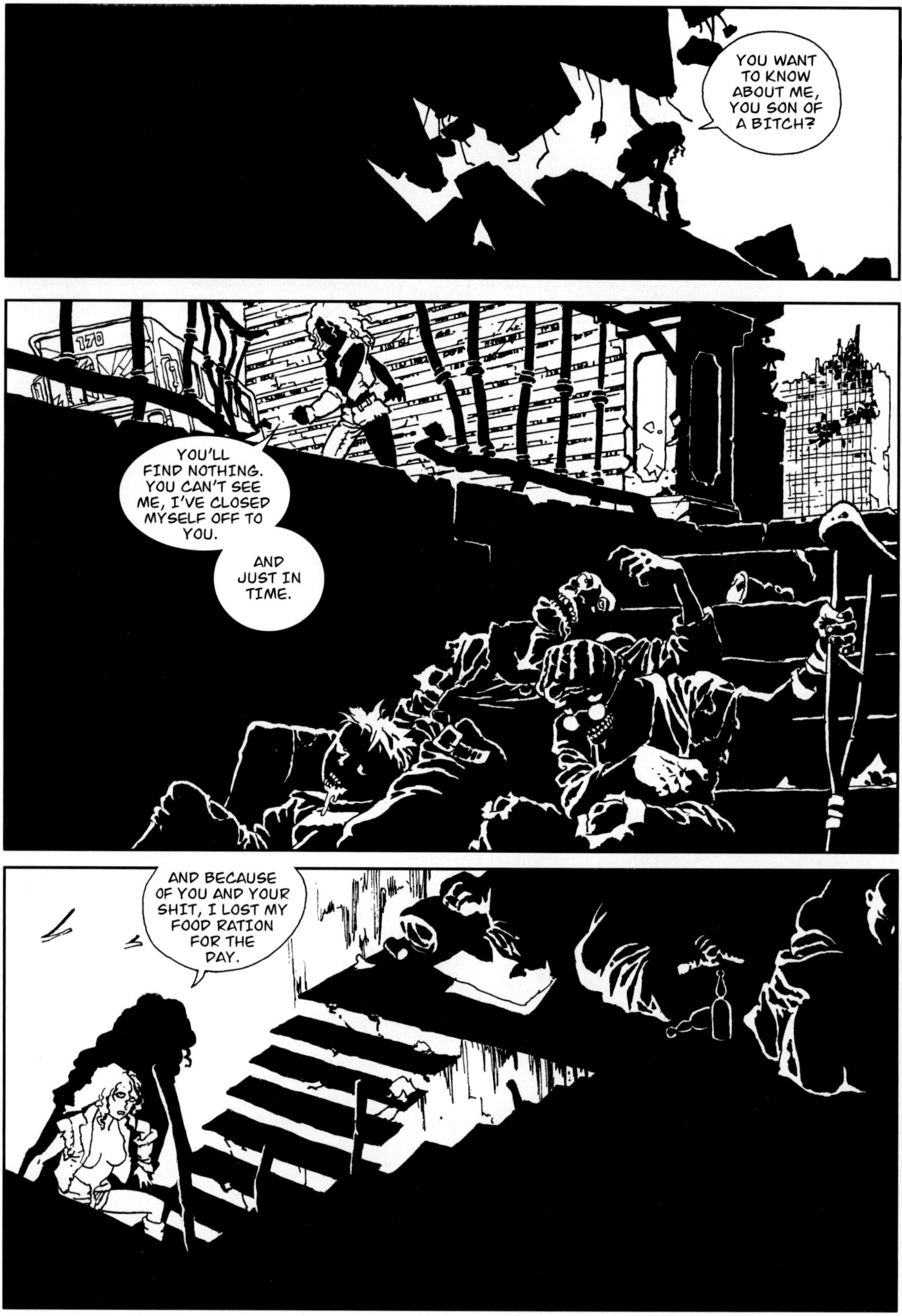

YOU WANT TO KNOW ABOUT ME, YOU SON OF A BITCH?
YOU'LL FIND NOTHING. YOU CAN'T SEE ME, I'VE CLOSED MYSELF OFF TO YOU.
AND JUST IN TIME.
AND BECAUSE OF YOU AND YOUR SHIT, I LOST MY FOOD RATION FOR THE DAY.

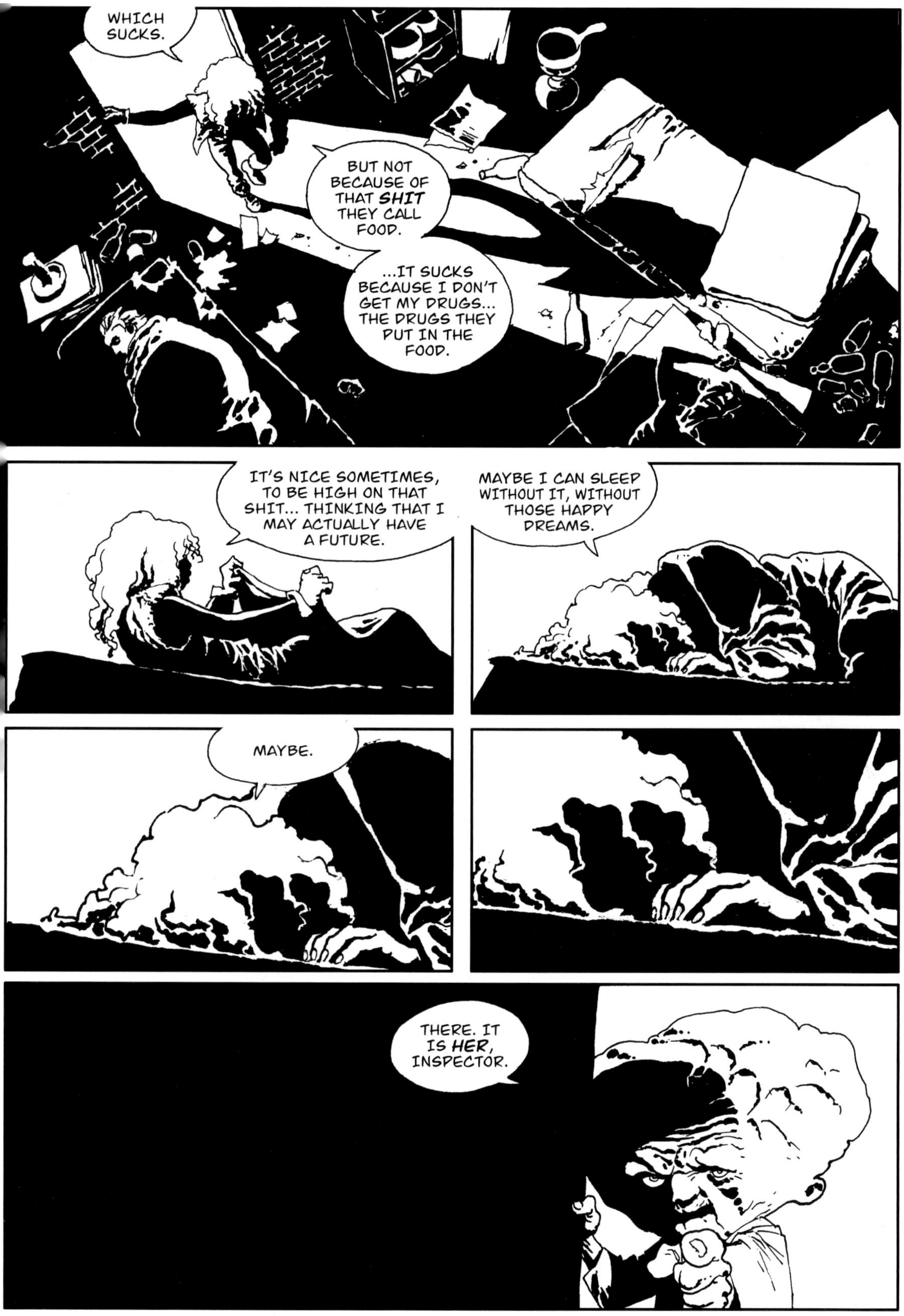
WHICH SUCKS.
BUT NOT BECAUSE OF THAT SHIT THEY CALL FOOD.
...IT SUCKS BECAUSE I DON'T GET MY DRUGS... THE DRUGS THEY PUT IN THE FOOD.
IT'S NICE SOMETIMES, TO BE HIGH ON THAT SHIT... THINKING THAT I MAY ACTUALLY HAVE A FUTURE.
MAYBE I CAN SLEEP WITHOUT IT, WITHOUT THOSE HAPPY DREAMS.
MAYBE.
THERE. IT IS HER, INSPECTOR.

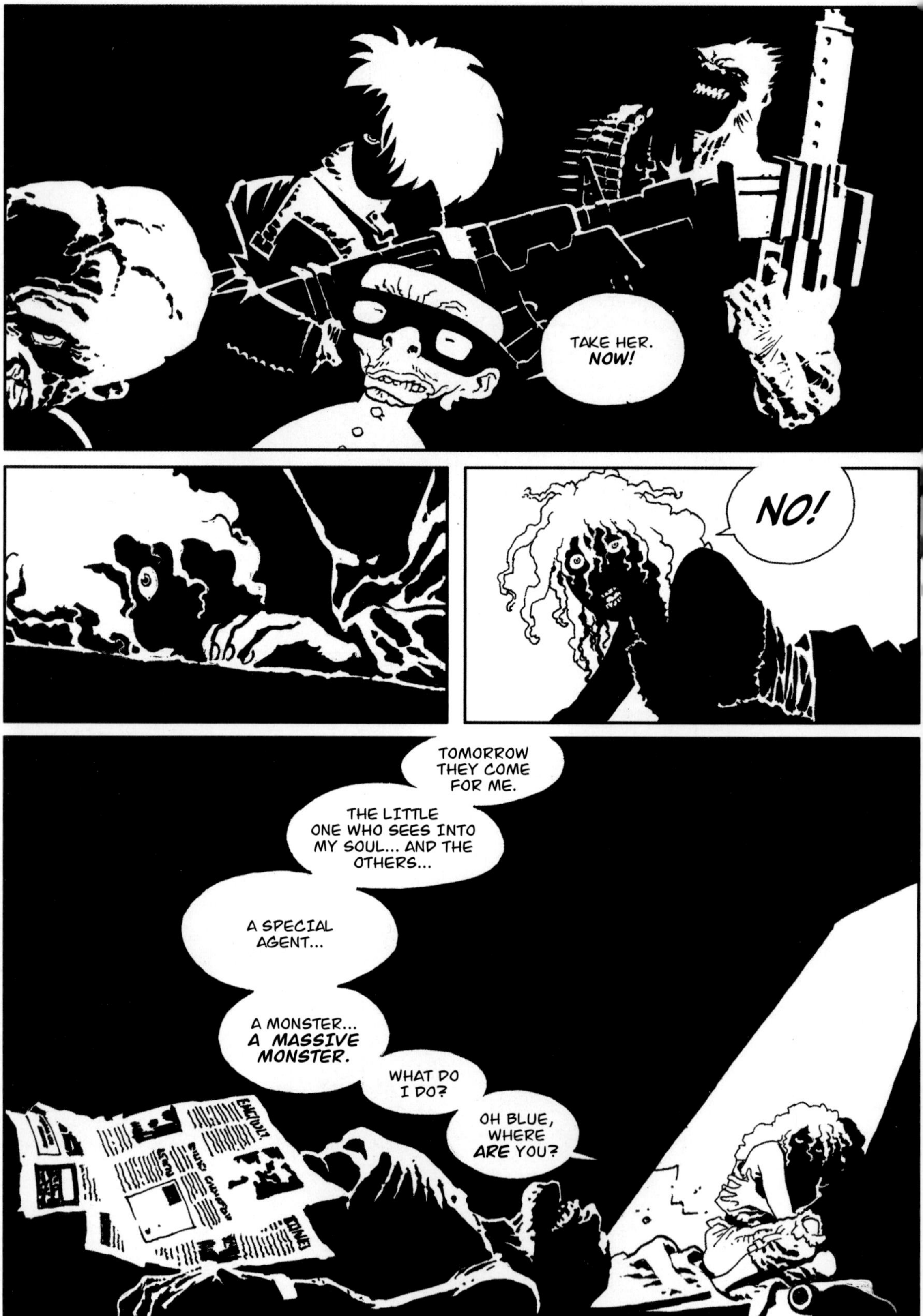
TAKE HER. *NOW!*
NO!
TOMORROW THEY COME FOR ME.
THE LITTLE ONE WHO SEES INTO MY SOUL... AND THE OTHERS...
A SPECIAL AGENT...
A MONSTER... *A MASSIVE MONSTER.*
WHAT DO I DO?
OH BLUE, WHERE *ARE* YOU?

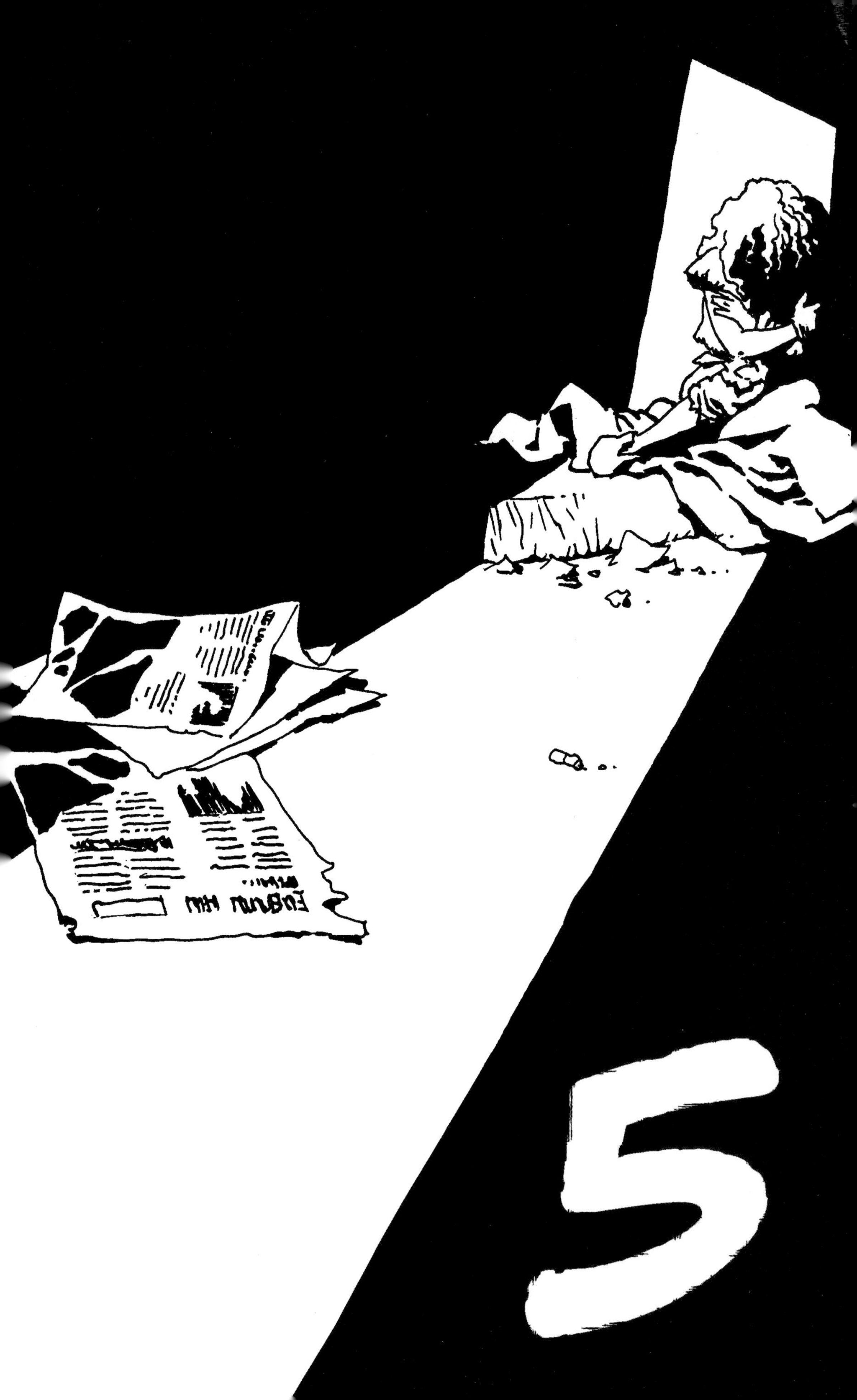
5

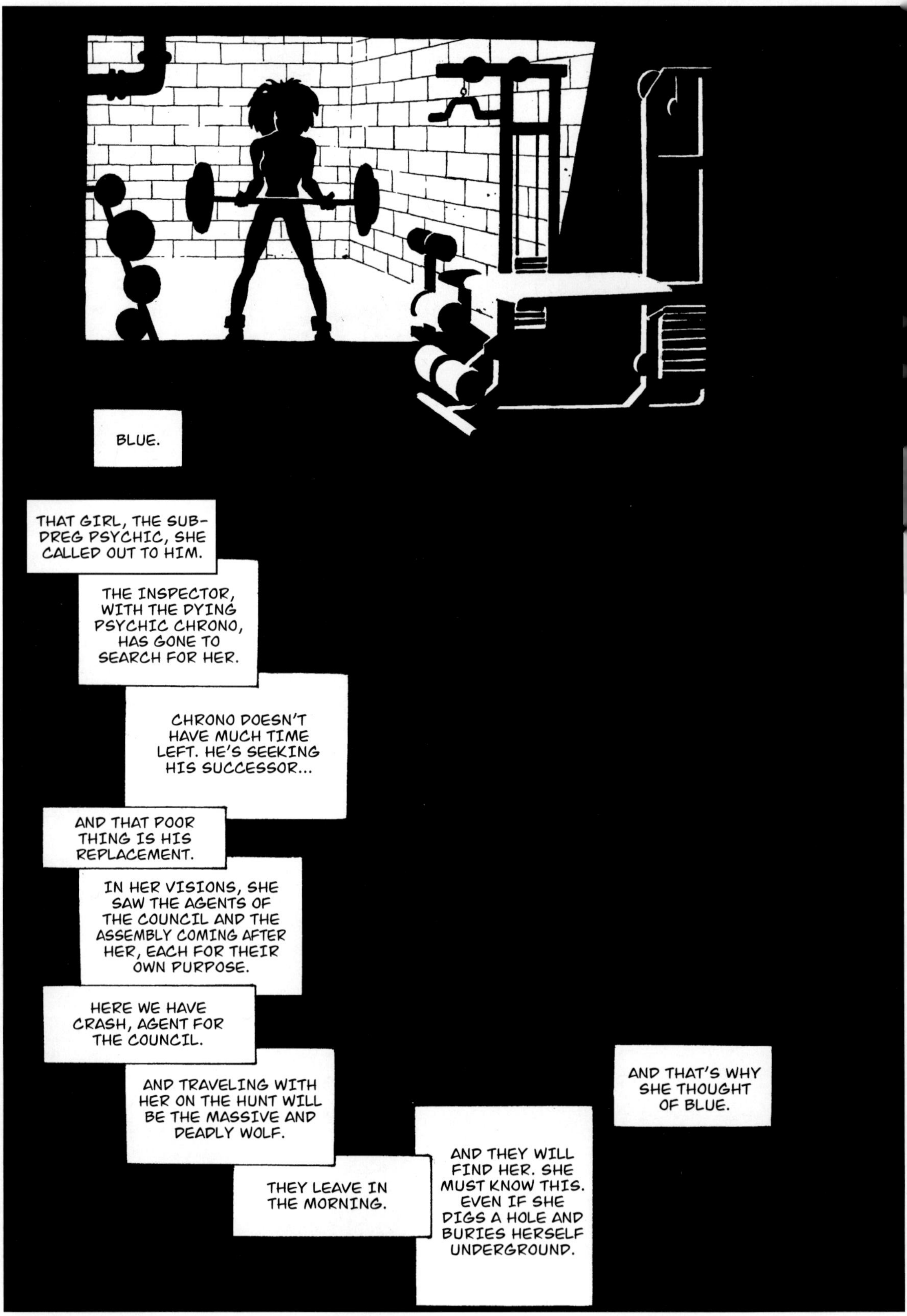

BLUE.
THAT GIRL, THE SUB-DREG PSYCHIC, SHE CALLED OUT TO HIM.
THE INSPECTOR, WITH THE DYING PSYCHIC CHRONO, HAS GONE TO SEARCH FOR HER.
CHRONO DOESN'T HAVE MUCH TIME LEFT. HE'S SEEKING HIS SUCCESSOR...
AND THAT POOR THING IS HIS REPLACEMENT.
IN HER VISIONS, SHE SAW THE AGENTS OF THE COUNCIL AND THE ASSEMBLY COMING AFTER HER, EACH FOR THEIR OWN PURPOSE.
HERE WE HAVE CRASH, AGENT FOR THE COUNCIL.
AND TRAVELING WITH HER ON THE HUNT WILL BE THE MASSIVE AND DEADLY WOLF.
THEY LEAVE IN THE MORNING.
AND THEY WILL FIND HER. SHE MUST KNOW THIS. EVEN IF SHE DIGS A HOLE AND BURIES HERSELF UNDERGROUND.
AND THAT'S WHY SHE THOUGHT OF BLUE.

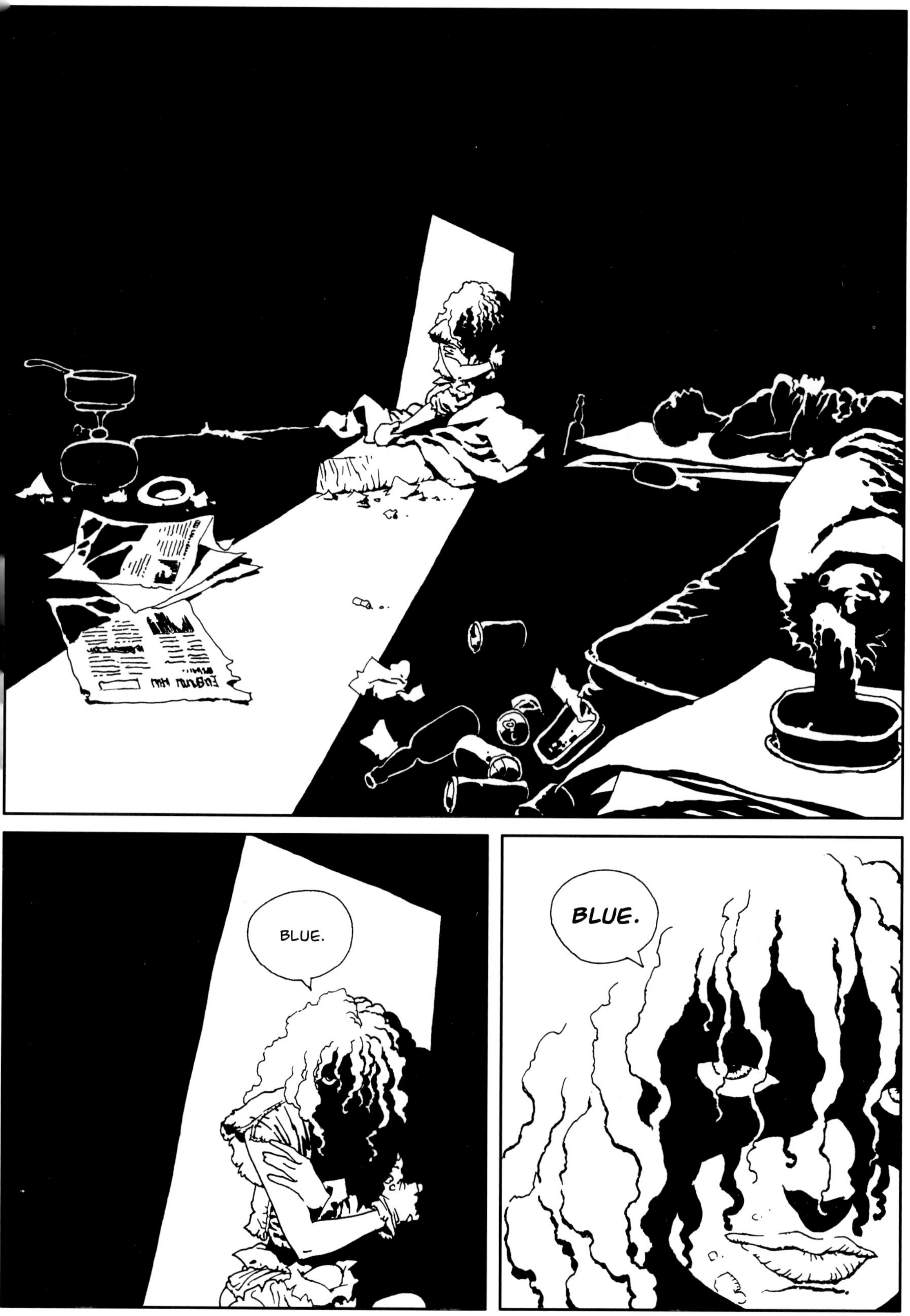
BLUE.
BLUE.

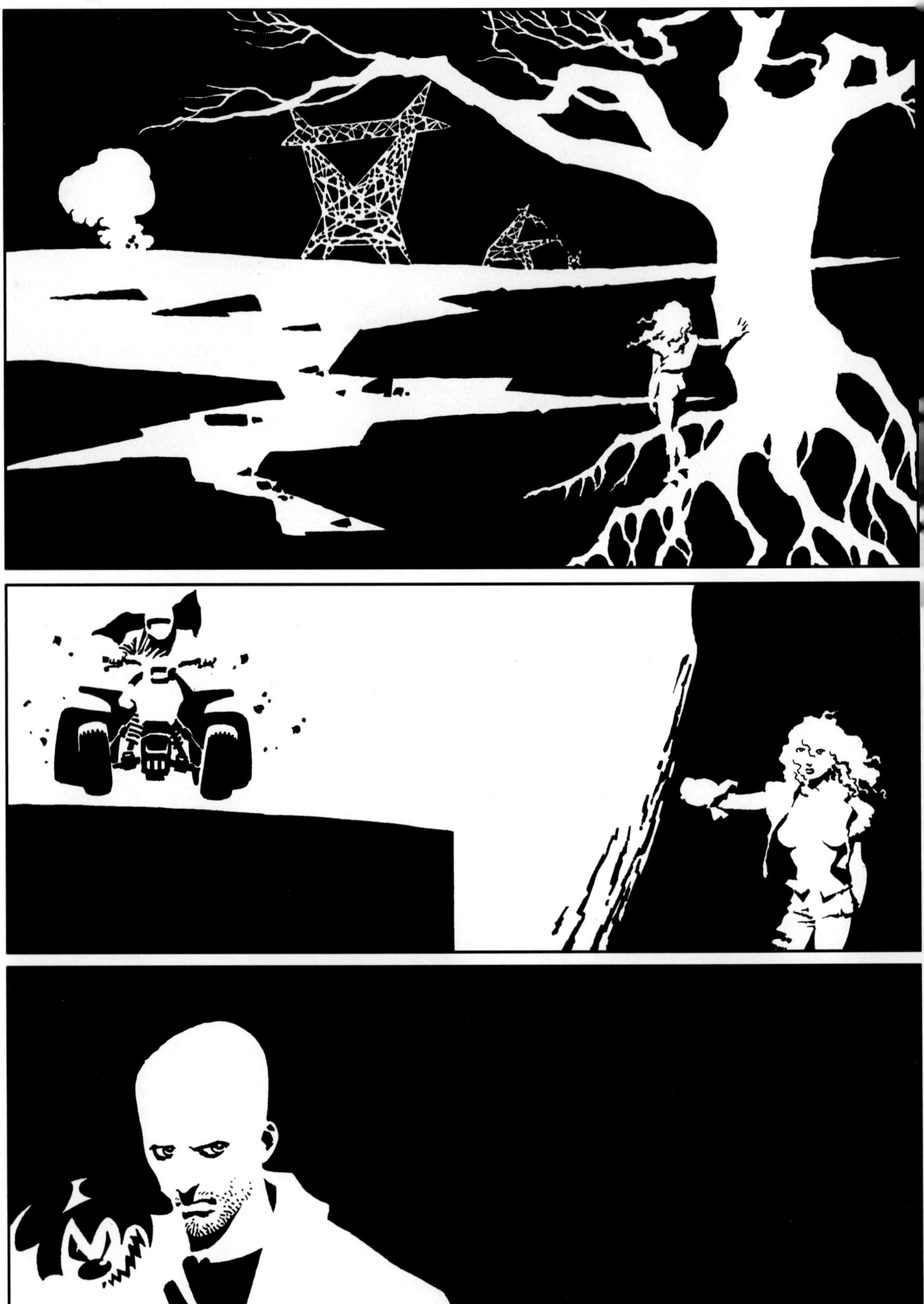

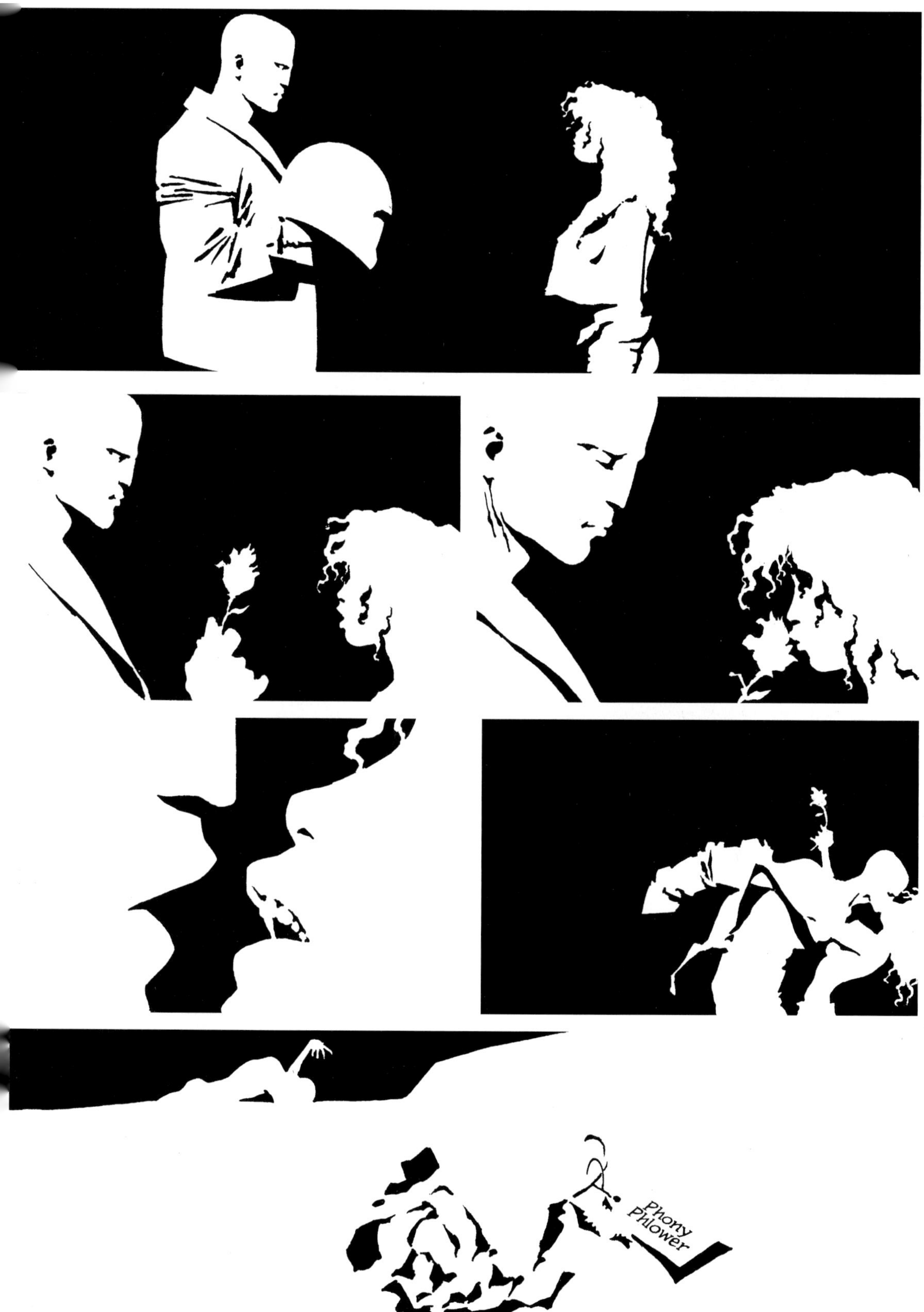
Phony Phlower

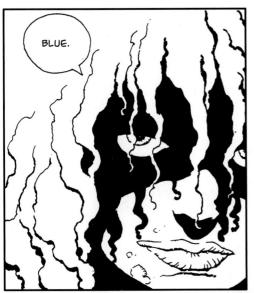

BLUE.

HOW CAN SOMEONE LIKE YOU, MAKE LOVE TO SOMEONE LIKE ME?

EVEN WITH ALL THE WORDS AND THOUGHTS WE EACH SAID TO EACH OTHER.

AND HE TOLD ME ALL ABOUT HIS PAST... HOW SAD.

ADDICTED TO THE DRUG ILLUSION, SELLING HIS GIRL'S ORGANS IN ORDER TO **FEED** THAT ADDICTION...

SHE WAS NOT LIKE ME, SHE WASN'T A SUB-DREG. THAT'S WHY SHE DID WELL ON THE ORGAN MARKET.

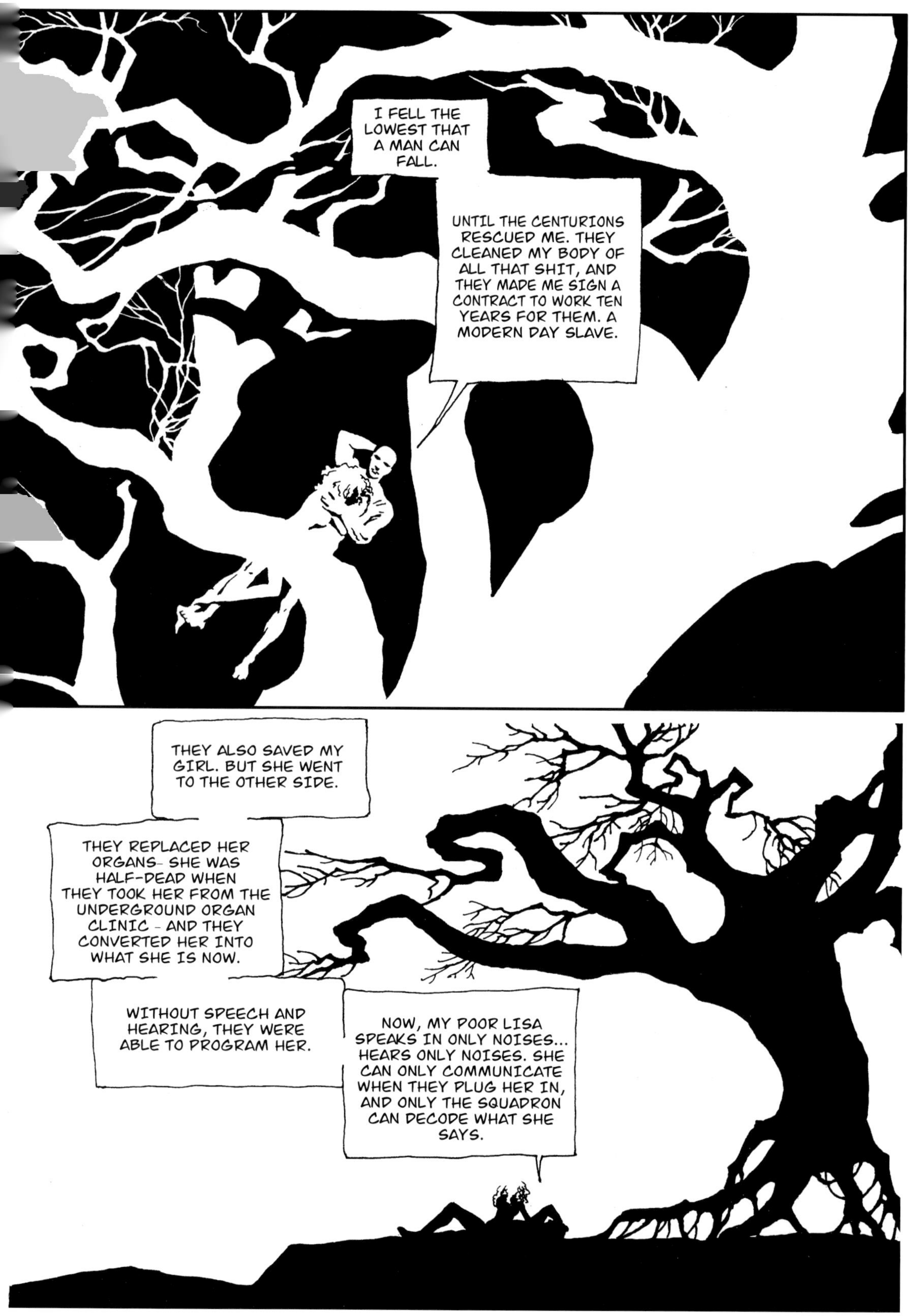
I FELL THE LOWEST THAT A MAN CAN FALL.
UNTIL THE CENTURIONS RESCUED ME. THEY CLEANED MY BODY OF ALL THAT SHIT, AND THEY MADE ME SIGN A CONTRACT TO WORK TEN YEARS FOR THEM. A MODERN DAY SLAVE.
THEY ALSO SAVED MY GIRL. BUT SHE WENT TO THE OTHER SIDE.
THEY REPLACED HER ORGANS- SHE WAS HALF-DEAD WHEN THEY TOOK HER FROM THE UNDERGROUND ORGAN CLINIC - AND THEY CONVERTED HER INTO WHAT SHE IS NOW.
WITHOUT SPEECH AND HEARING, THEY WERE ABLE TO PROGRAM HER.
NOW, MY POOR LISA SPEAKS IN ONLY NOISES... HEARS ONLY NOISES. SHE CAN ONLY COMMUNICATE WHEN THEY PLUG HER IN, AND ONLY THE SQUADRON CAN DECODE WHAT SHE SAYS.

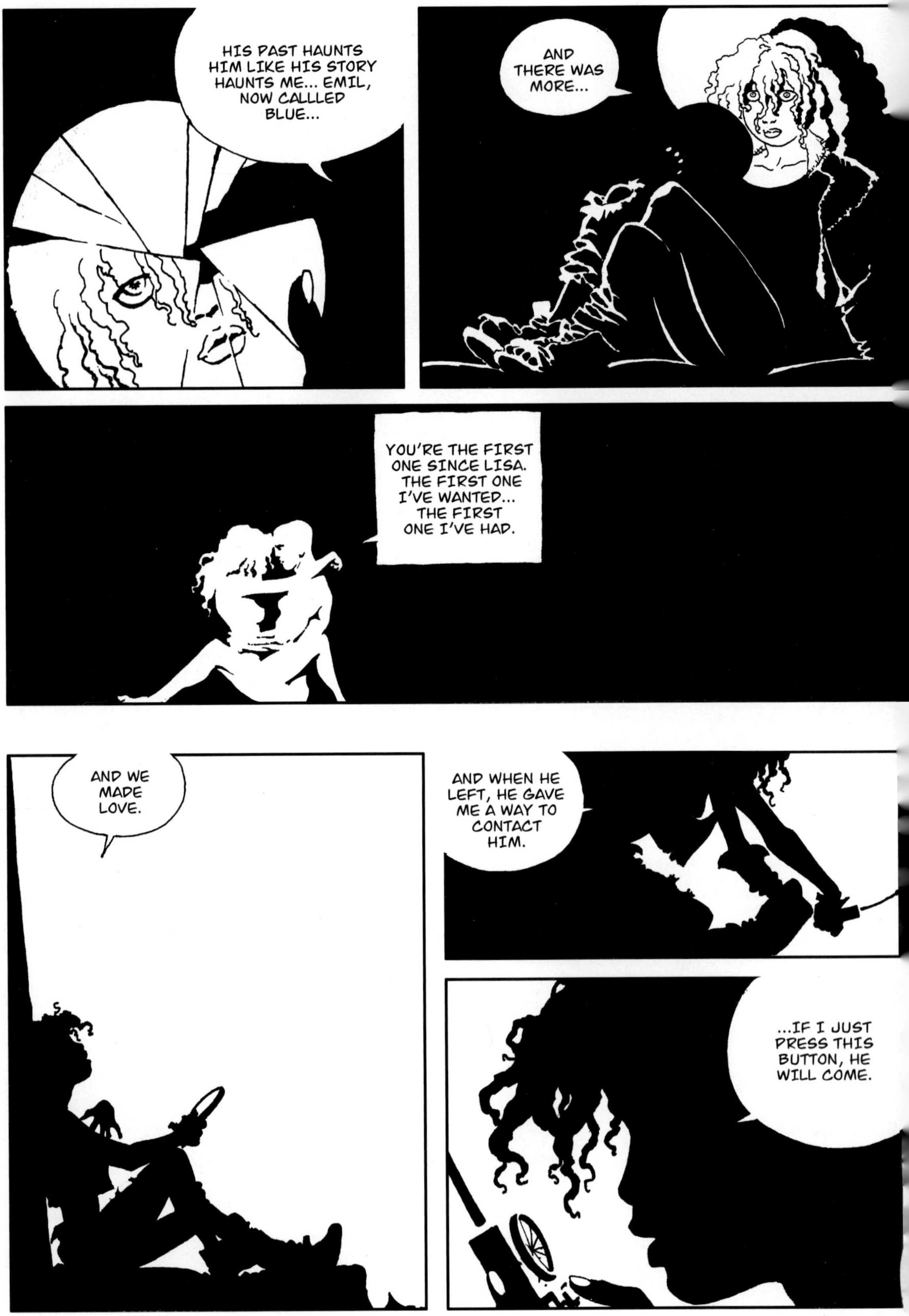
HIS PAST HAUNTS HIM LIKE HIS STORY HAUNTS ME... EMIL, NOW CALLLED BLUE...
AND THERE WAS MORE...
YOU'RE THE FIRST ONE SINCE LISA. THE FIRST ONE I'VE WANTED... THE FIRST ONE I'VE HAD.
AND WE MADE LOVE.
AND WHEN HE LEFT, HE GAVE ME A WAY TO CONTACT HIM.
...IF I JUST PRESS THIS BUTTON, HE WILL COME.

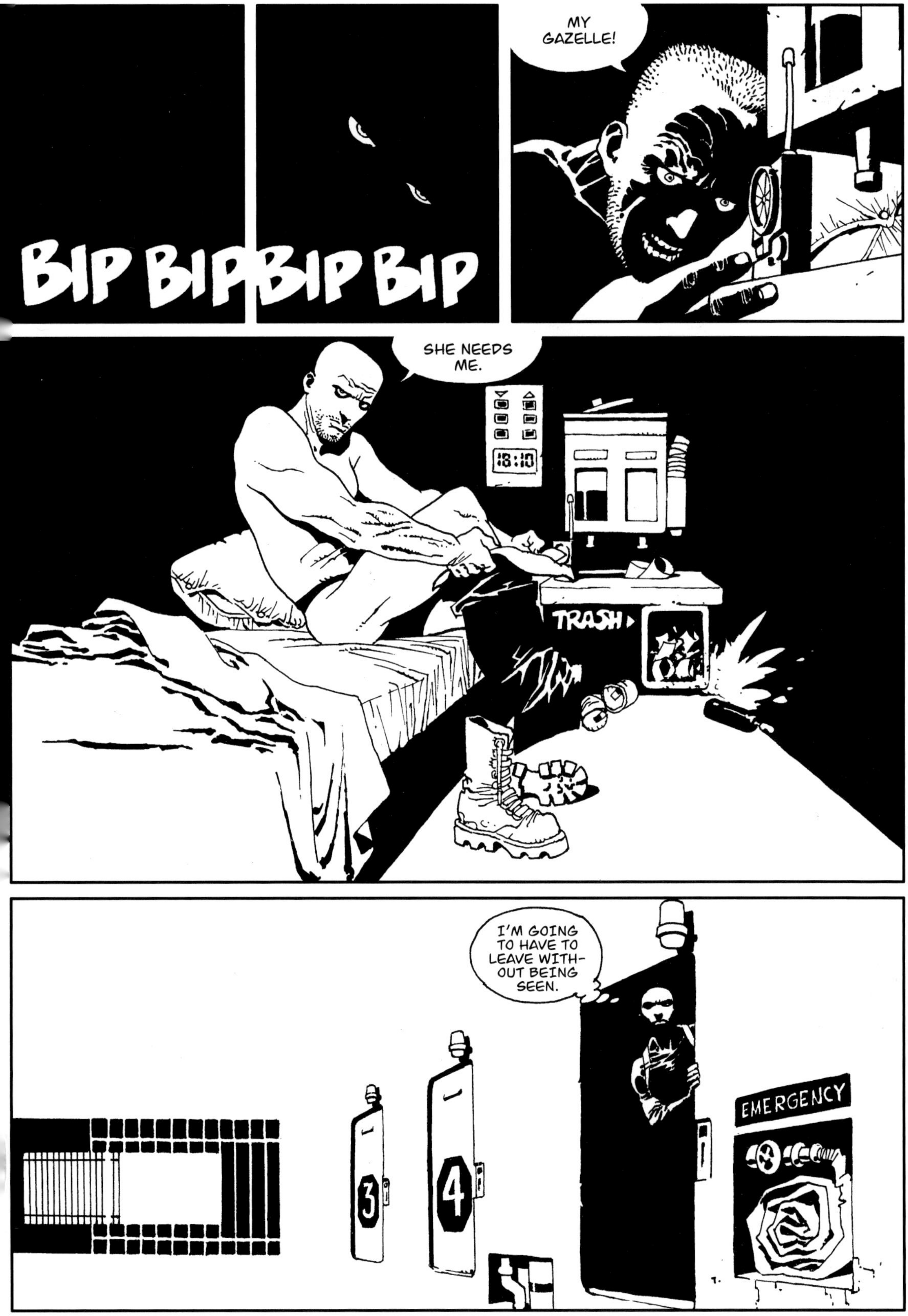
BIP BIP BIP BIP
MY GAZELLE!
SHE NEEDS ME.
18:10
TRASH
I'M GOING TO HAVE TO LEAVE WITH-OUT BEING SEEN.
3
4
EMERGENCY

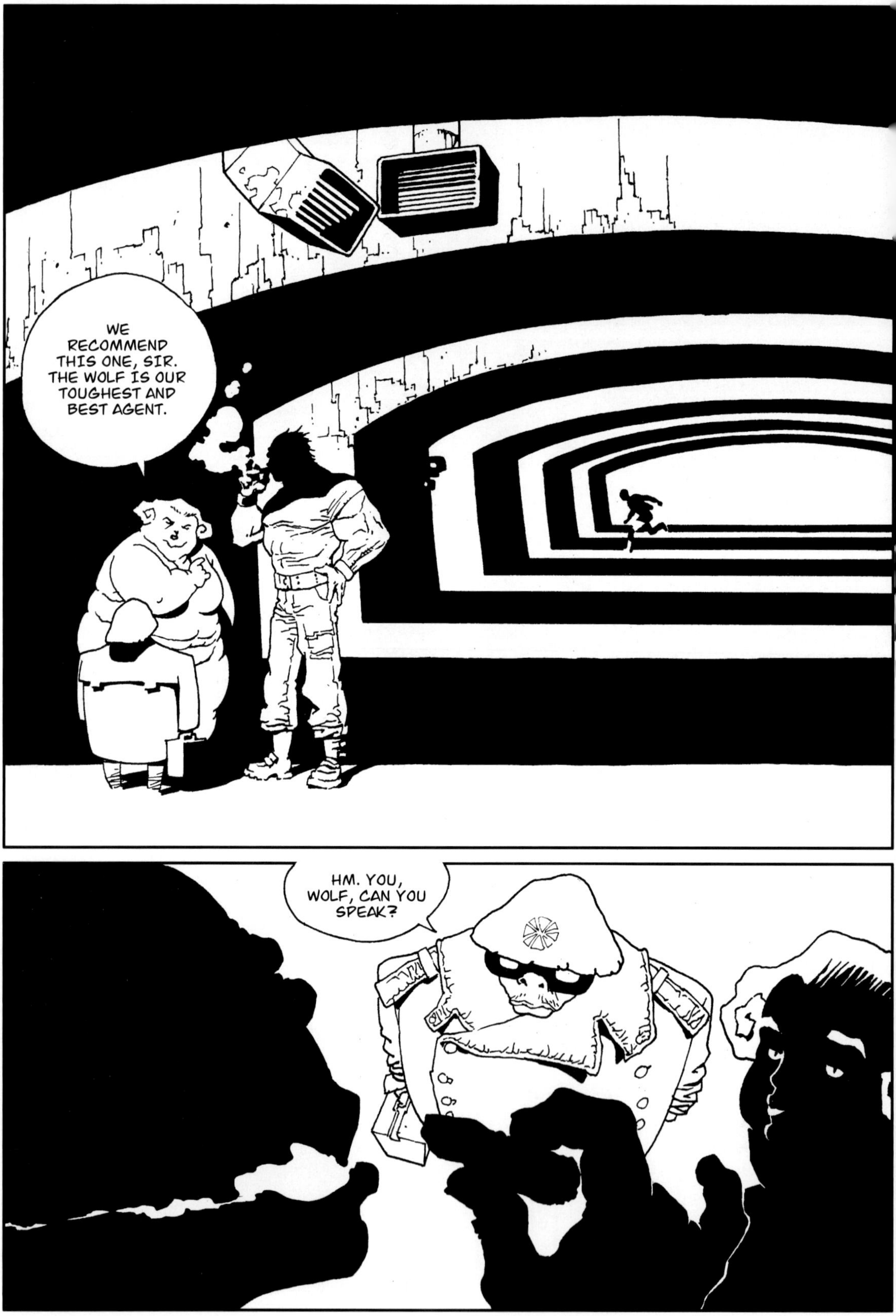
WE RECOMMEND THIS ONE, SIR. THE WOLF IS OUR TOUGHEST AND BEST AGENT.
HM. YOU, WOLF, CAN YOU SPEAK?

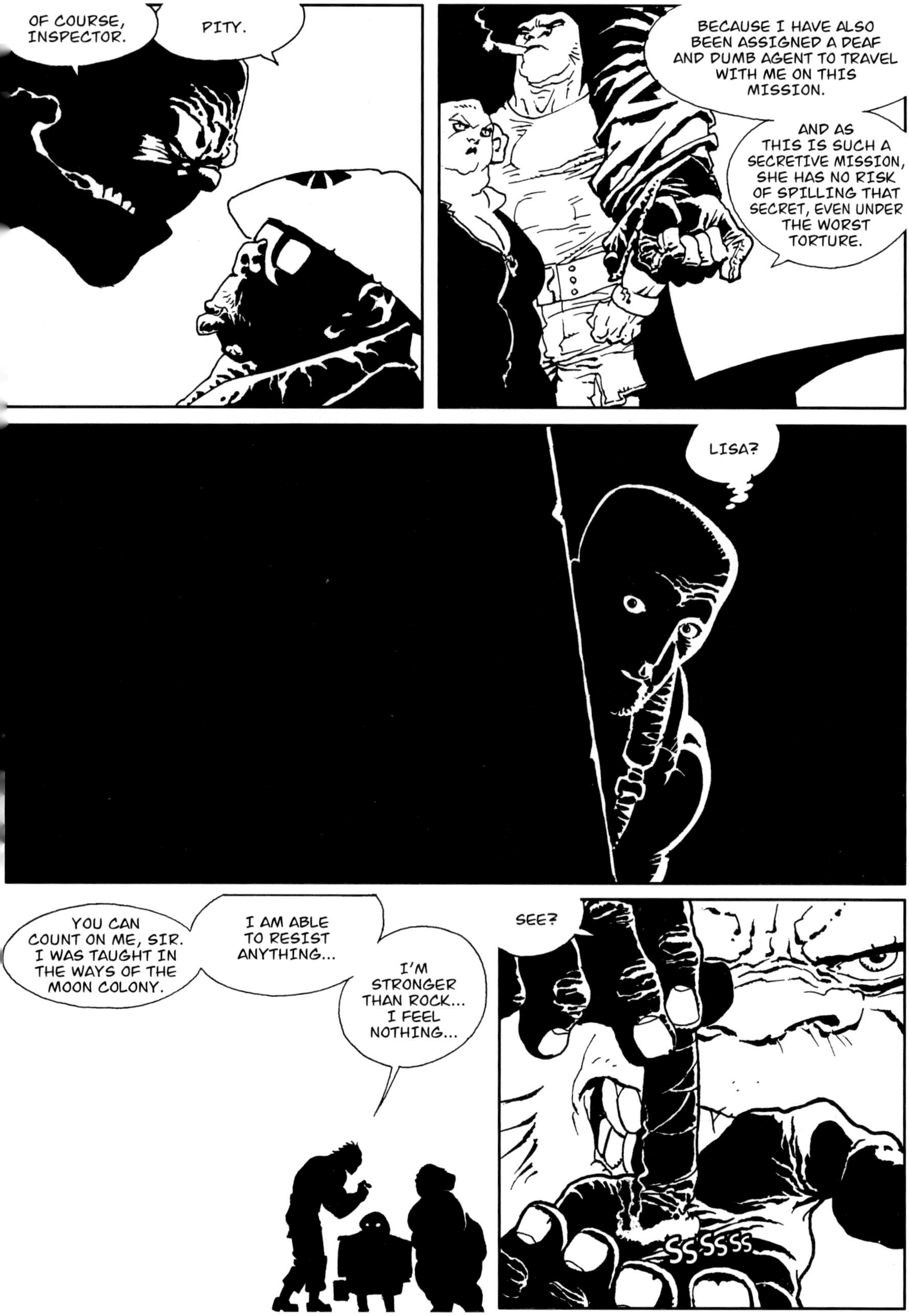
OF COURSE, INSPECTOR.
PITY.
BECAUSE I HAVE ALSO BEEN ASSIGNED A DEAF AND DUMB AGENT TO TRAVEL WITH ME ON THIS MISSION.
AND AS THIS IS SUCH A SECRETIVE MISSION, SHE HAS NO RISK OF SPILLING THAT SECRET, EVEN UNDER THE WORST TORTURE.
LISA?
YOU CAN COUNT ON ME, SIR. I WAS TAUGHT IN THE WAYS OF THE MOON COLONY.
I AM ABLE TO RESIST ANYTHING...
I'M STRONGER THAN ROCK... I FEEL NOTHING...
SEE?
SSSSSS

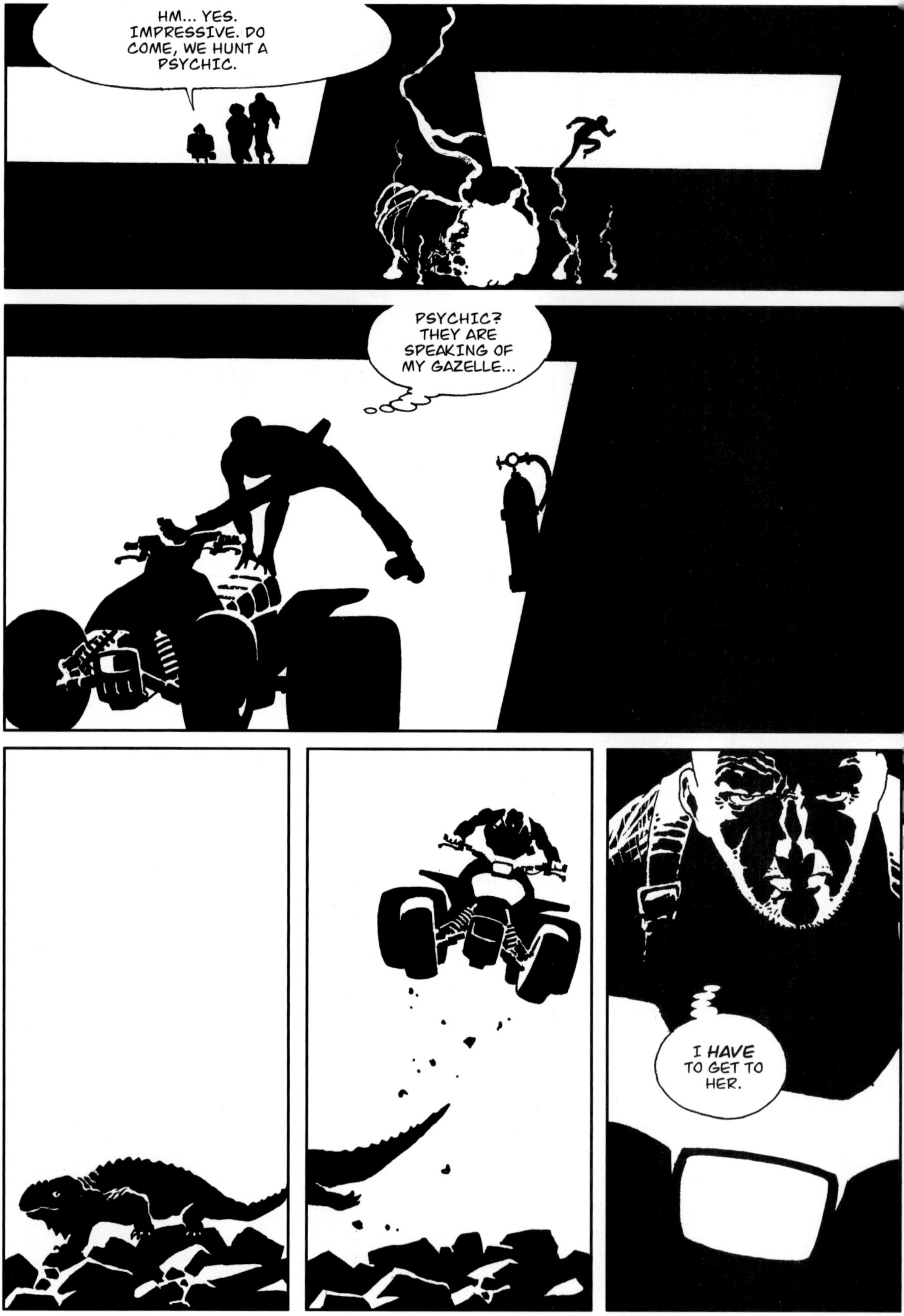
HM... YES. IMPRESSIVE. DO COME, WE HUNT A PSYCHIC.
PSYCHIC? THEY ARE SPEAKING OF MY GAZELLE...
I HAVE TO GET TO HER.

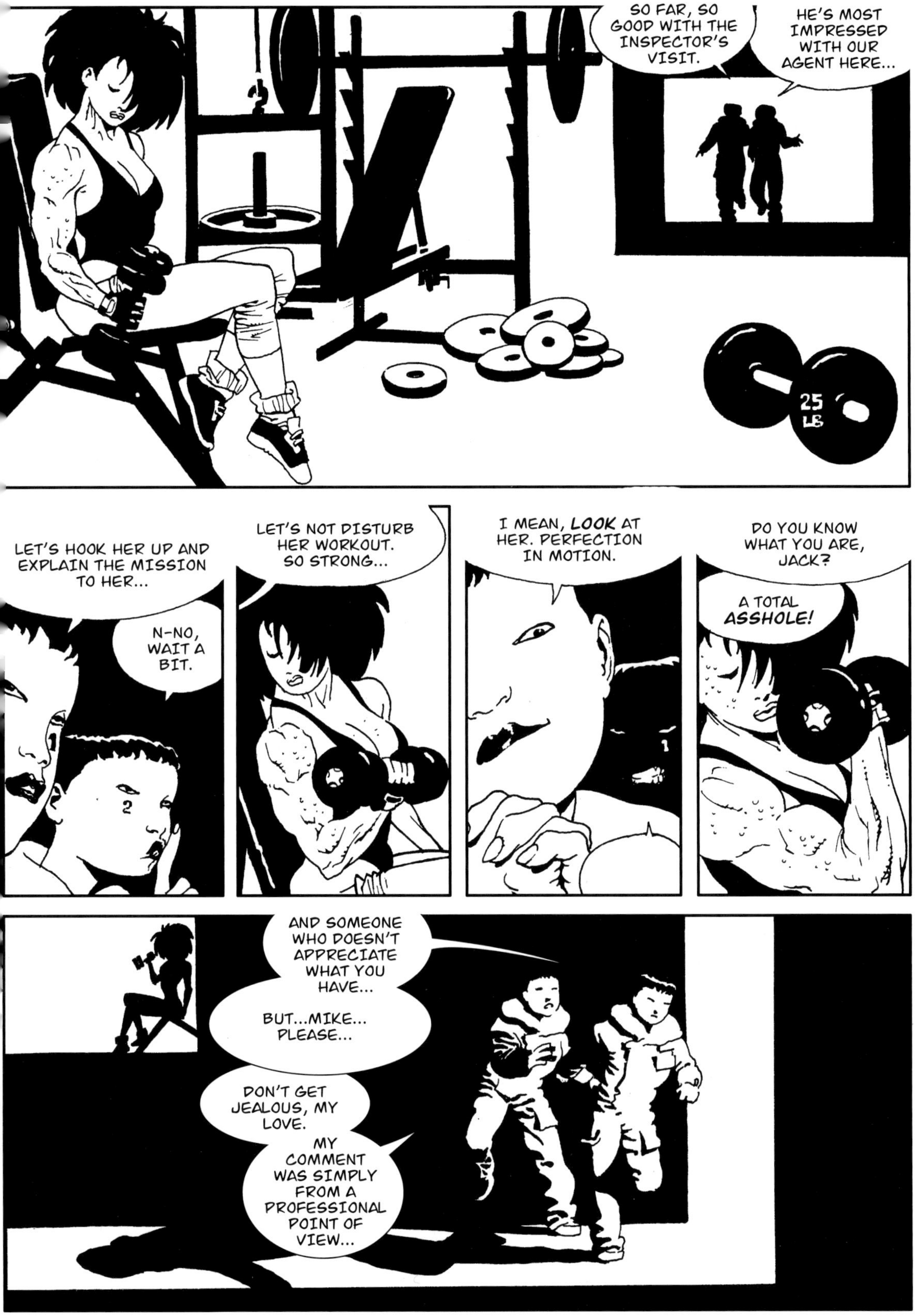
SO FAR, SO GOOD WITH THE INSPECTOR'S VISIT.
HE'S MOST IMPRESSED WITH OUR AGENT HERE...
25 LB
LET'S HOOK HER UP AND EXPLAIN THE MISSION TO HER...
N-NO, WAIT A BIT.
LET'S NOT DISTURB HER WORKOUT. SO STRONG...
I MEAN, LOOK AT HER. PERFECTION IN MOTION.
DO YOU KNOW WHAT YOU ARE, JACK?
A TOTAL ASSHOLE!
AND SOMEONE WHO DOESN'T APPRECIATE WHAT YOU HAVE...
BUT...MIKE... PLEASE...
DON'T GET JEALOUS, MY LOVE.
MY COMMENT WAS SIMPLY FROM A PROFESSIONAL POINT OF VIEW...

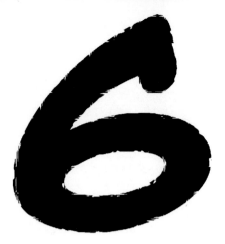

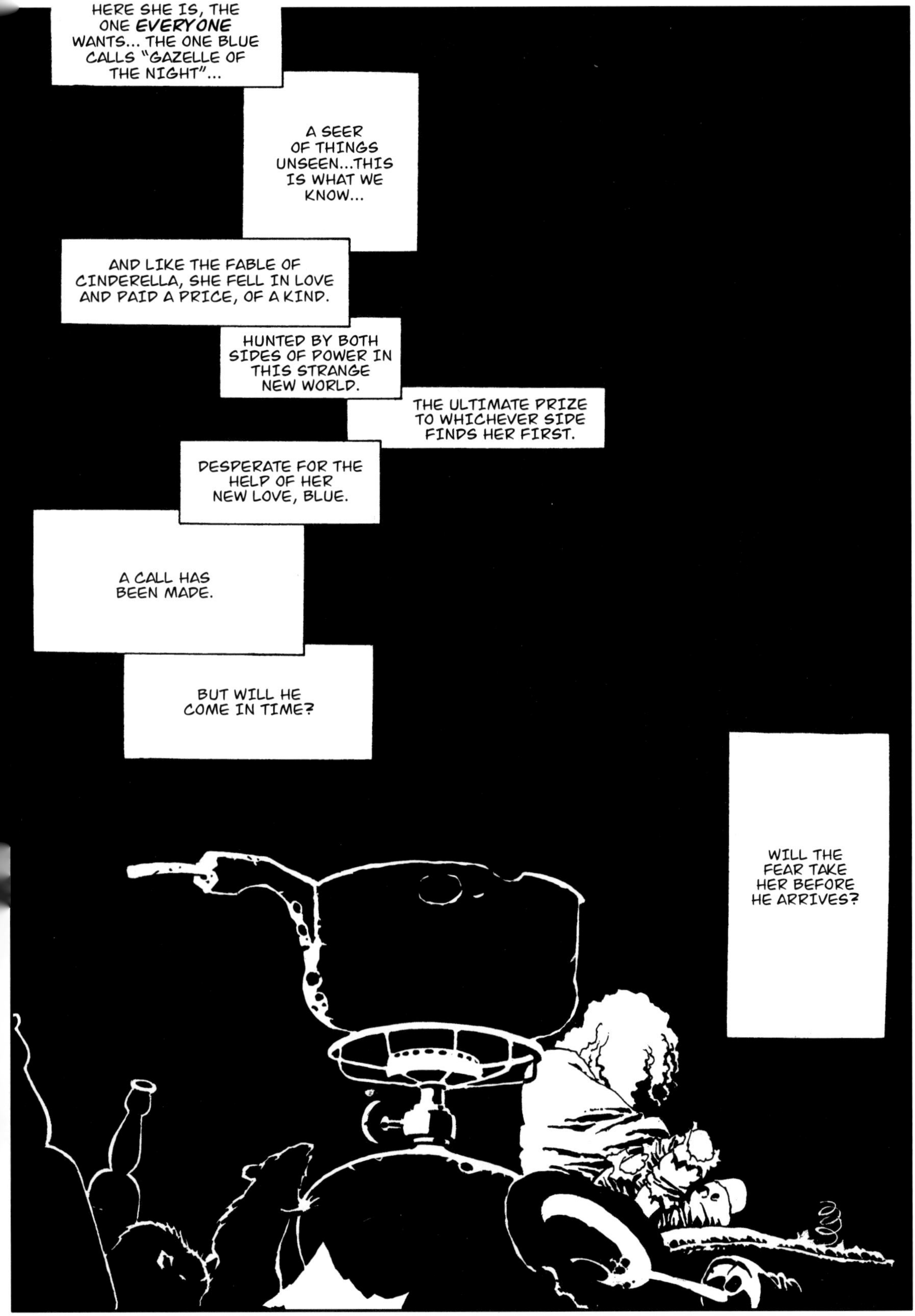
HERE SHE IS, THE ONE **EVERYONE** WANTS... THE ONE BLUE CALLS "GAZELLE OF THE NIGHT"...
A SEER OF THINGS UNSEEN...THIS IS WHAT WE KNOW...
AND LIKE THE FABLE OF CINDERELLA, SHE FELL IN LOVE AND PAID A PRICE, OF A KIND.
HUNTED BY BOTH SIDES OF POWER IN THIS STRANGE NEW WORLD.
THE ULTIMATE PRIZE TO WHICHEVER SIDE FINDS HER FIRST.
DESPERATE FOR THE HELP OF HER NEW LOVE, BLUE.
A CALL HAS BEEN MADE.
BUT WILL HE COME IN TIME?
WILL THE FEAR TAKE HER BEFORE HE ARRIVES?

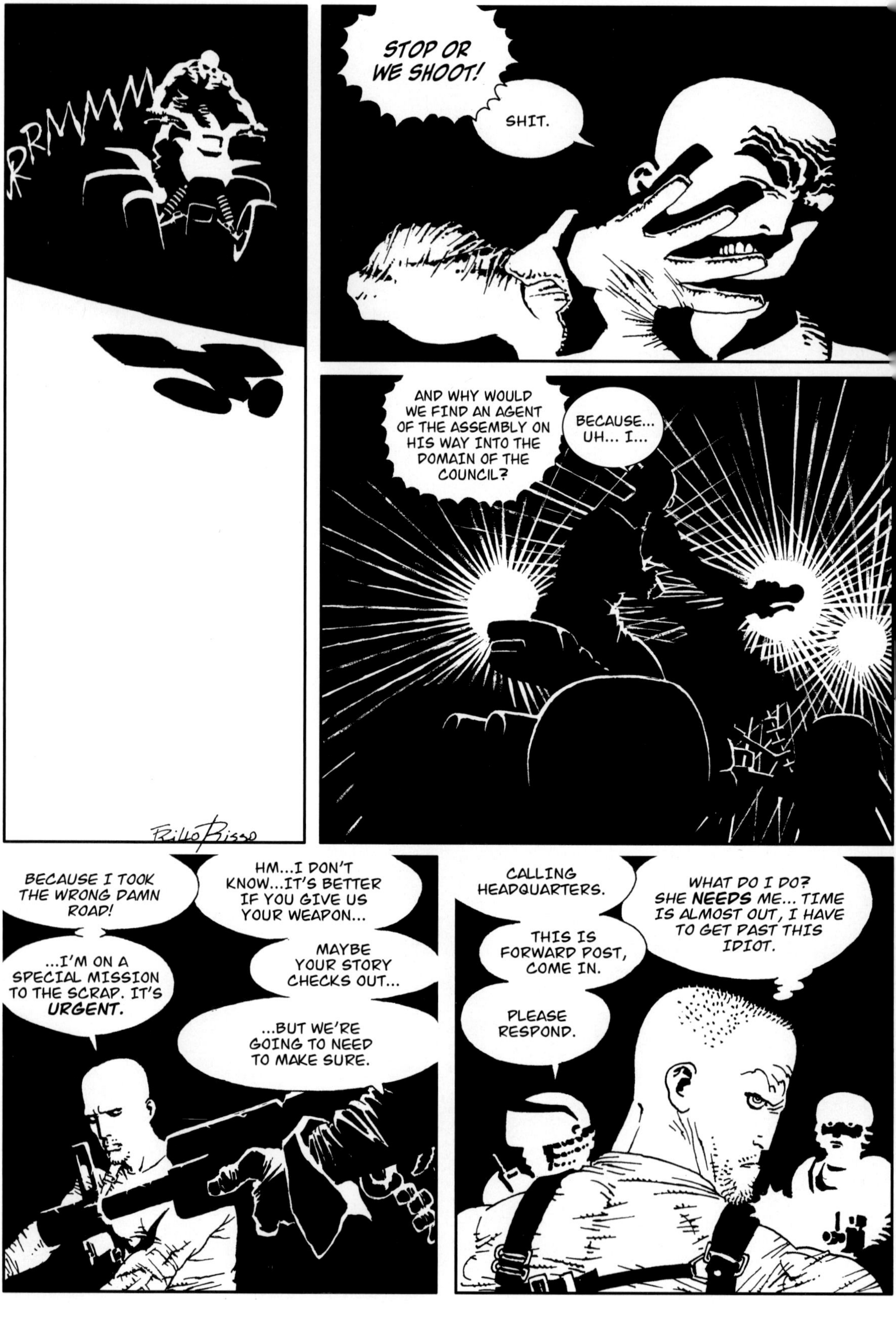
RRMMMM
STOP OR WE SHOOT!
SHIT.
AND WHY WOULD WE FIND AN AGENT OF THE ASSEMBLY ON HIS WAY INTO THE DOMAIN OF THE COUNCIL?
BECAUSE... UH... I...
BECAUSE I TOOK THE WRONG DAMN ROAD!
...I'M ON A SPECIAL MISSION TO THE SCRAP. IT'S URGENT.
HM...I DON'T KNOW...IT'S BETTER IF YOU GIVE US YOUR WEAPON...
MAYBE YOUR STORY CHECKS OUT...
...BUT WE'RE GOING TO NEED TO MAKE SURE.
CALLING HEADQUARTERS.
THIS IS FORWARD POST, COME IN.
PLEASE RESPOND.
WHAT DO I DO? SHE NEEDS ME... TIME IS ALMOST OUT, I HAVE TO GET PAST THIS IDIOT.

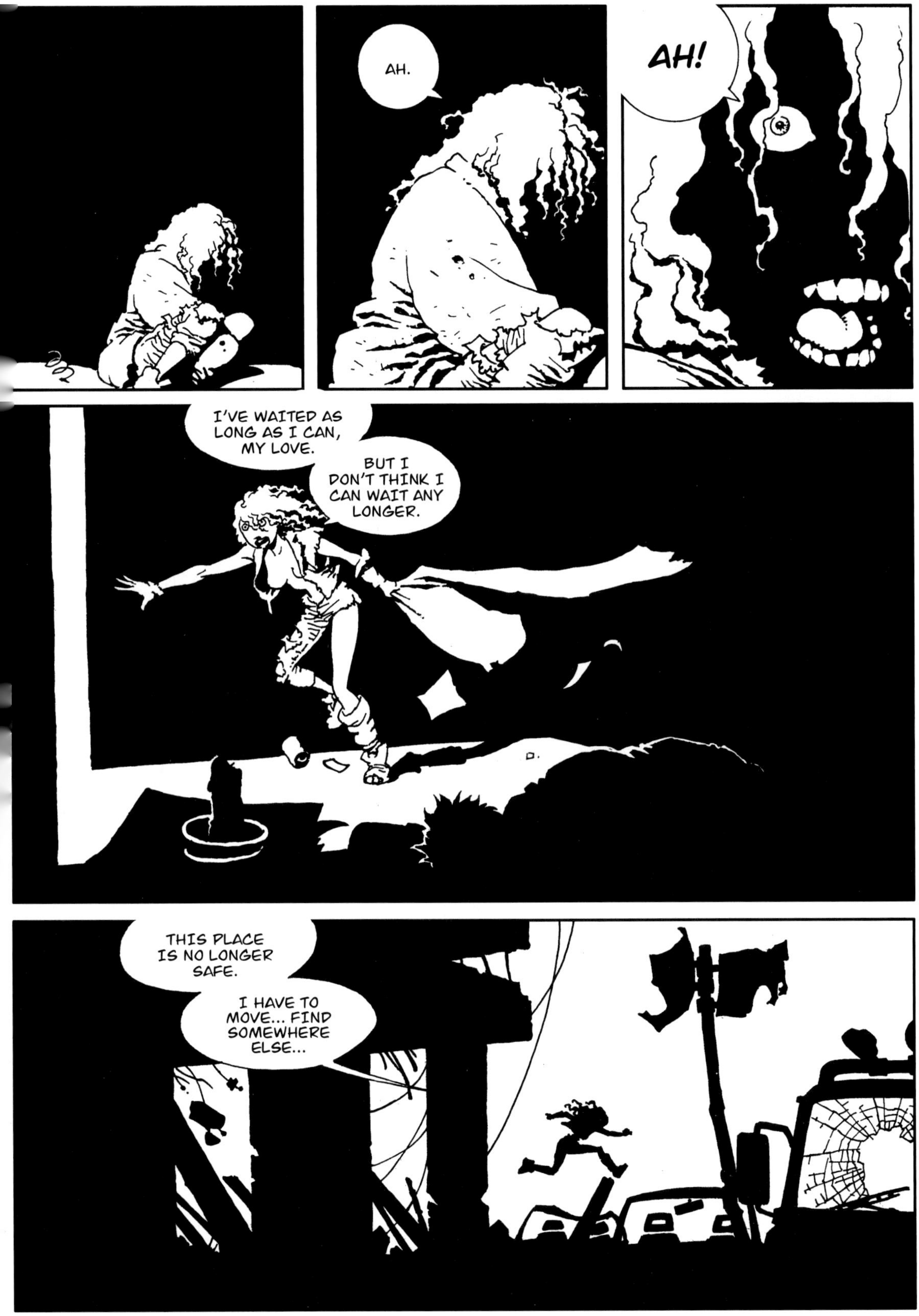
AH.
AH!
I'VE WAITED AS LONG AS I CAN, MY LOVE.
BUT I DON'T THINK I CAN WAIT ANY LONGER.
THIS PLACE IS NO LONGER SAFE.
I HAVE TO MOVE... FIND SOMEWHERE ELSE...

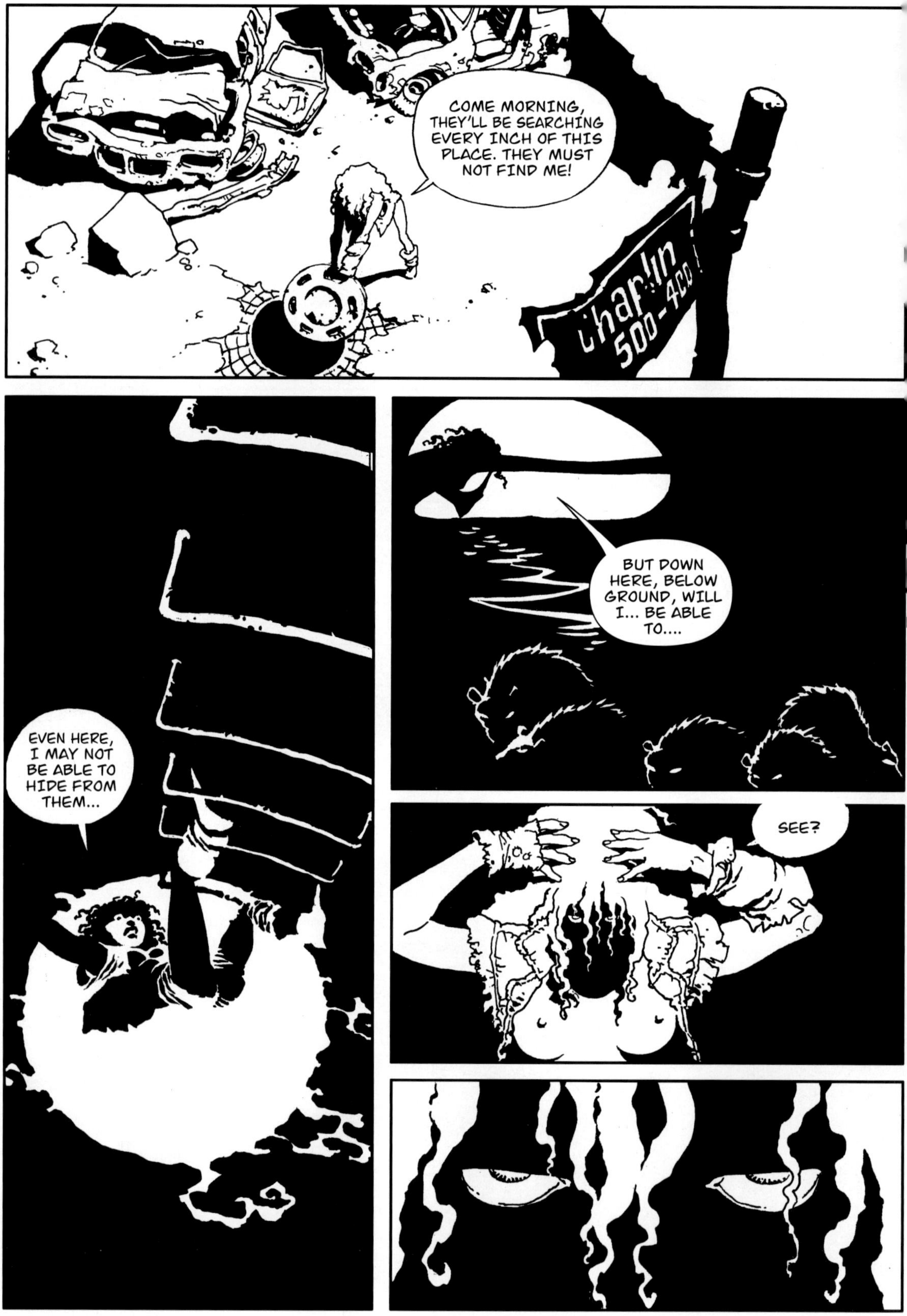
COME MORNING, THEY'LL BE SEARCHING EVERY INCH OF THIS PLACE. THEY MUST NOT FIND ME!
chaplin
500-400
EVEN HERE, I MAY NOT BE ABLE TO HIDE FROM THEM...
BUT DOWN HERE, BELOW GROUND, WILL I... BE ABLE TO....
SEE?

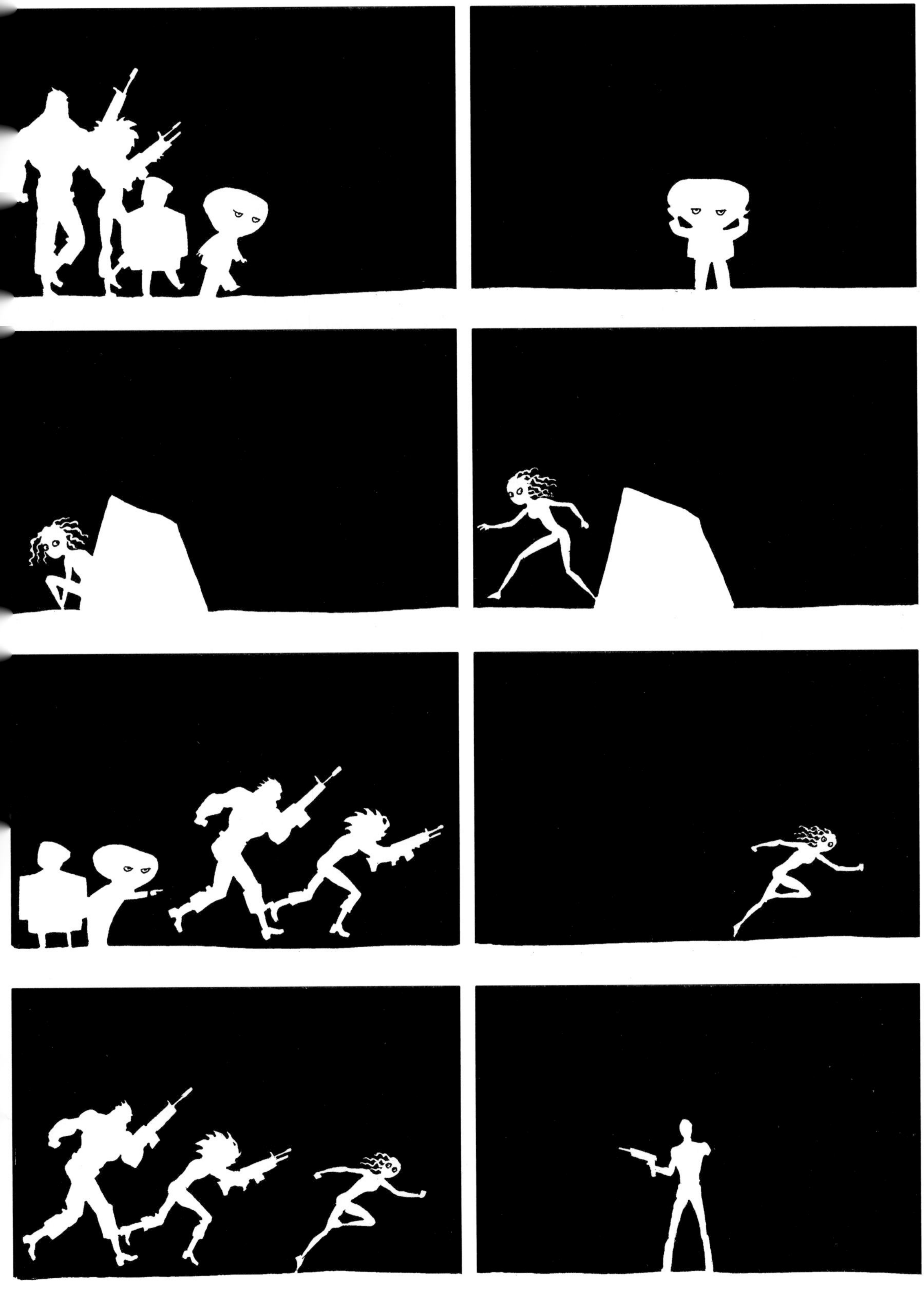

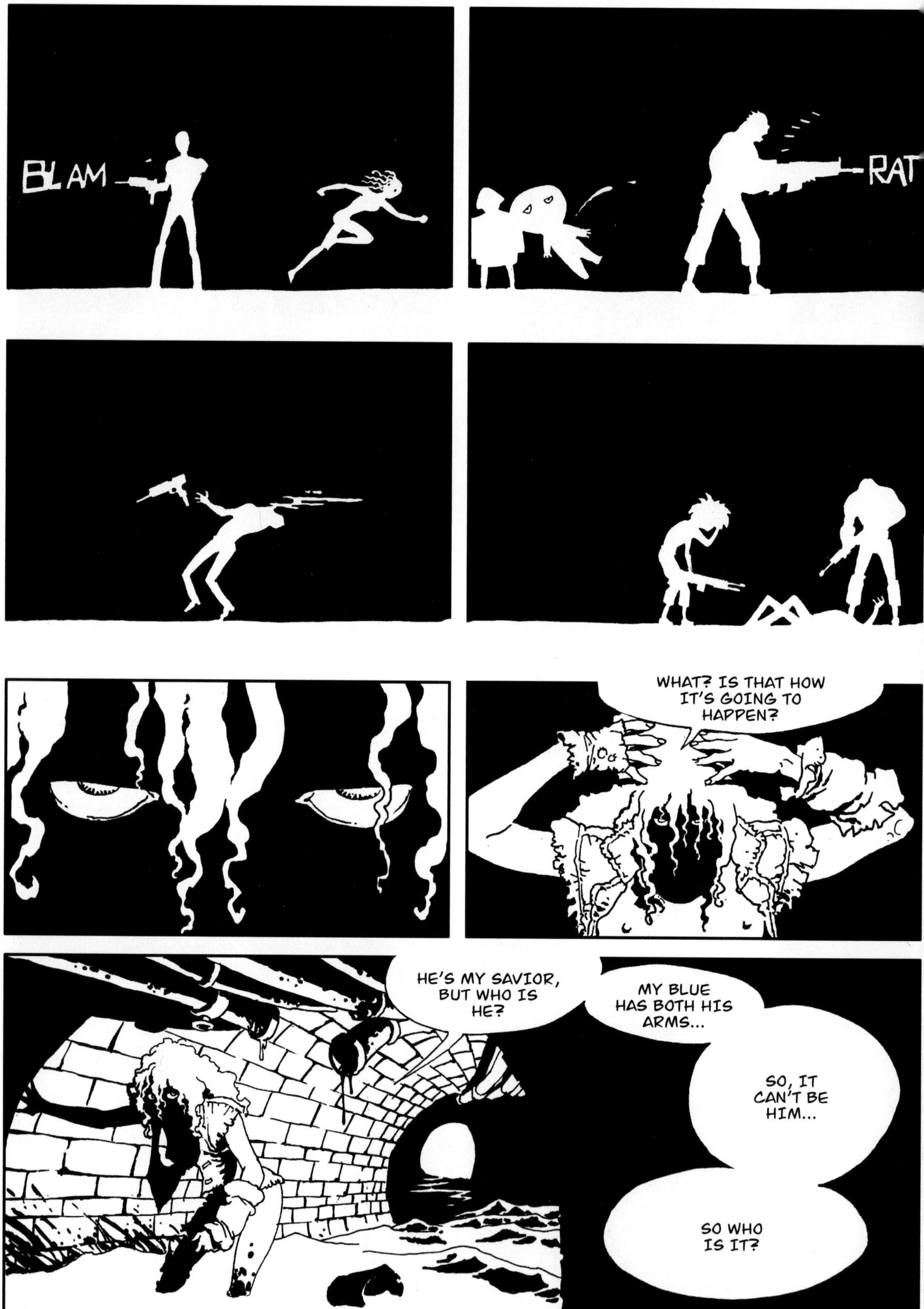

BLAM
RAT
WHAT? IS THAT HOW IT'S GOING TO HAPPEN?
HE'S MY SAVIOR, BUT WHO IS HE?
MY BLUE HAS BOTH HIS ARMS...
SO, IT CAN'T BE HIM...
SO WHO IS IT?

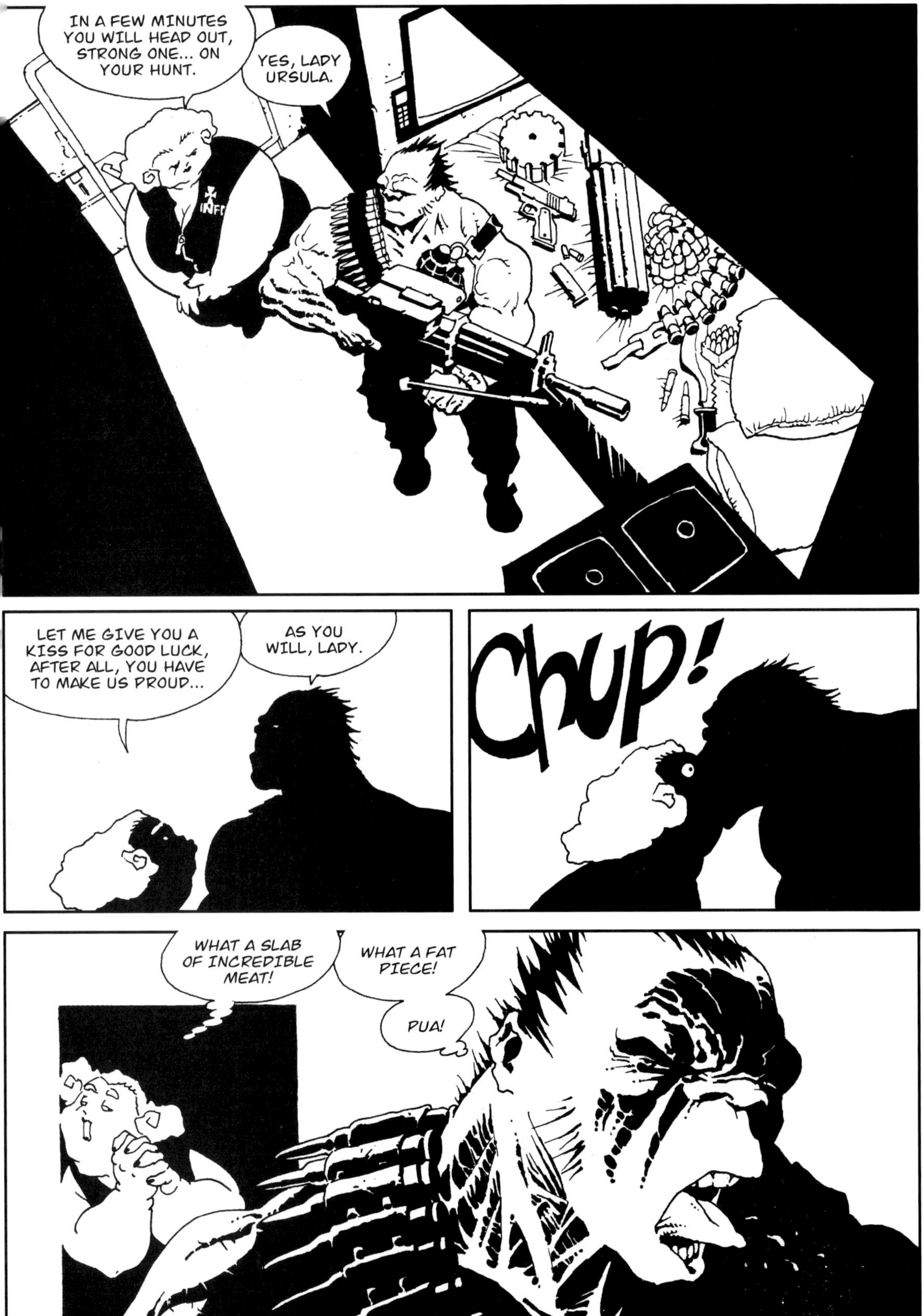
IN A FEW MINUTES YOU WILL HEAD OUT, STRONG ONE... ON YOUR HUNT.
YES, LADY URSULA.
LET ME GIVE YOU A KISS FOR GOOD LUCK, AFTER ALL, YOU HAVE TO MAKE US PROUD...
AS YOU WILL, LADY.
CHUP!
WHAT A SLAB OF INCREDIBLE MEAT!
WHAT A FAT PIECE!
PUA!

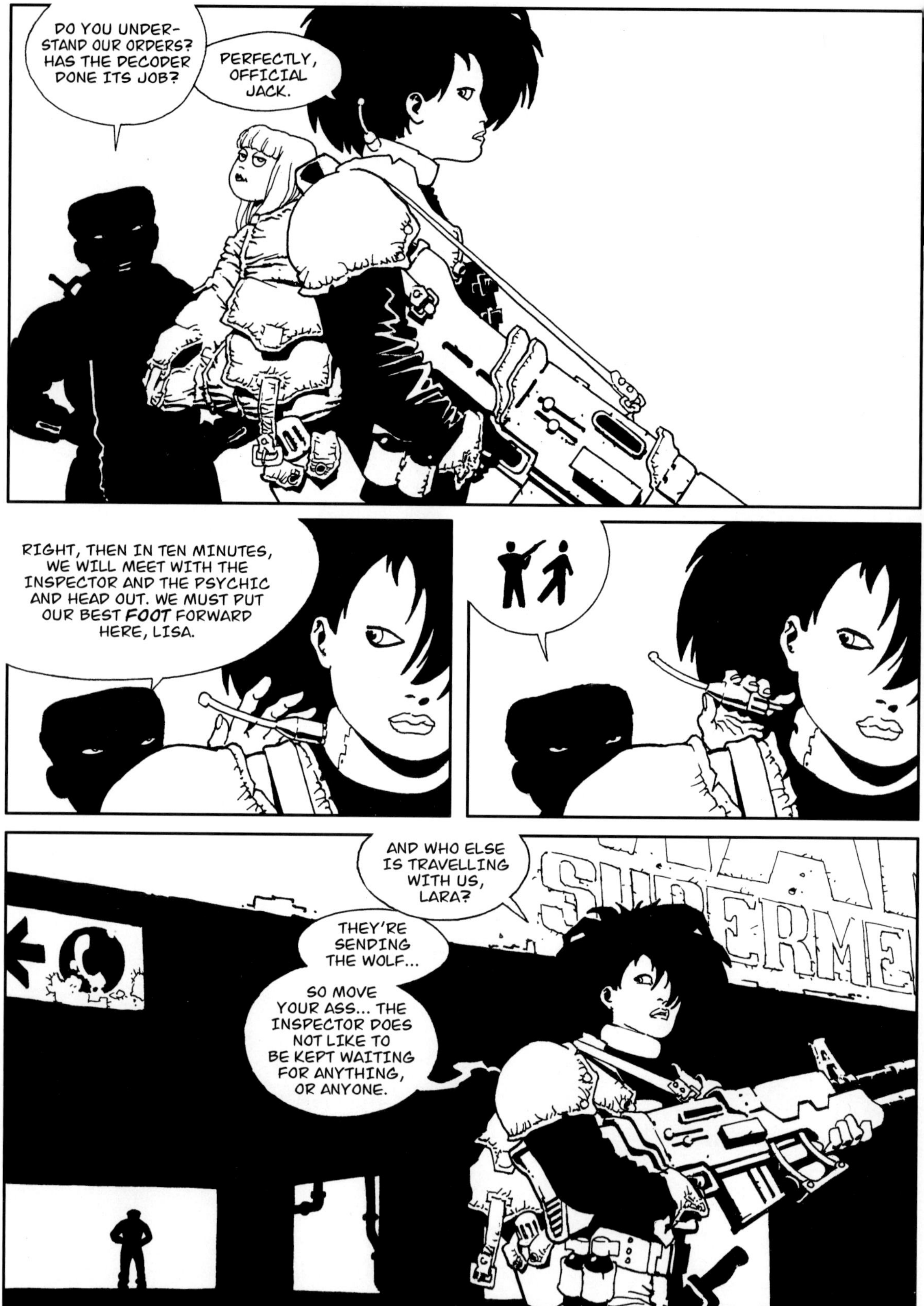
DO YOU UNDERSTAND OUR ORDERS? HAS THE DECODER DONE ITS JOB?
PERFECTLY, OFFICIAL JACK.
RIGHT, THEN IN TEN MINUTES, WE WILL MEET WITH THE INSPECTOR AND THE PSYCHIC AND HEAD OUT. WE MUST PUT OUR BEST *FOOT* FORWARD HERE, LISA.
AND WHO ELSE IS TRAVELLING WITH US, LARA?
THEY'RE SENDING THE WOLF...
SO MOVE YOUR ASS... THE INSPECTOR DOES NOT LIKE TO BE KEPT WAITING FOR ANYTHING, OR ANYONE.

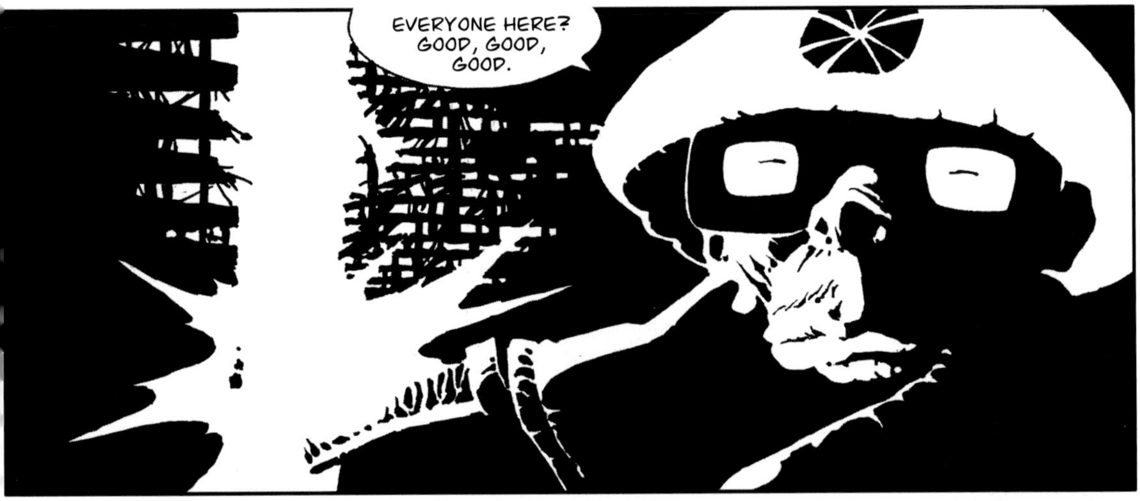
EVERYONE HERE? GOOD, GOOD, GOOD.

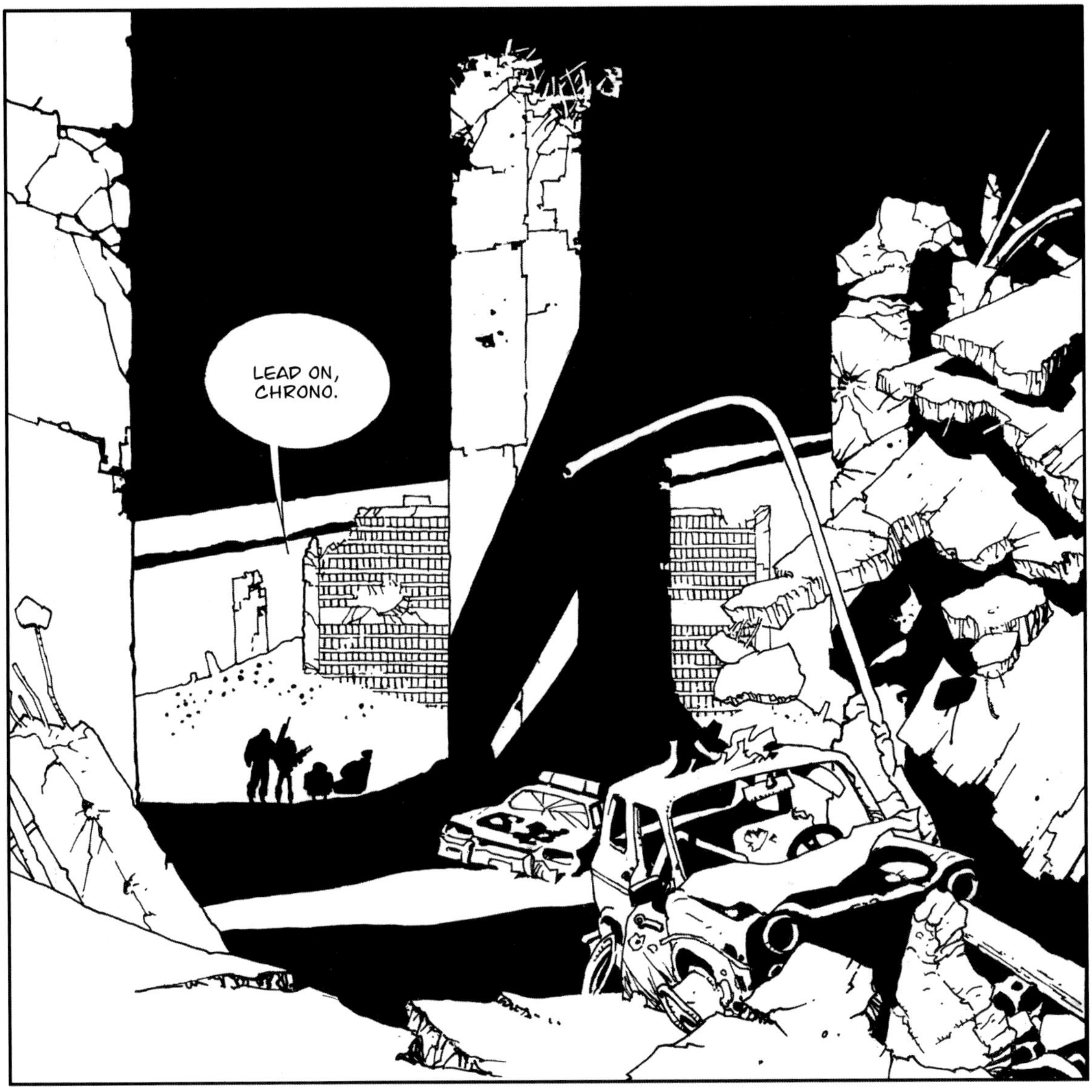
LEAD ON, CHRONO.

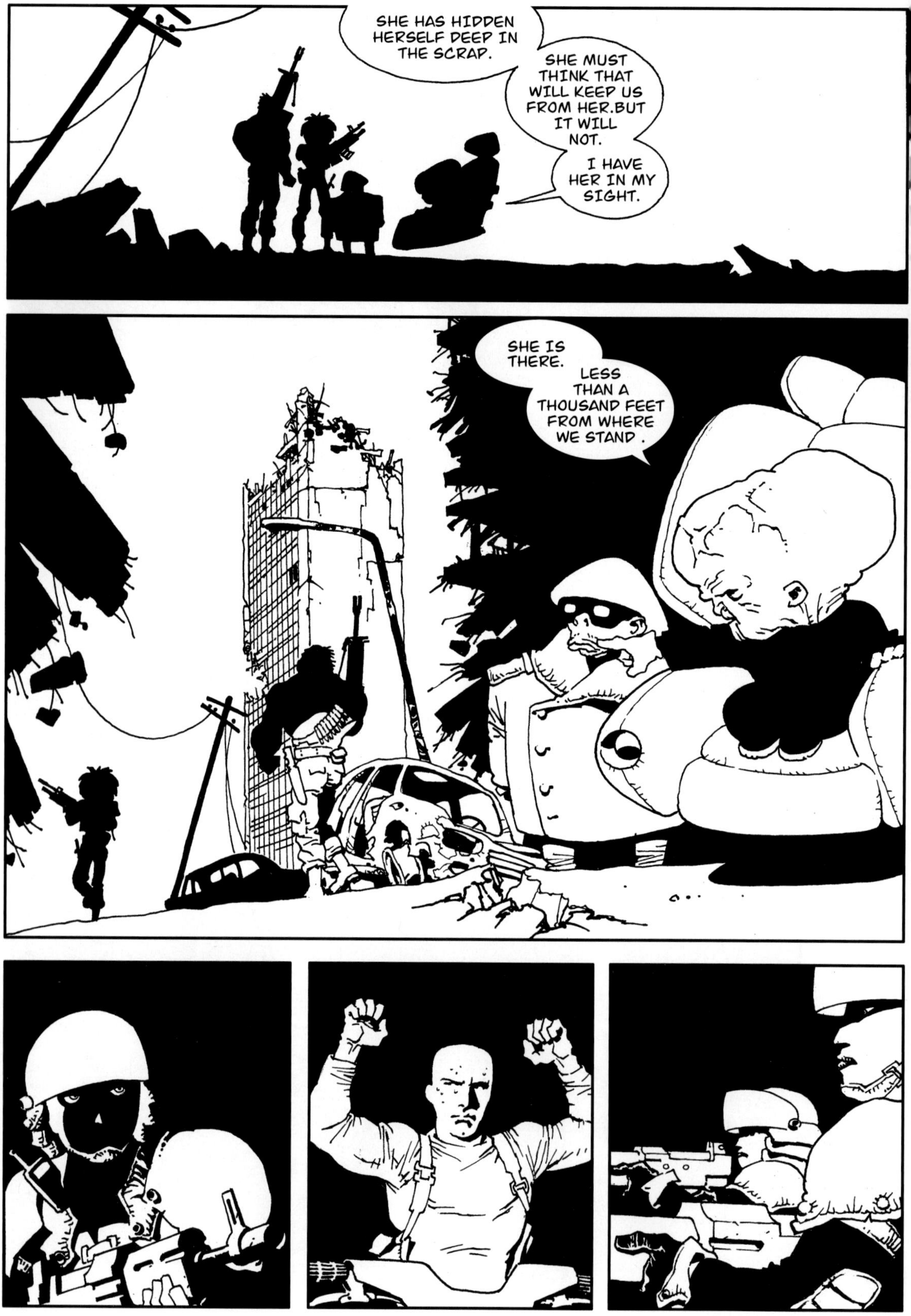
SHE HAS HIDDEN HERSELF DEEP IN THE SCRAP.
SHE MUST THINK THAT WILL KEEP US FROM HER.BUT IT WILL NOT.
I HAVE HER IN MY SIGHT.
SHE IS THERE.
LESS THAN A THOUSAND FEET FROM WHERE WE STAND .

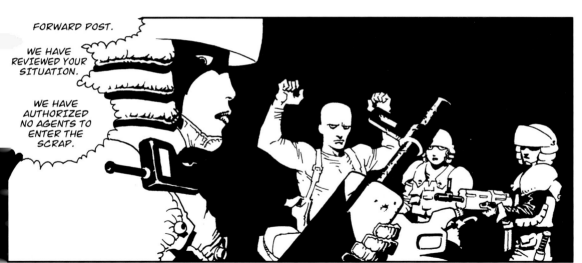

FORWARD POST.

WE HAVE REVIEWED YOUR SITUATION.

WE HAVE AUTHORIZED NO AGENTS TO ENTER THE SCRAP.

PLACE HIM IN CUSTODY IMMEDIATELY. WE WILL DEAL WITH IT.

WELL, THAT ANSWERS THAT... SO NOW I FIGHT.

...FOR...

...MY LIFE AND THE LIFE OF MY LOVE.

EH!

I'LL TAKE THAT!

WHAT ARE YOU DOING YOU CRAZY—

ISN'T IT CLEAR?

BRAKA BRAKA BRAKA

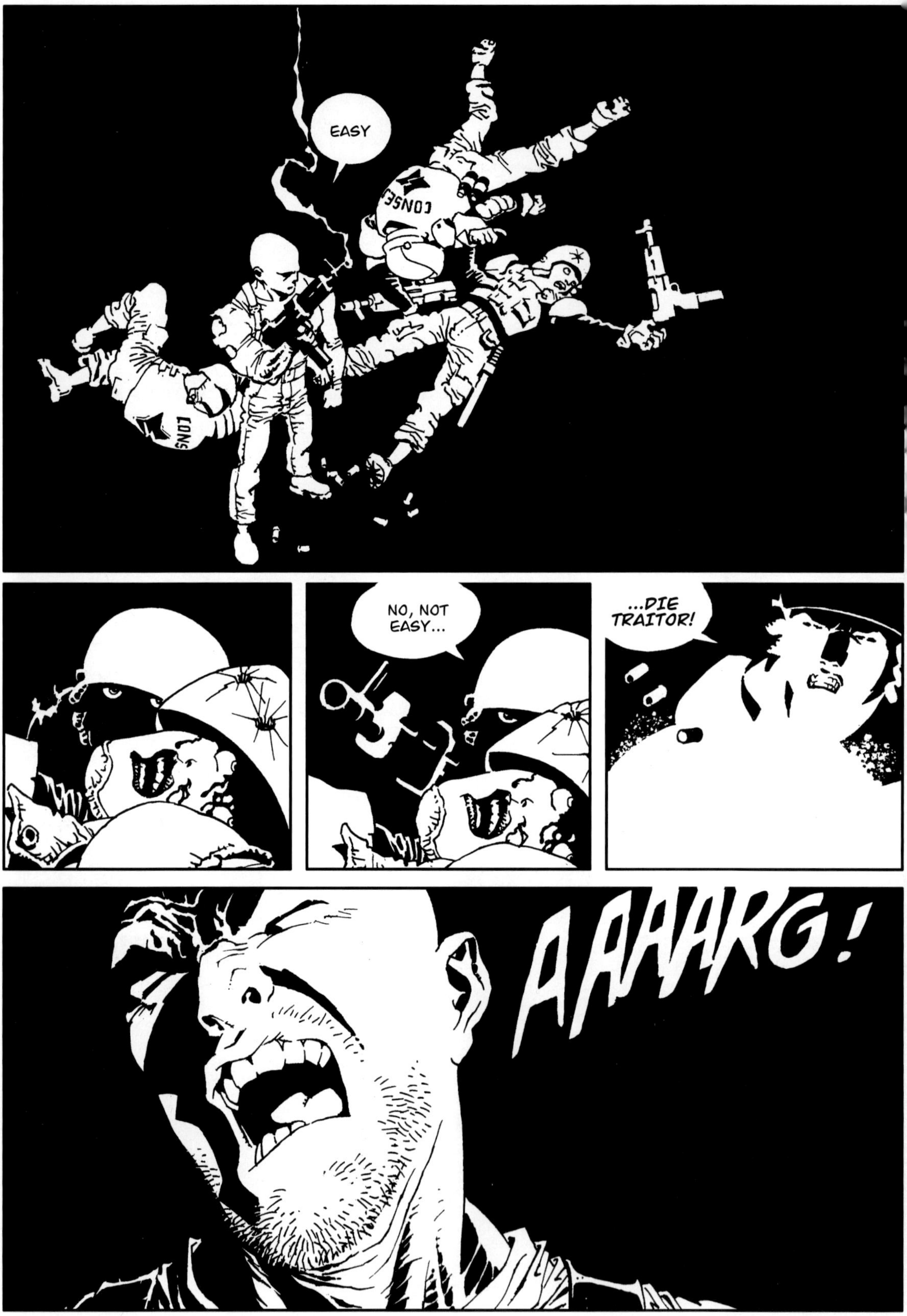
EASY
NO, NOT EASY...
...DIE TRAITOR!
AAAARG!

7

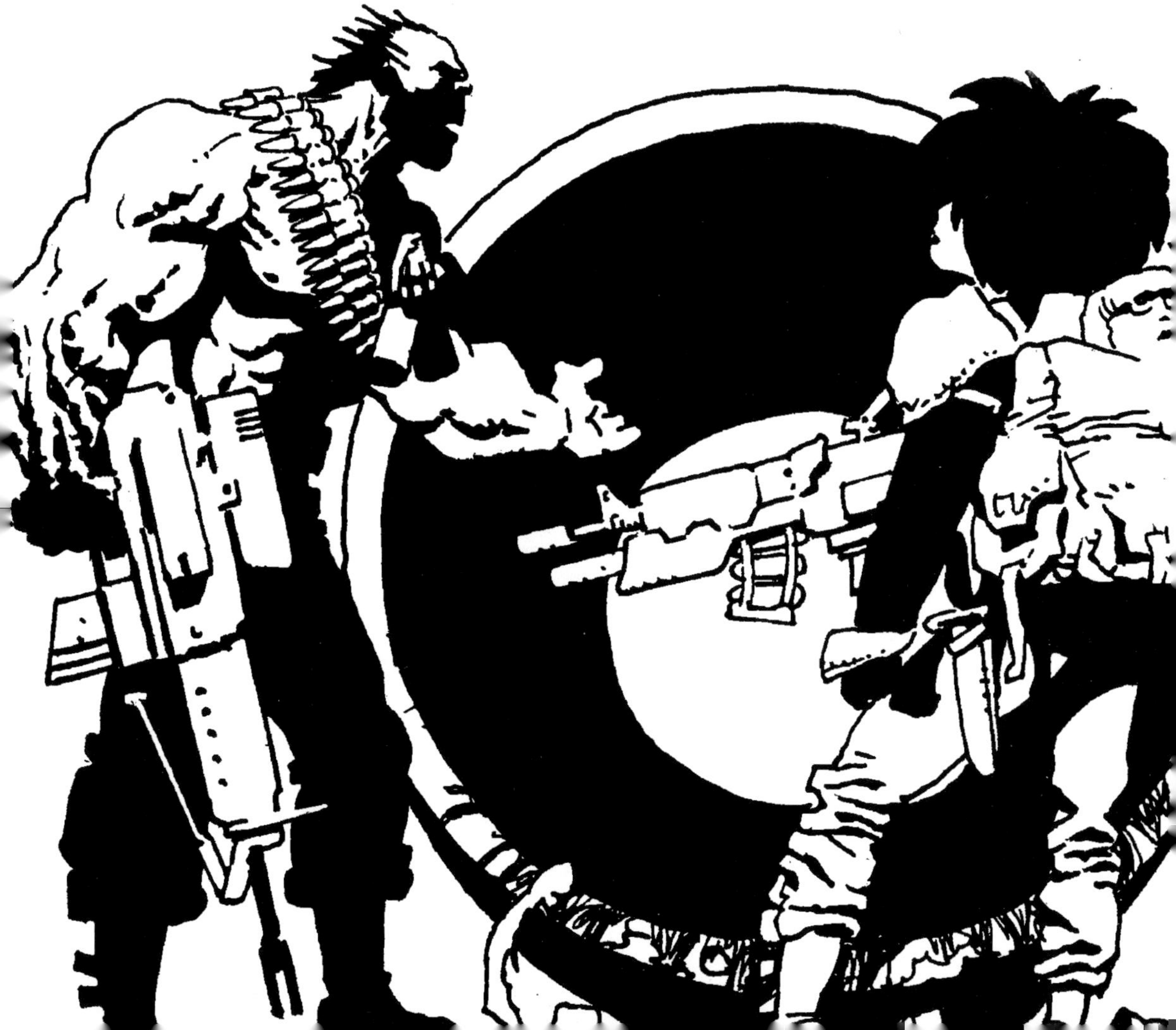

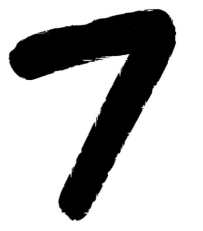

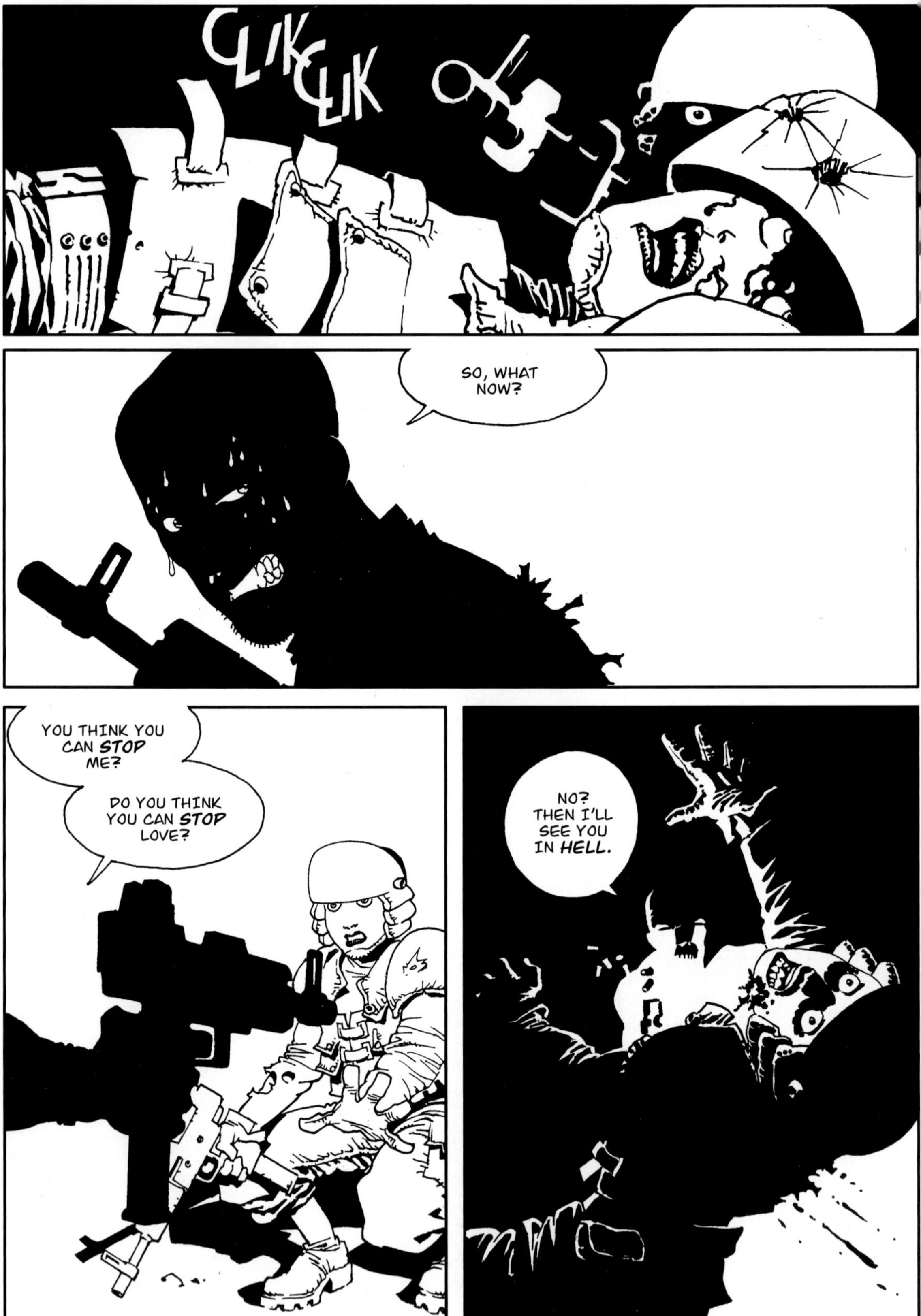
CLIK CLIK
SO, WHAT NOW?
YOU THINK YOU CAN STOP ME?
DO YOU THINK YOU CAN STOP LOVE?
NO? THEN I'LL SEE YOU IN HELL.

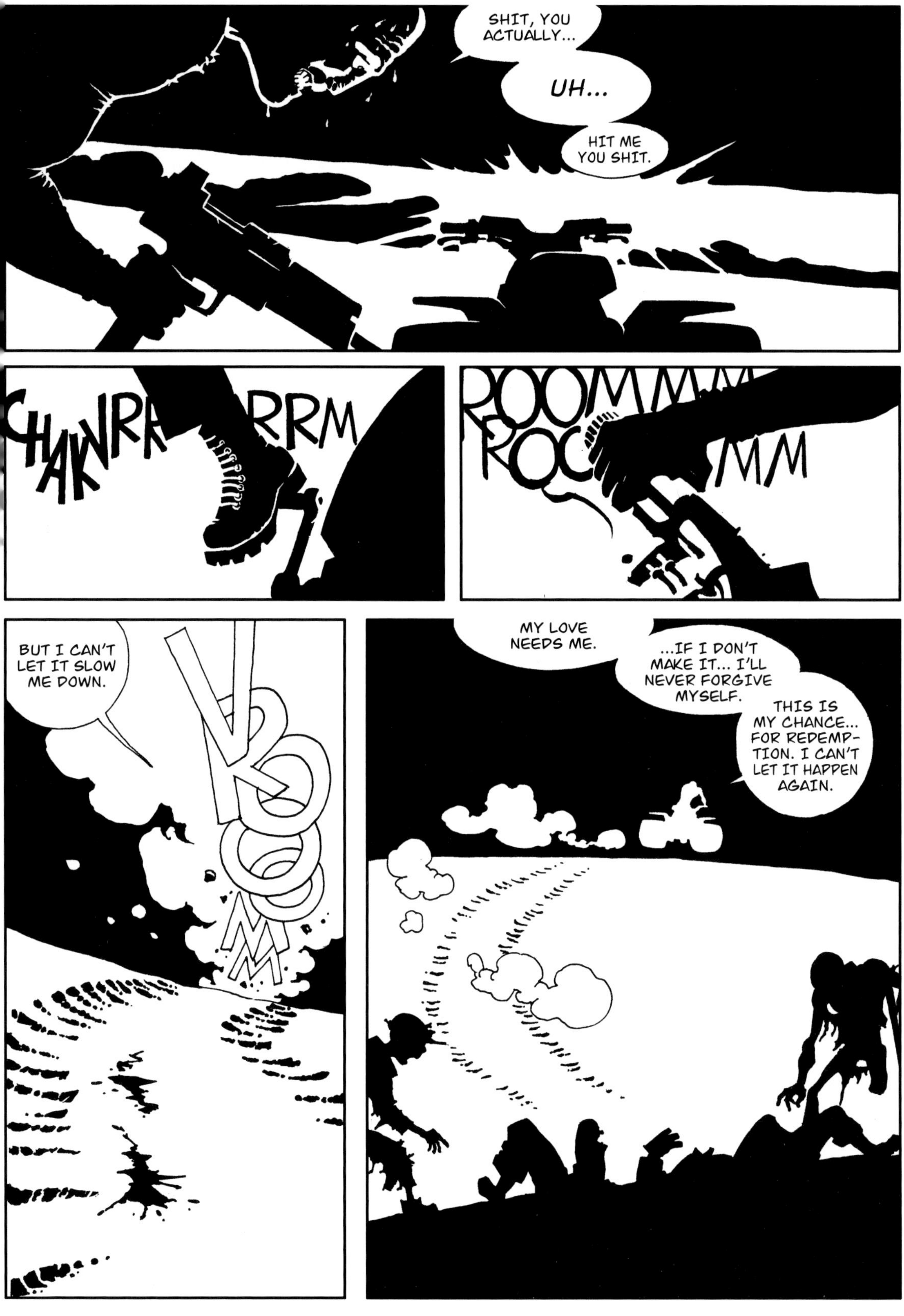
SHIT, YOU ACTUALLY...
UH...
HIT ME YOU SHIT.
CHAKVRRRRRM
ROOMMM ROOMM
BUT I CAN'T LET IT SLOW ME DOWN.
VROOOM
MY LOVE NEEDS ME.
...IF I DON'T MAKE IT... I'LL NEVER FORGIVE MYSELF.
THIS IS MY CHANCE... FOR REDEMPTION. I CAN'T LET IT HAPPEN AGAIN.

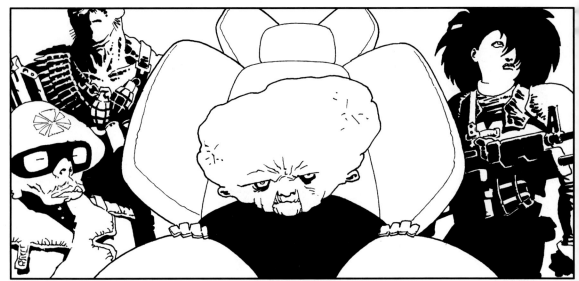

OVER THERE.

DOWN IN THE SEWERS.

THAT'S WHERE YOU'LL FIND HER.

WELL? WHAT ARE YOU *WAITING* FOR... GET IN THERE!

COUGH COUGH COUGH

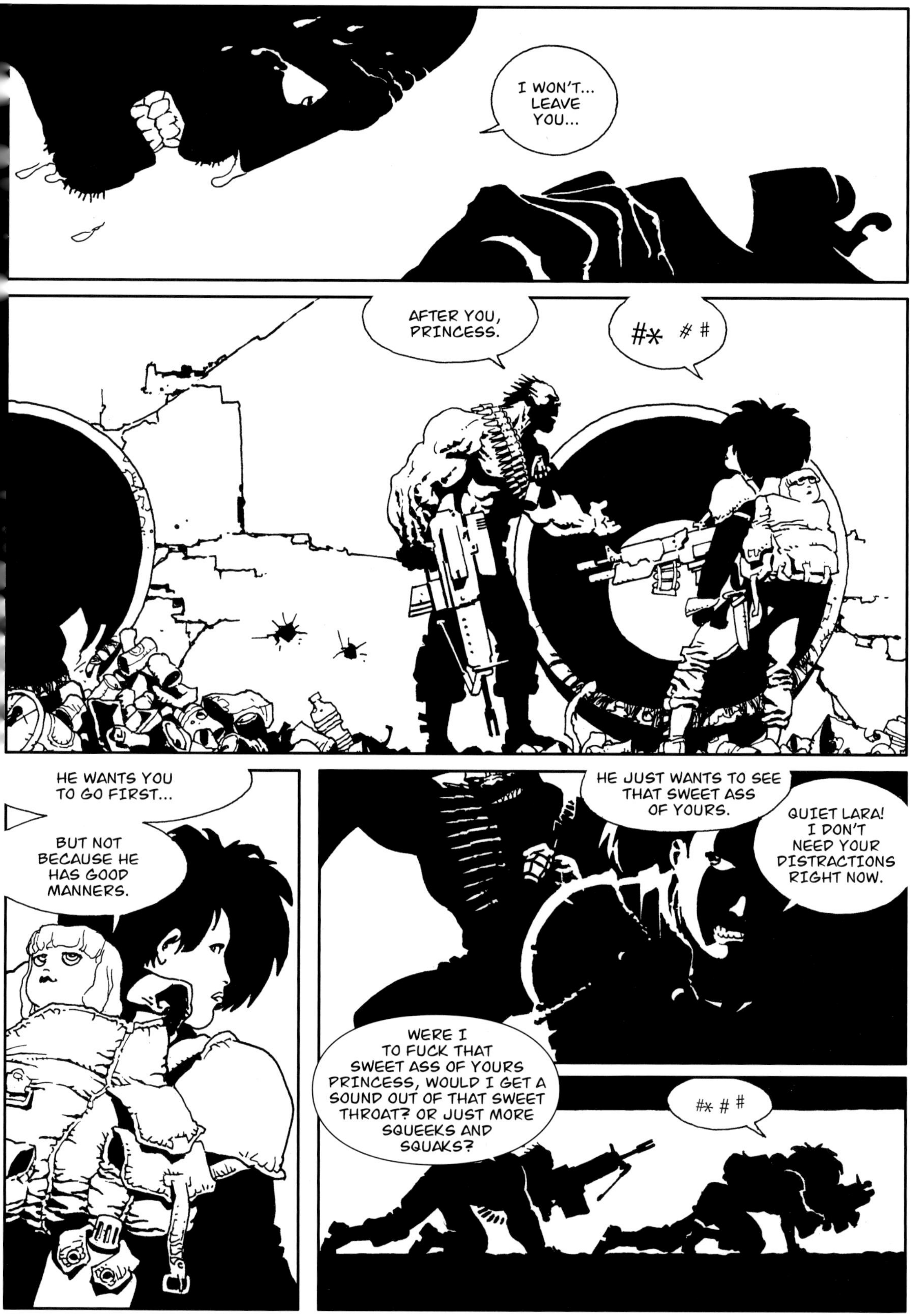
I WON'T... LEAVE YOU...
AFTER YOU, PRINCESS.
#* # #
HE WANTS YOU TO GO FIRST...
BUT NOT BECAUSE HE HAS GOOD MANNERS.
HE JUST WANTS TO SEE THAT SWEET ASS OF YOURS.
QUIET LARA! I DON'T NEED YOUR DISTRACTIONS RIGHT NOW.
WERE I TO FUCK THAT SWEET ASS OF YOURS PRINCESS, WOULD I GET A SOUND OUT OF THAT SWEET THROAT? OR JUST MORE SQUEEKS AND SQUAKS?
#* # #

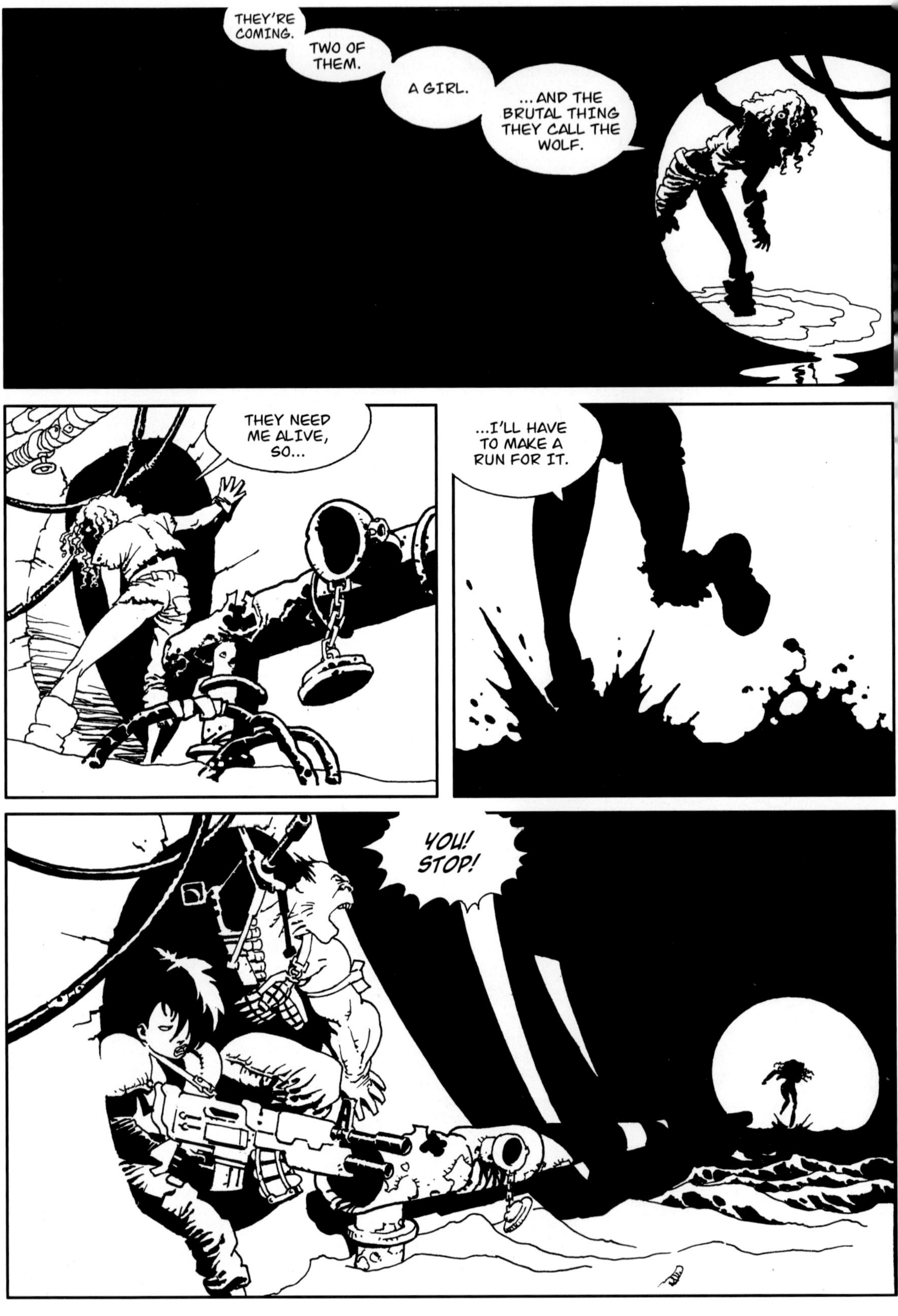
THEY'RE COMING.
TWO OF THEM.
A GIRL.
...AND THE BRUTAL THING THEY CALL THE WOLF.
THEY NEED ME ALIVE, SO...
...I'LL HAVE TO MAKE A RUN FOR IT.
YOU! STOP!

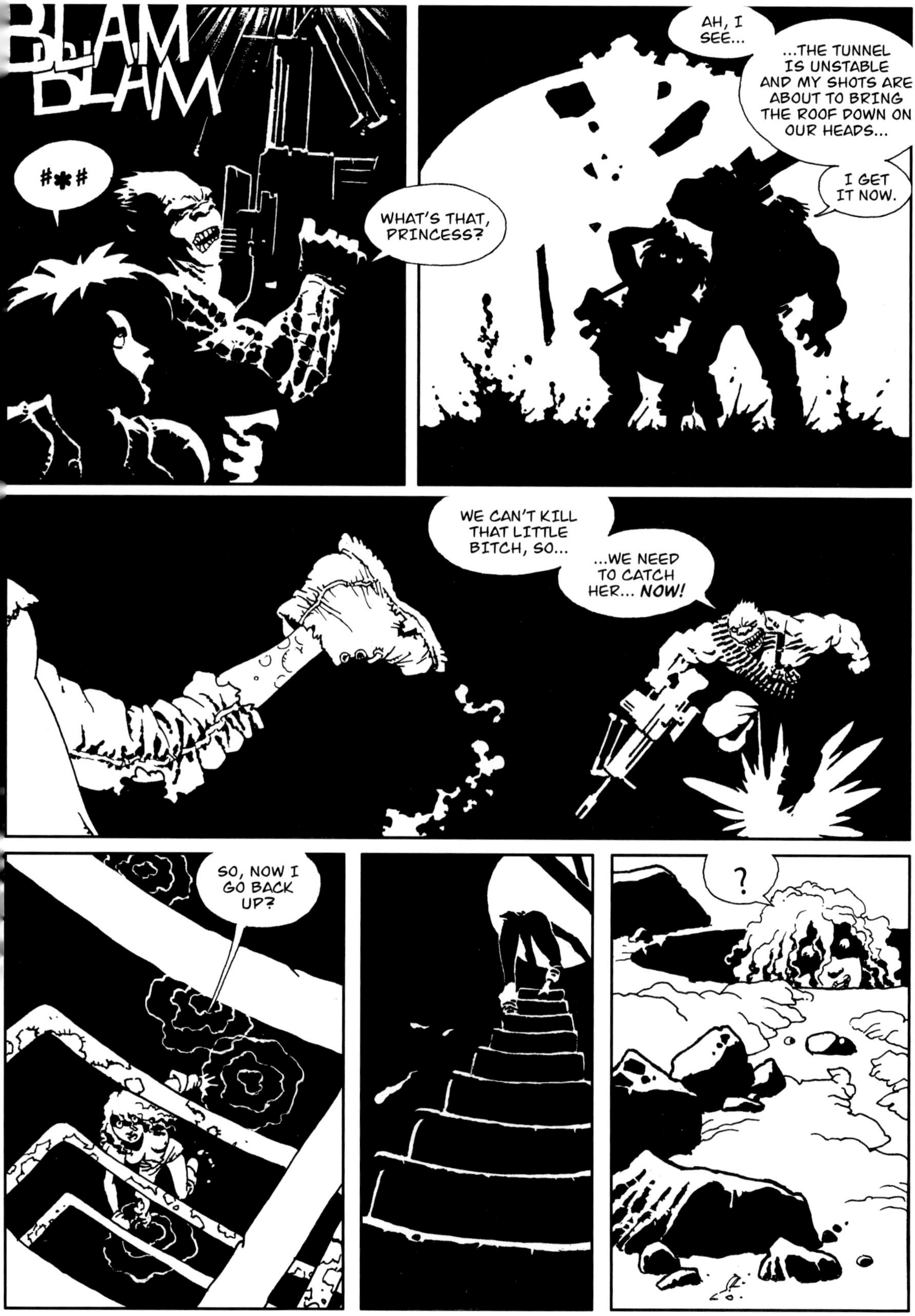
BLAM BLAM
#✱#
WHAT'S THAT, PRINCESS?
AH, I SEE...
...THE TUNNEL IS UNSTABLE AND MY SHOTS ARE ABOUT TO BRING THE ROOF DOWN ON OUR HEADS...
I GET IT NOW.
WE CAN'T KILL THAT LITTLE BITCH, SO...
...WE NEED TO CATCH HER... NOW!
SO, NOW I GO BACK UP?
?

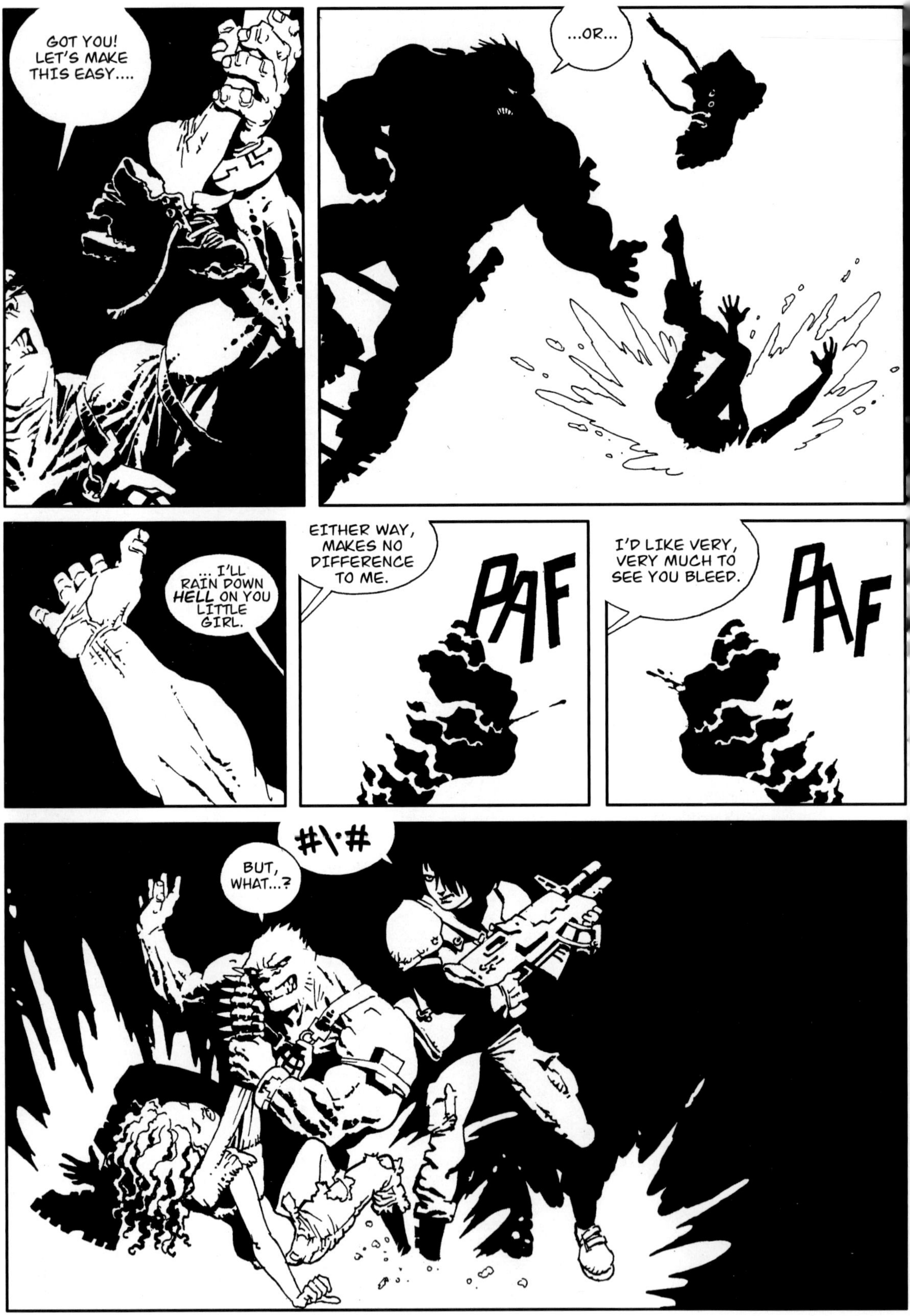
GOT YOU! LET'S MAKE THIS EASY....
...OR...
... I'LL RAIN DOWN **HELL** ON YOU LITTLE GIRL.
EITHER WAY, MAKES NO DIFFERENCE TO ME.
PAF
I'D LIKE VERY, VERY MUCH TO SEE YOU BLEED.
PAF
BUT, WHAT...?
#\:#

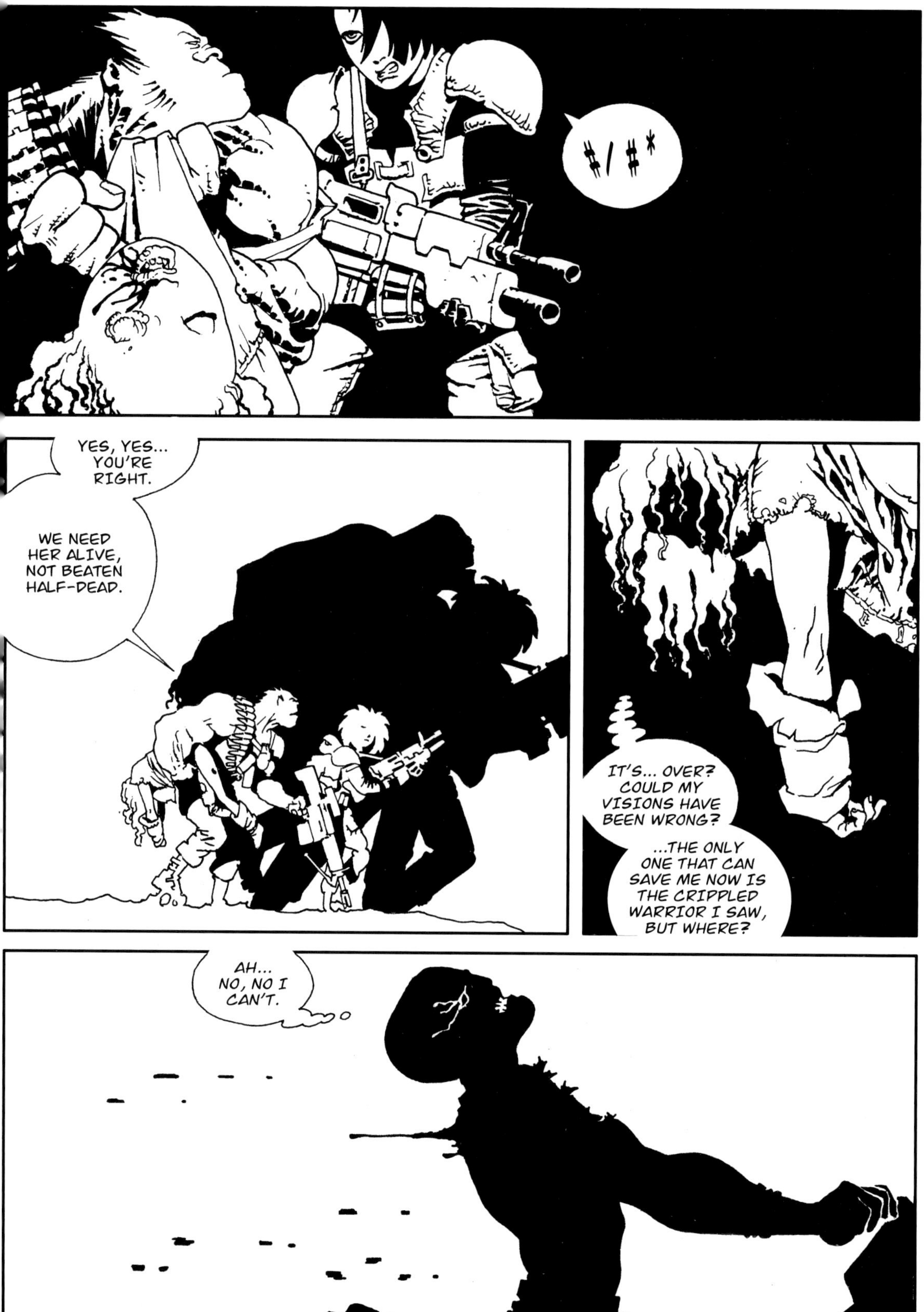
#/#*
YES, YES... YOU'RE RIGHT.
WE NEED HER ALIVE, NOT BEATEN HALF-DEAD.
IT'S... OVER? COULD MY VISIONS HAVE BEEN WRONG?
...THE ONLY ONE THAT CAN SAVE ME NOW IS THE CRIPPLED WARRIOR I SAW, BUT WHERE?
AH... NO, NO I CAN'T.

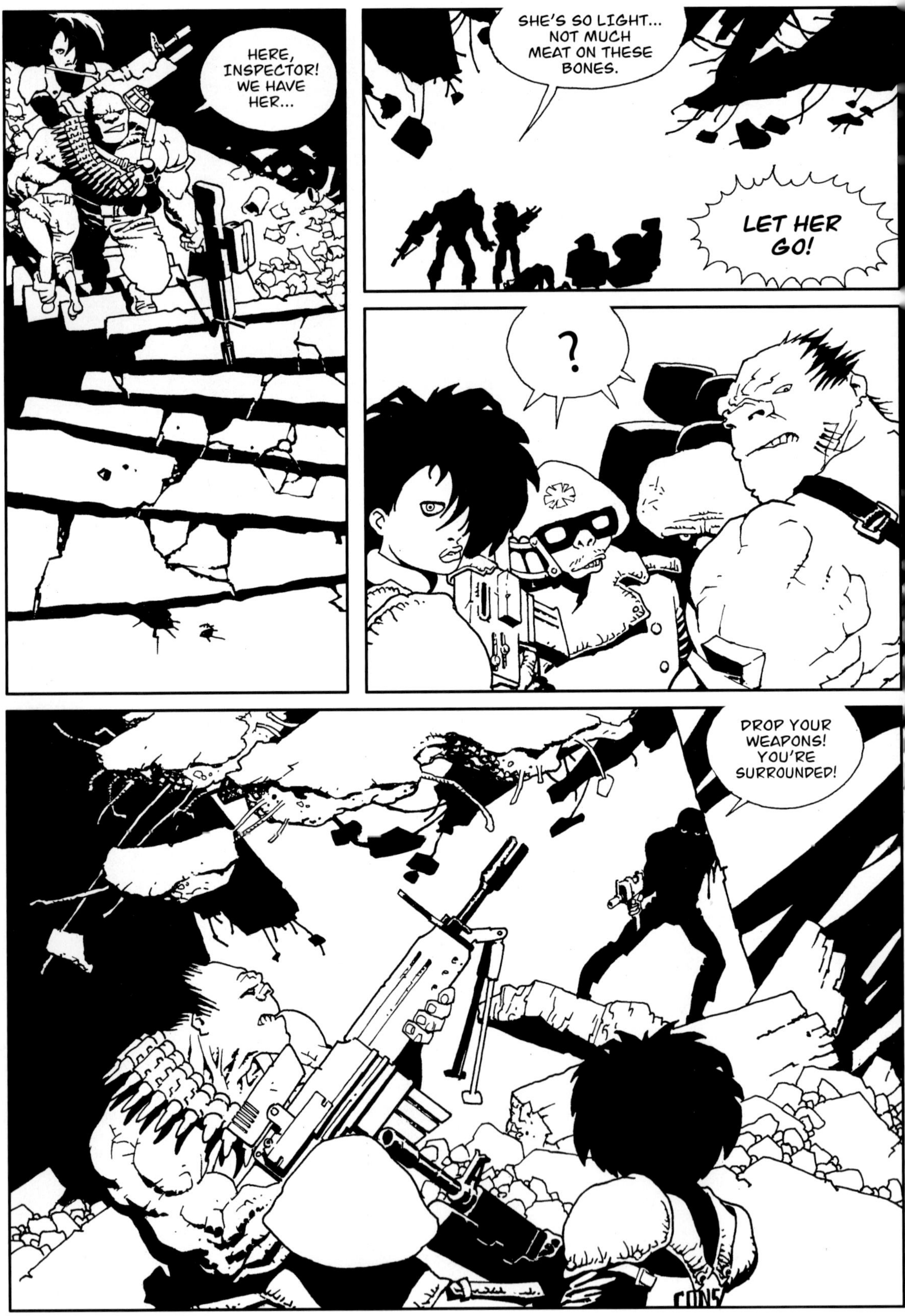
HERE, INSPECTOR! WE HAVE HER...
SHE'S SO LIGHT... NOT MUCH MEAT ON THESE BONES.
LET HER GO!
?
DROP YOUR WEAPONS! YOU'RE SURROUNDED!

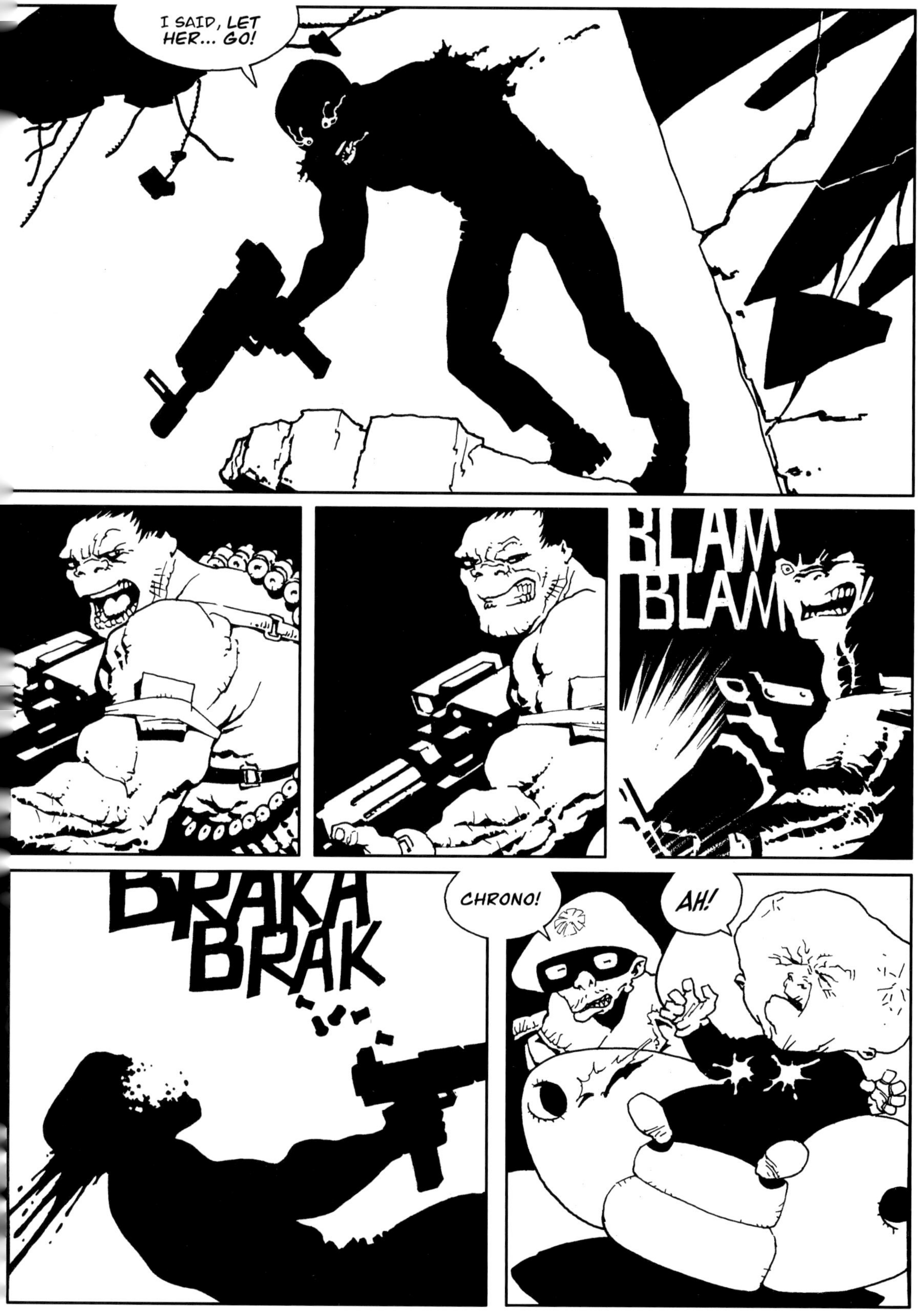
I SAID, LET HER... GO!
BLAM
BLAM
BRAKA
BRAK
CHRONO!
AH!

STOP HER! SHE'S GETTING AWAY!

YES...

BUT...

...WHERE DID SHE GO?

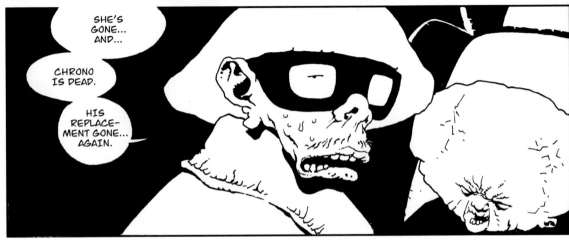

SHE'S GONE... AND...

CHRONO IS DEAD.

HIS REPLACEMENT GONE... AGAIN.

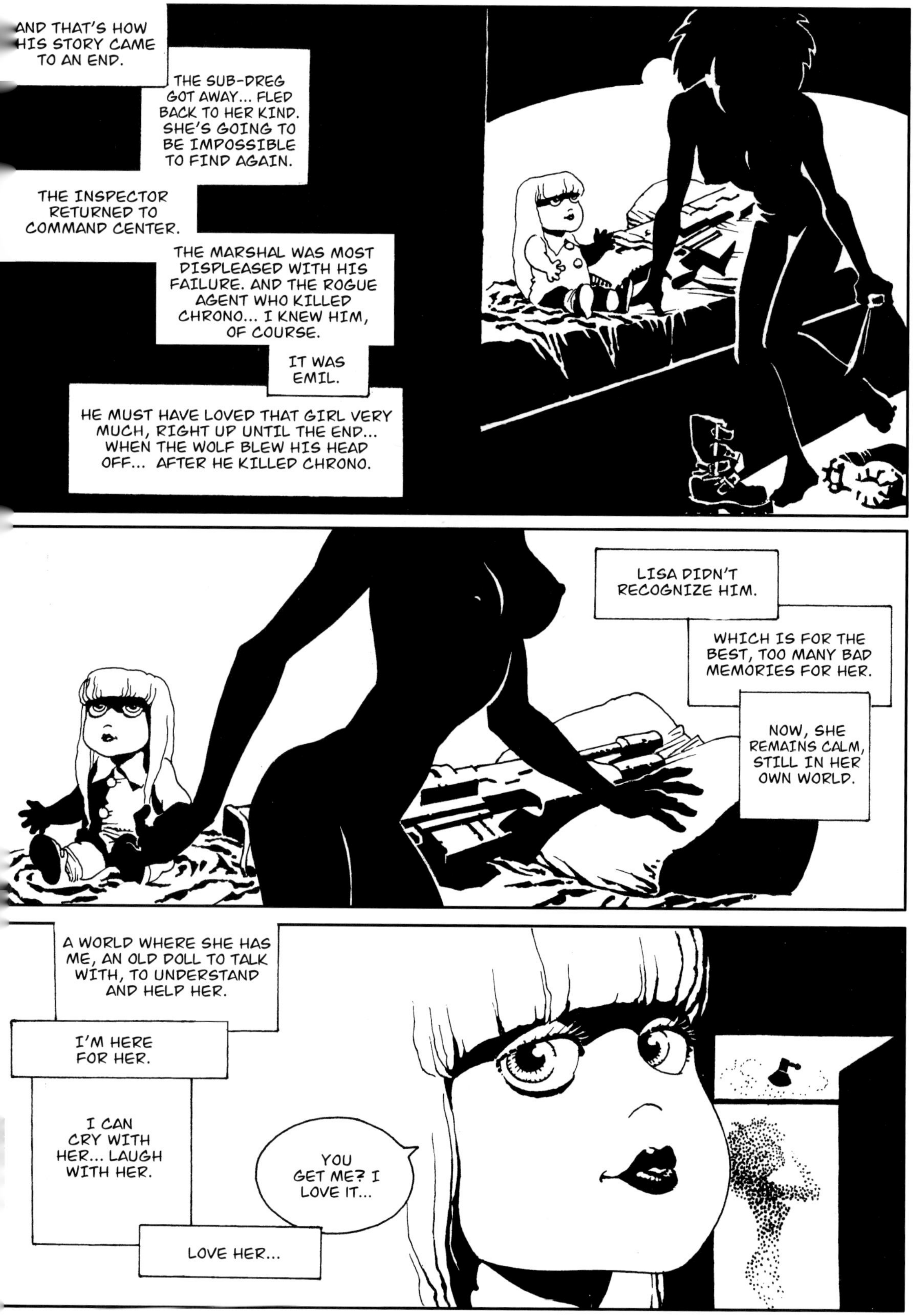
AND THAT'S HOW HIS STORY CAME TO AN END.
THE SUB-DREG GOT AWAY... FLED BACK TO HER KIND. SHE'S GOING TO BE IMPOSSIBLE TO FIND AGAIN.
THE INSPECTOR RETURNED TO COMMAND CENTER.
THE MARSHAL WAS MOST DISPLEASED WITH HIS FAILURE. AND THE ROGUE AGENT WHO KILLED CHRONO... I KNEW HIM, OF COURSE.
IT WAS EMIL.
HE MUST HAVE LOVED THAT GIRL VERY MUCH, RIGHT UP UNTIL THE END... WHEN THE WOLF BLEW HIS HEAD OFF... AFTER HE KILLED CHRONO.
LISA DIDN'T RECOGNIZE HIM.
WHICH IS FOR THE BEST, TOO MANY BAD MEMORIES FOR HER.
NOW, SHE REMAINS CALM, STILL IN HER OWN WORLD.
A WORLD WHERE SHE HAS ME, AN OLD DOLL TO TALK WITH, TO UNDERSTAND AND HELP HER.
I'M HERE FOR HER.
I CAN CRY WITH HER... LAUGH WITH HER.
YOU GET ME? I LOVE IT...
LOVE HER...

8

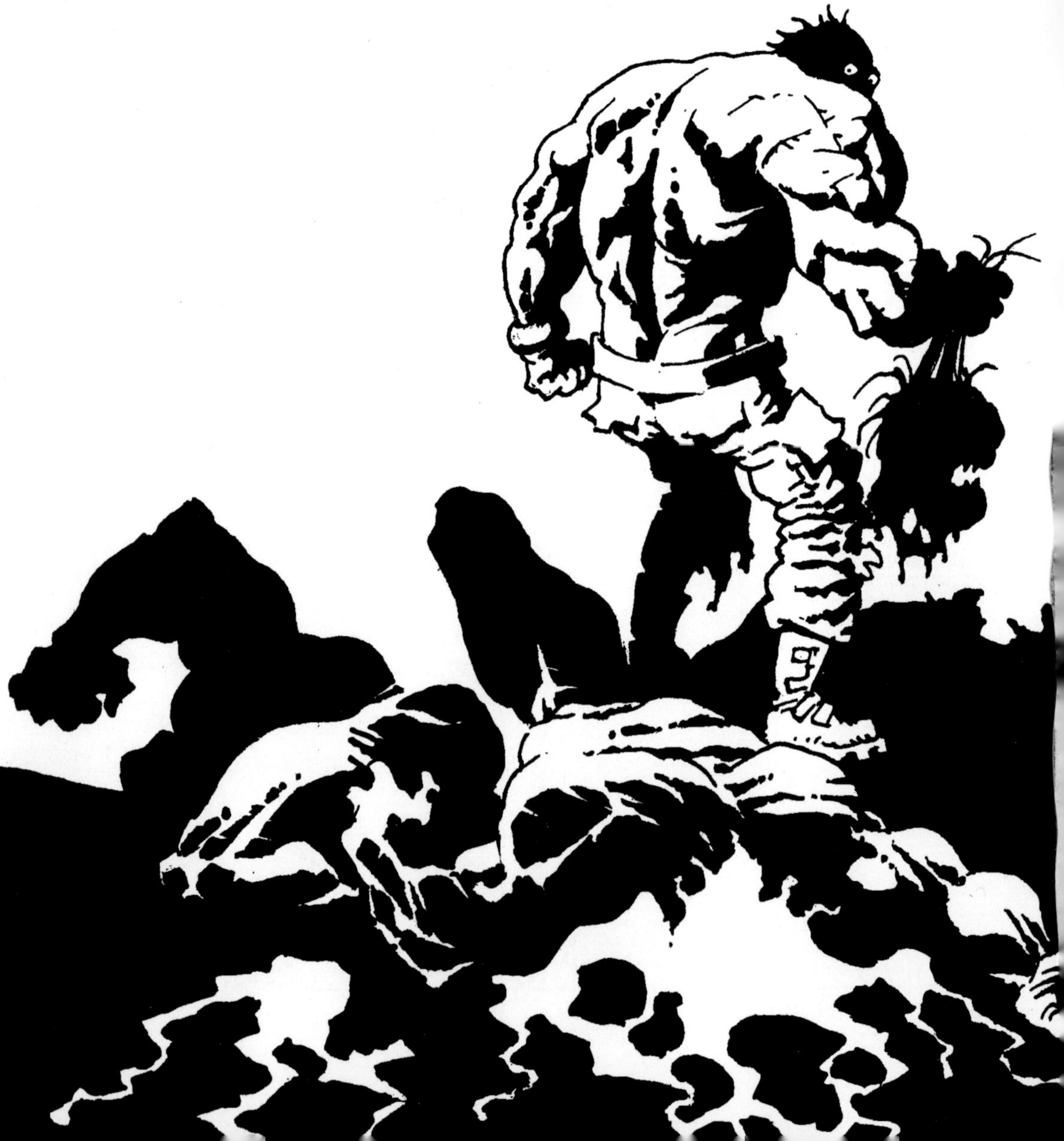

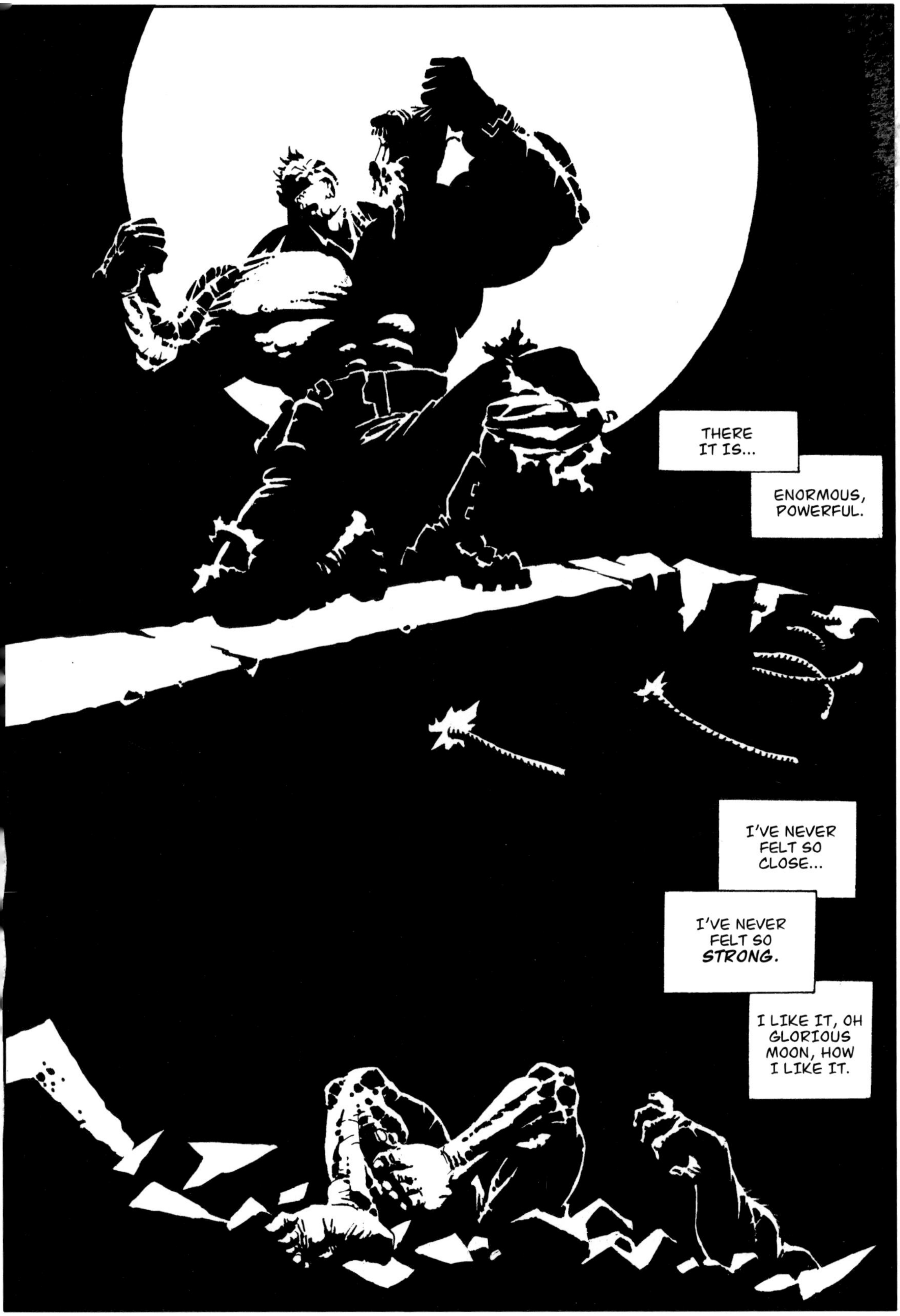
THERE IT IS...
ENORMOUS, POWERFUL.
I'VE NEVER FELT SO CLOSE...
I'VE NEVER FELT SO STRONG.
I LIKE IT, OH GLORIOUS MOON, HOW I LIKE IT.

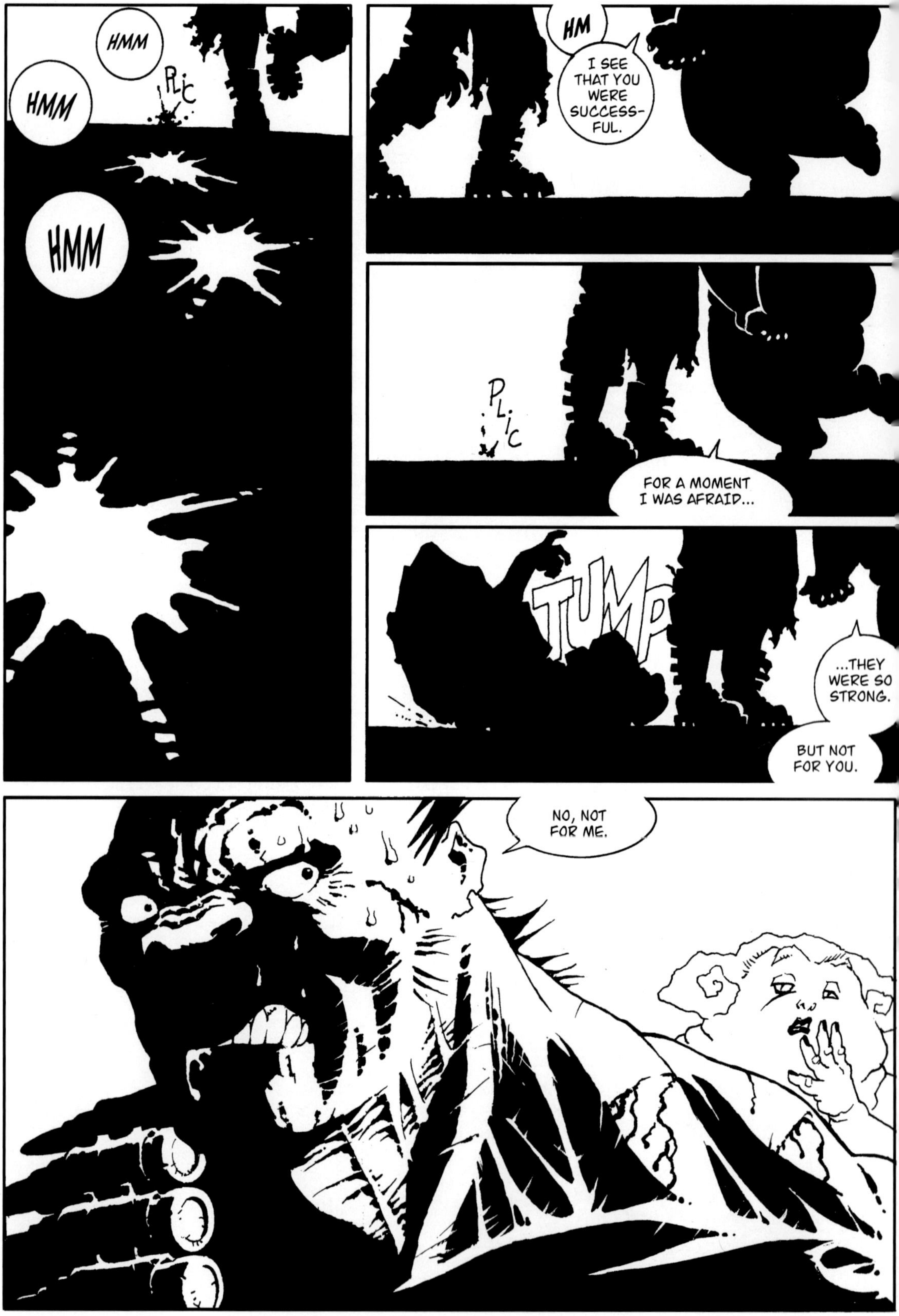
HMM
HMM
PLIC
HMM
HM
I SEE THAT YOU WERE SUCCESS-FUL.
PLIC
FOR A MOMENT I WAS AFRAID...
TUMP
...THEY WERE SO STRONG.
BUT NOT FOR YOU.
NO, NOT FOR ME.

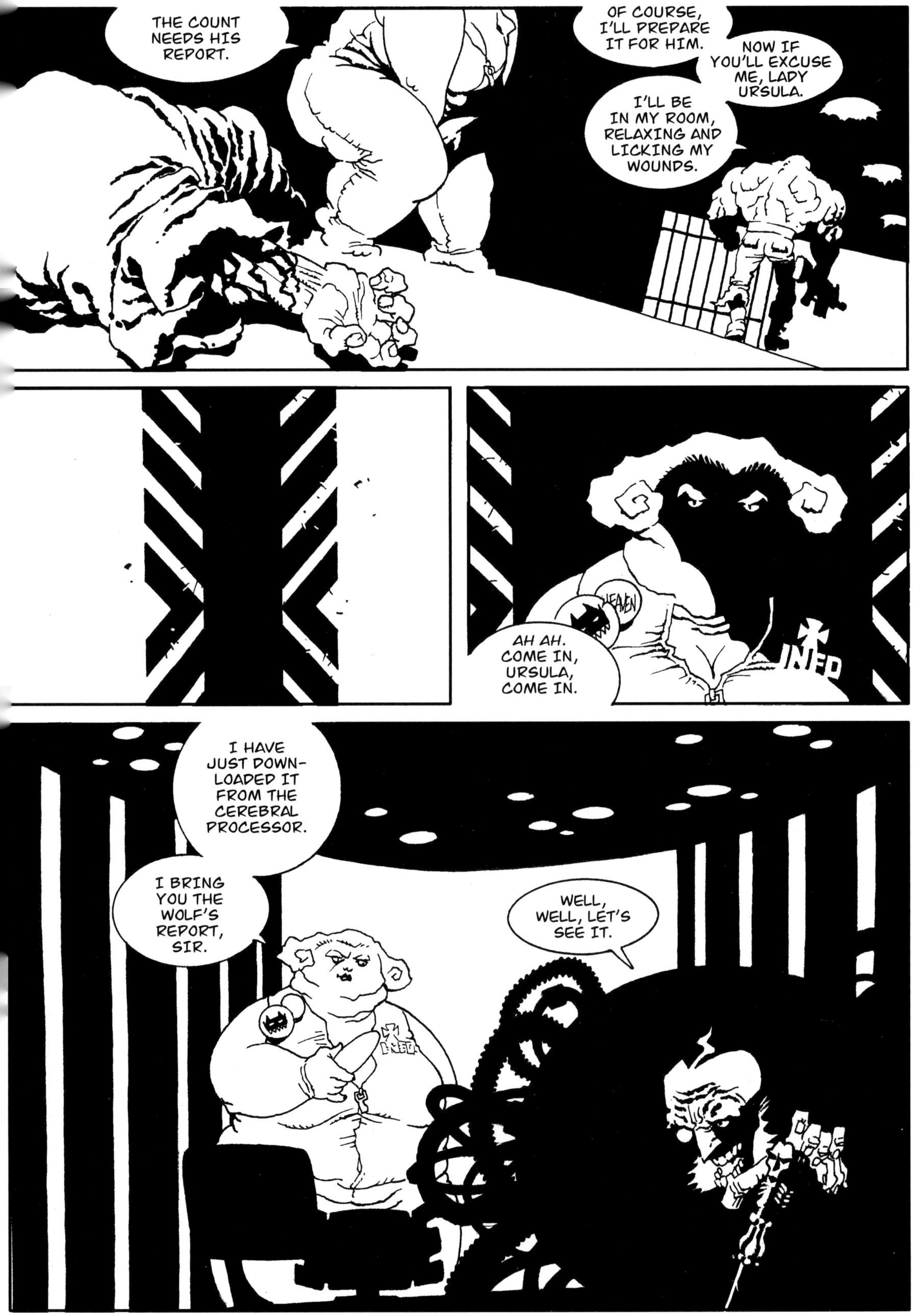
THE COUNT NEEDS HIS REPORT.
OF COURSE, I'LL PREPARE IT FOR HIM.
NOW IF YOU'LL EXCUSE ME, LADY URSULA.
I'LL BE IN MY ROOM, RELAXING AND LICKING MY WOUNDS.
AH AH. COME IN, URSULA, COME IN.
I BRING YOU THE WOLF'S REPORT, SIR.
I HAVE JUST DOWN-LOADED IT FROM THE CEREBRAL PROCESSOR.
WELL, WELL, LET'S SEE IT.

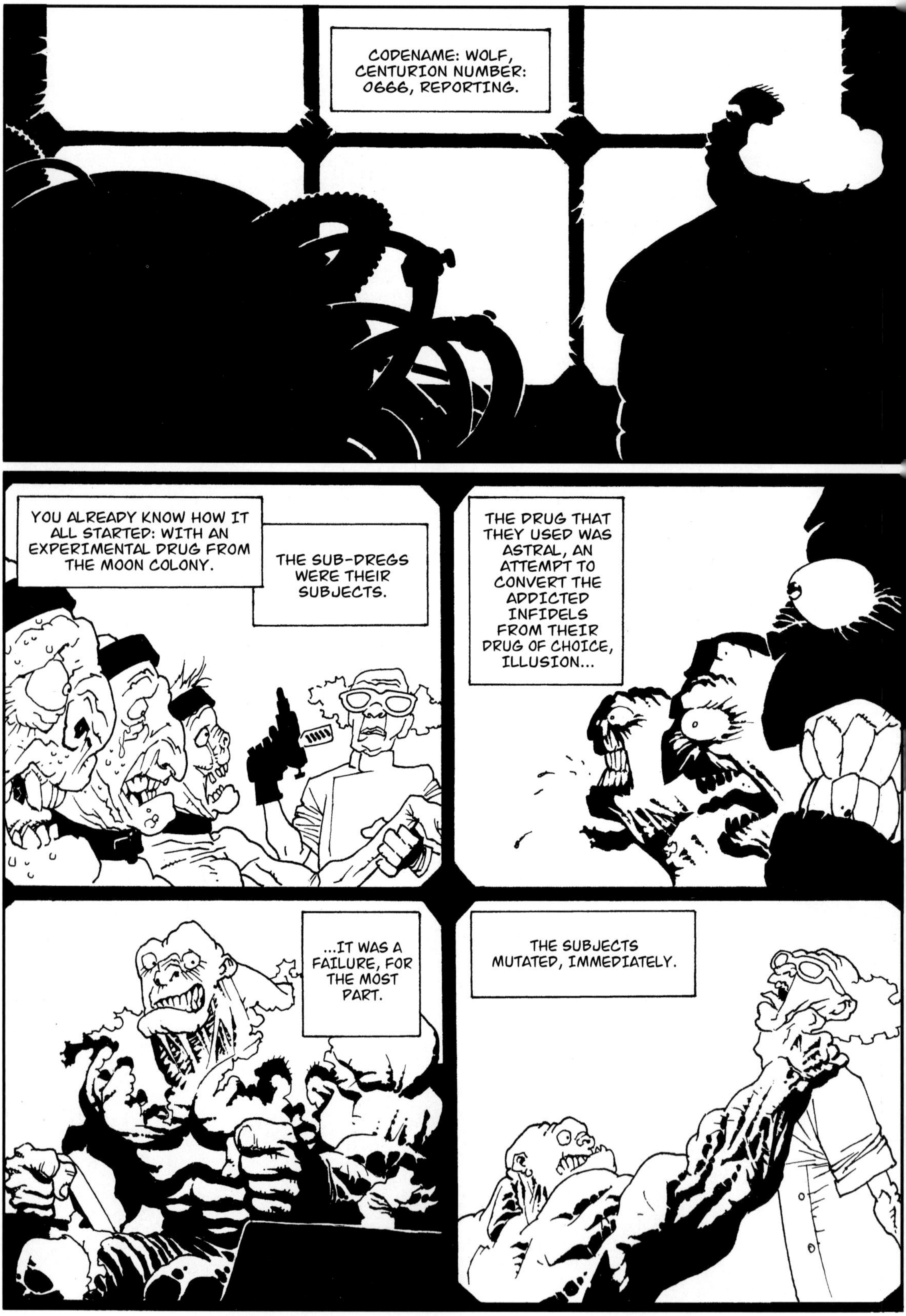
CODENAME: WOLF, CENTURION NUMBER: 0666, REPORTING.
YOU ALREADY KNOW HOW IT ALL STARTED: WITH AN EXPERIMENTAL DRUG FROM THE MOON COLONY.
THE SUB-DREGS WERE THEIR SUBJECTS.
THE DRUG THAT THEY USED WAS ASTRAL, AN ATTEMPT TO CONVERT THE ADDICTED INFIDELS FROM THEIR DRUG OF CHOICE, ILLUSION...
...IT WAS A FAILURE, FOR THE MOST PART.
THE SUBJECTS MUTATED, IMMEDIATELY.

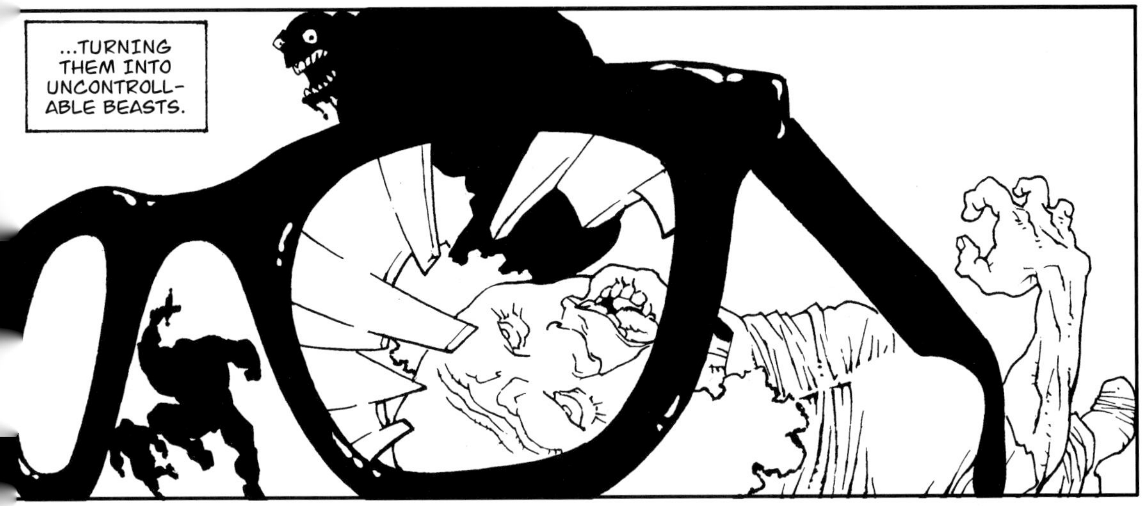
...TURNING THEM INTO UNCONTROLL-ABLE BEASTS.

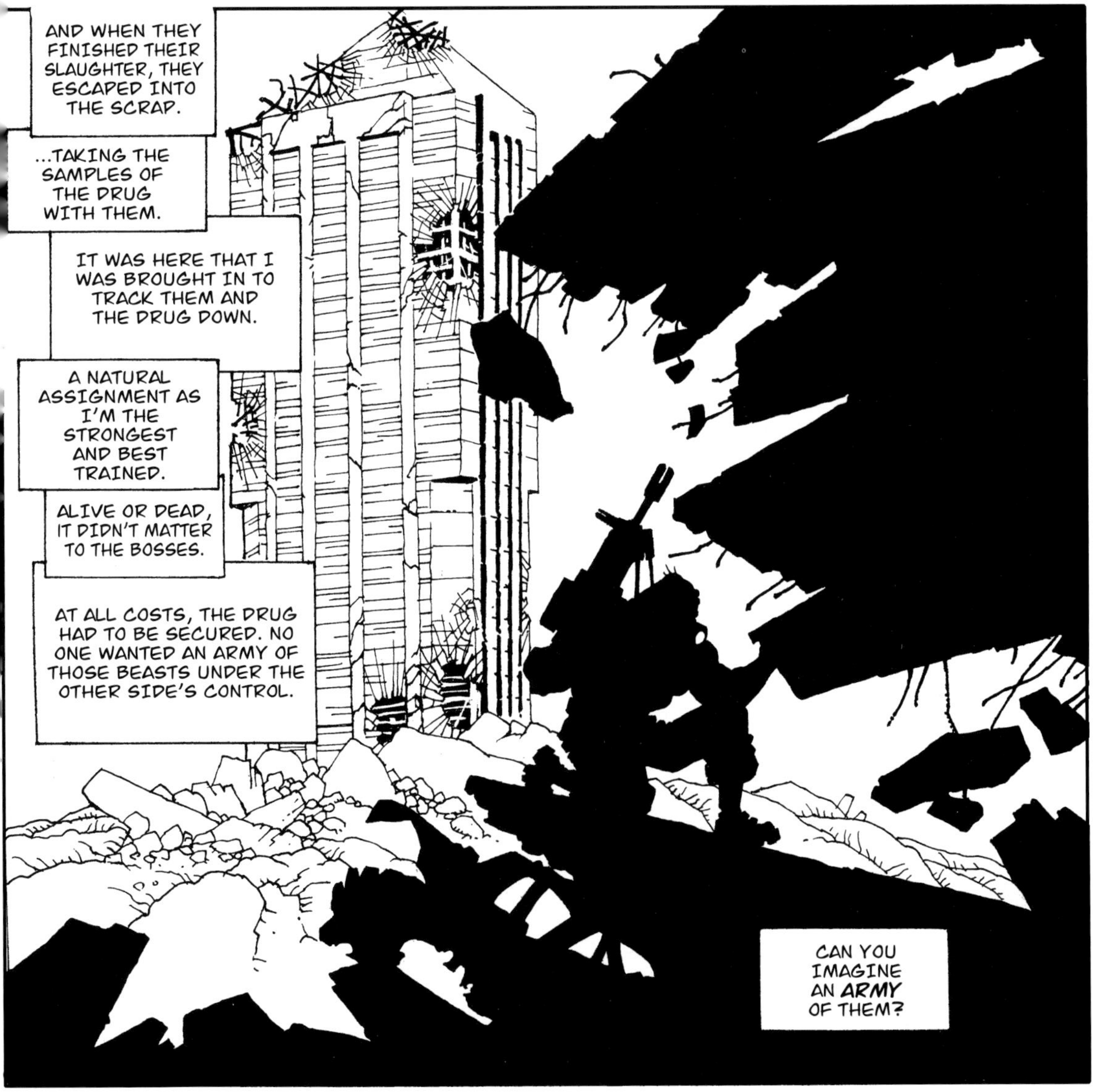
AND WHEN THEY FINISHED THEIR SLAUGHTER, THEY ESCAPED INTO THE SCRAP.
...TAKING THE SAMPLES OF THE DRUG WITH THEM.
IT WAS HERE THAT I WAS BROUGHT IN TO TRACK THEM AND THE DRUG DOWN.
A NATURAL ASSIGNMENT AS I'M THE STRONGEST AND BEST TRAINED.
ALIVE OR DEAD, IT DIDN'T MATTER TO THE BOSSES.
AT ALL COSTS, THE DRUG HAD TO BE SECURED. NO ONE WANTED AN ARMY OF THOSE BEASTS UNDER THE OTHER SIDE'S CONTROL.
CAN YOU IMAGINE AN ***ARMY*** OF THEM?

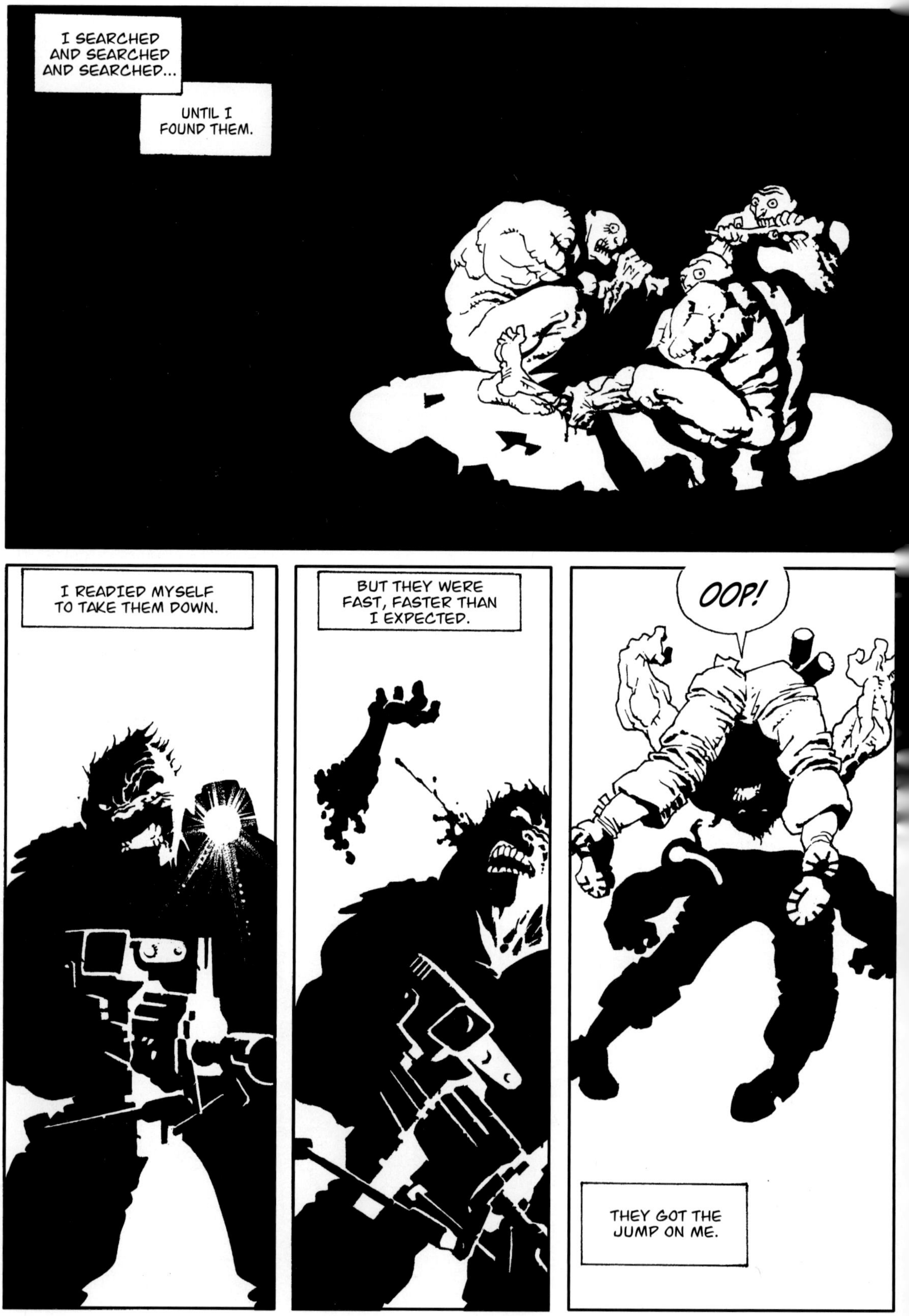
I SEARCHED AND SEARCHED AND SEARCHED...
UNTIL I FOUND THEM.
I READIED MYSELF TO TAKE THEM DOWN.
BUT THEY WERE FAST, FASTER THAN I EXPECTED.
OOP!
THEY GOT THE JUMP ON ME.

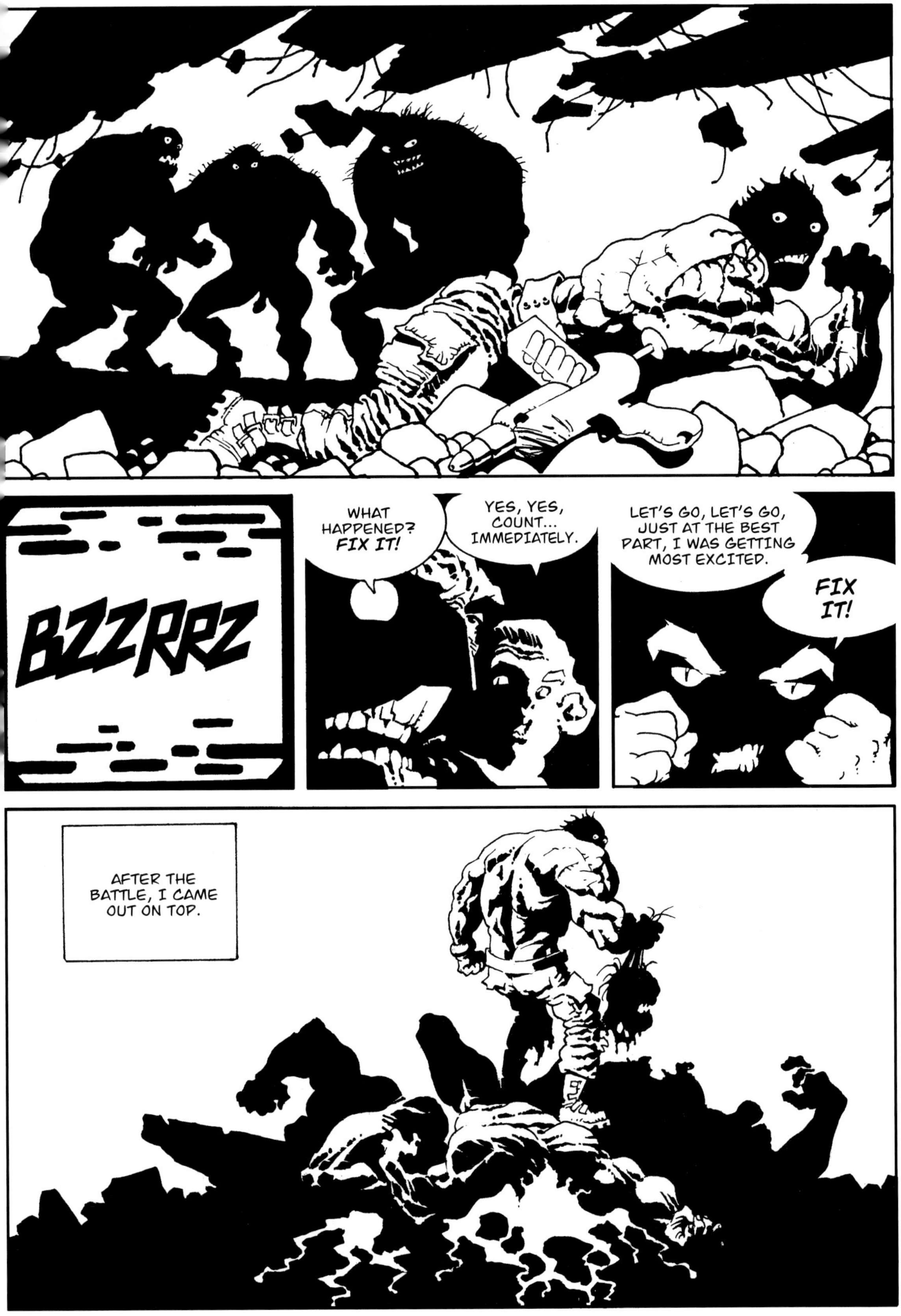
BZZRRZ
WHAT HAPPENED? FIX IT!
YES, YES, COUNT... IMMEDIATELY.
LET'S GO, LET'S GO, JUST AT THE BEST PART, I WAS GETTING MOST EXCITED.
FIX IT!
AFTER THE BATTLE, I CAME OUT ON TOP.

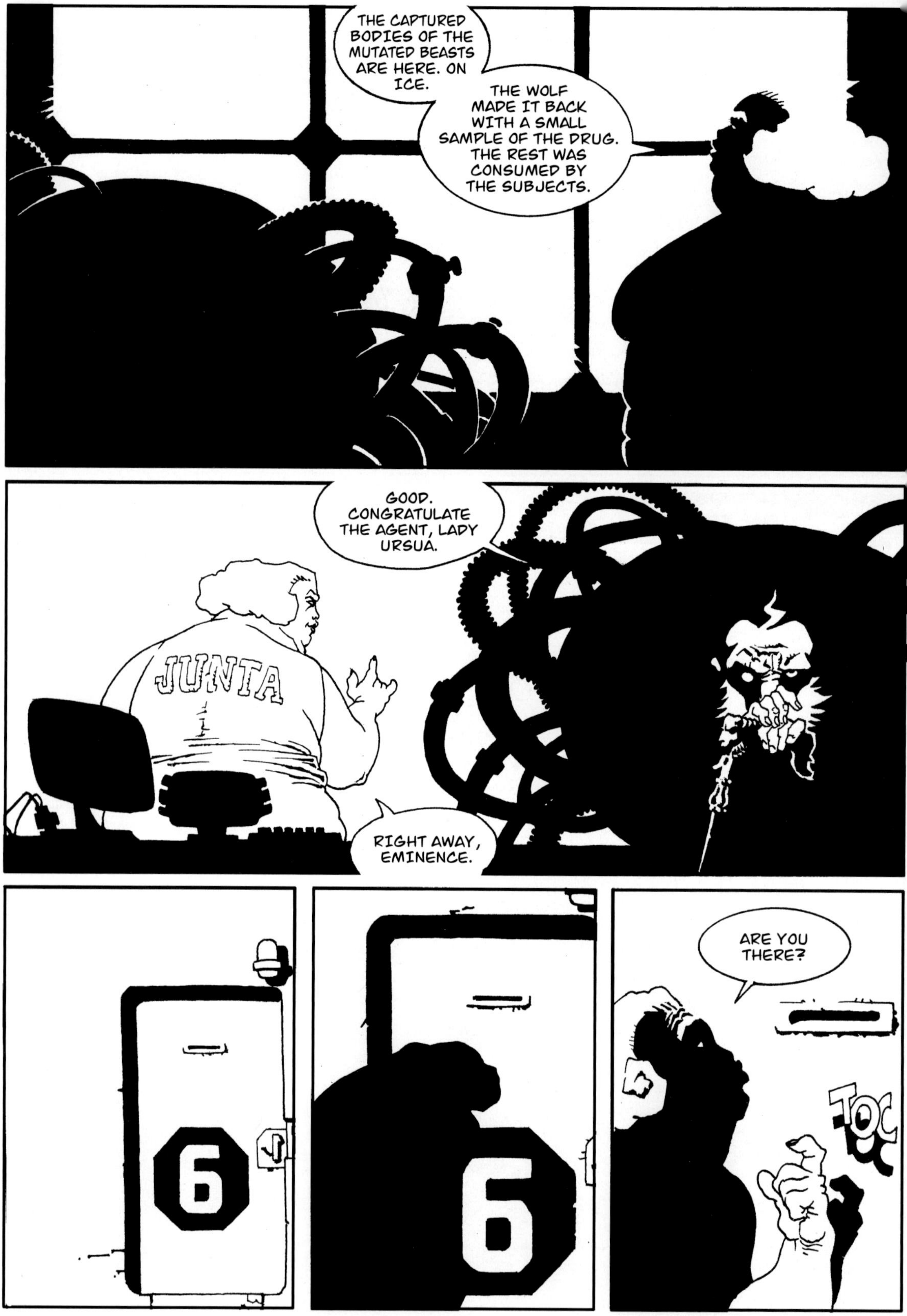
THE CAPTURED BODIES OF THE MUTATED BEASTS ARE HERE. ON ICE.
THE WOLF MADE IT BACK WITH A SMALL SAMPLE OF THE DRUG. THE REST WAS CONSUMED BY THE SUBJECTS.
GOOD. CONGRATULATE THE AGENT, LADY URSUA.
JUNTA
RIGHT AWAY, EMINENCE.
6
6
ARE YOU THERE?
TOC TOC

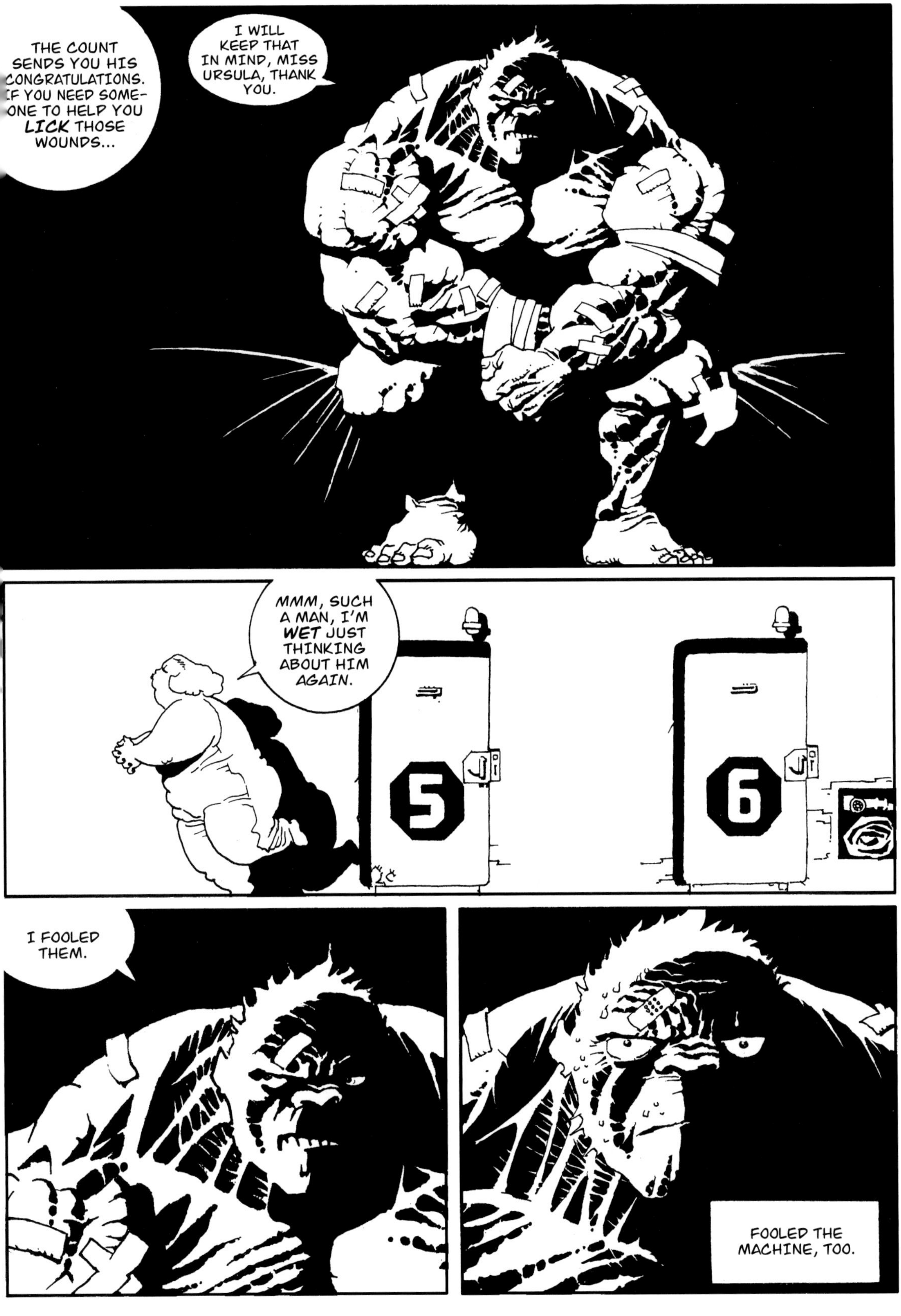
THE COUNT SENDS YOU HIS CONGRATULATIONS. IF YOU NEED SOME-ONE TO HELP YOU LICK THOSE WOUNDS...
I WILL KEEP THAT IN MIND, MISS URSULA, THANK YOU.
MMM, SUCH A MAN, I'M WET JUST THINKING ABOUT HIM AGAIN.
5
6
I FOOLED THEM.
FOOLED THE MACHINE, TOO.

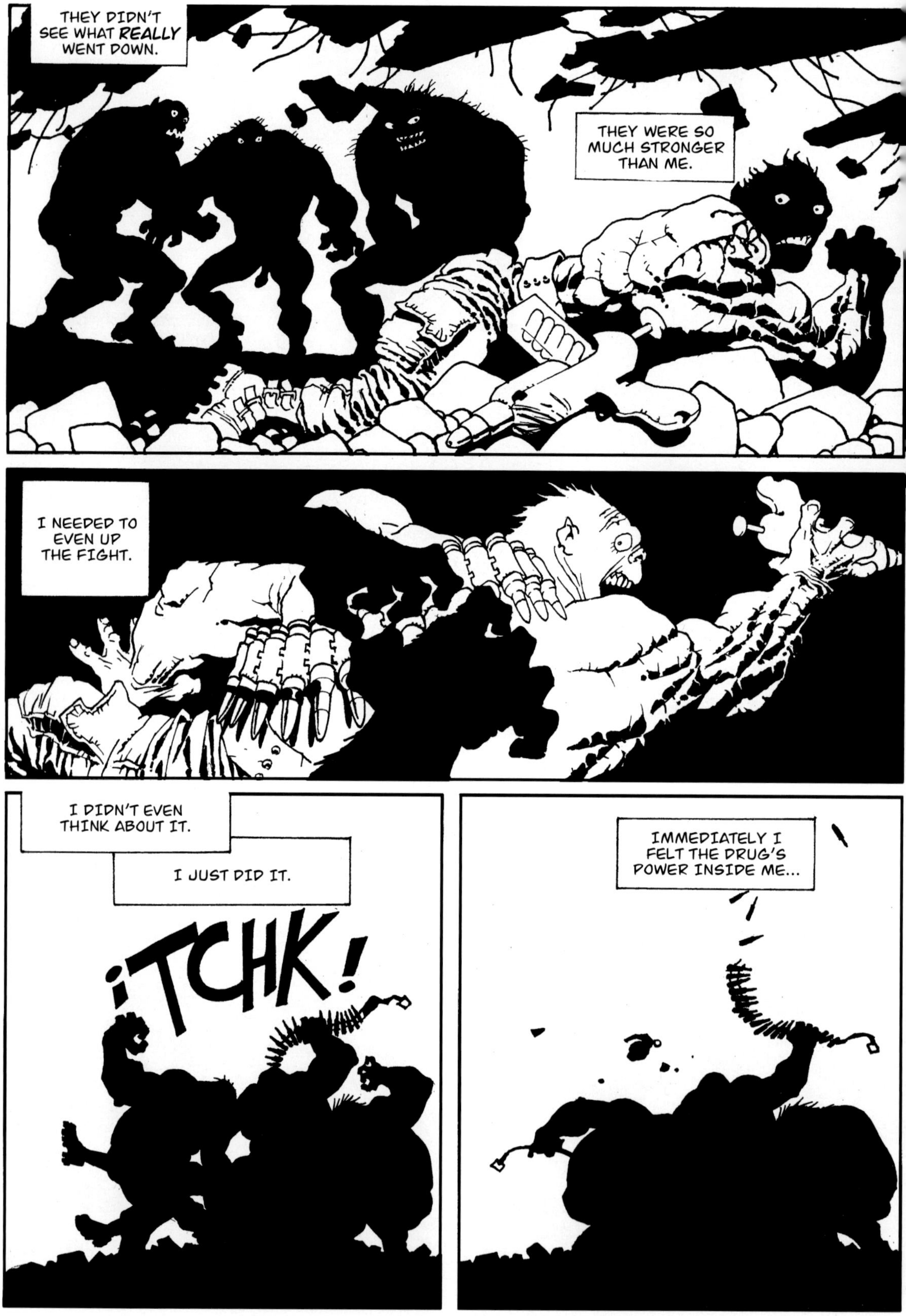
THEY DIDN'T SEE WHAT REALLY WENT DOWN.
THEY WERE SO MUCH STRONGER THAN ME.
I NEEDED TO EVEN UP THE FIGHT.
I DIDN'T EVEN THINK ABOUT IT.
I JUST DID IT.
¡TCHK!
IMMEDIATELY I FELT THE DRUG'S POWER INSIDE ME...

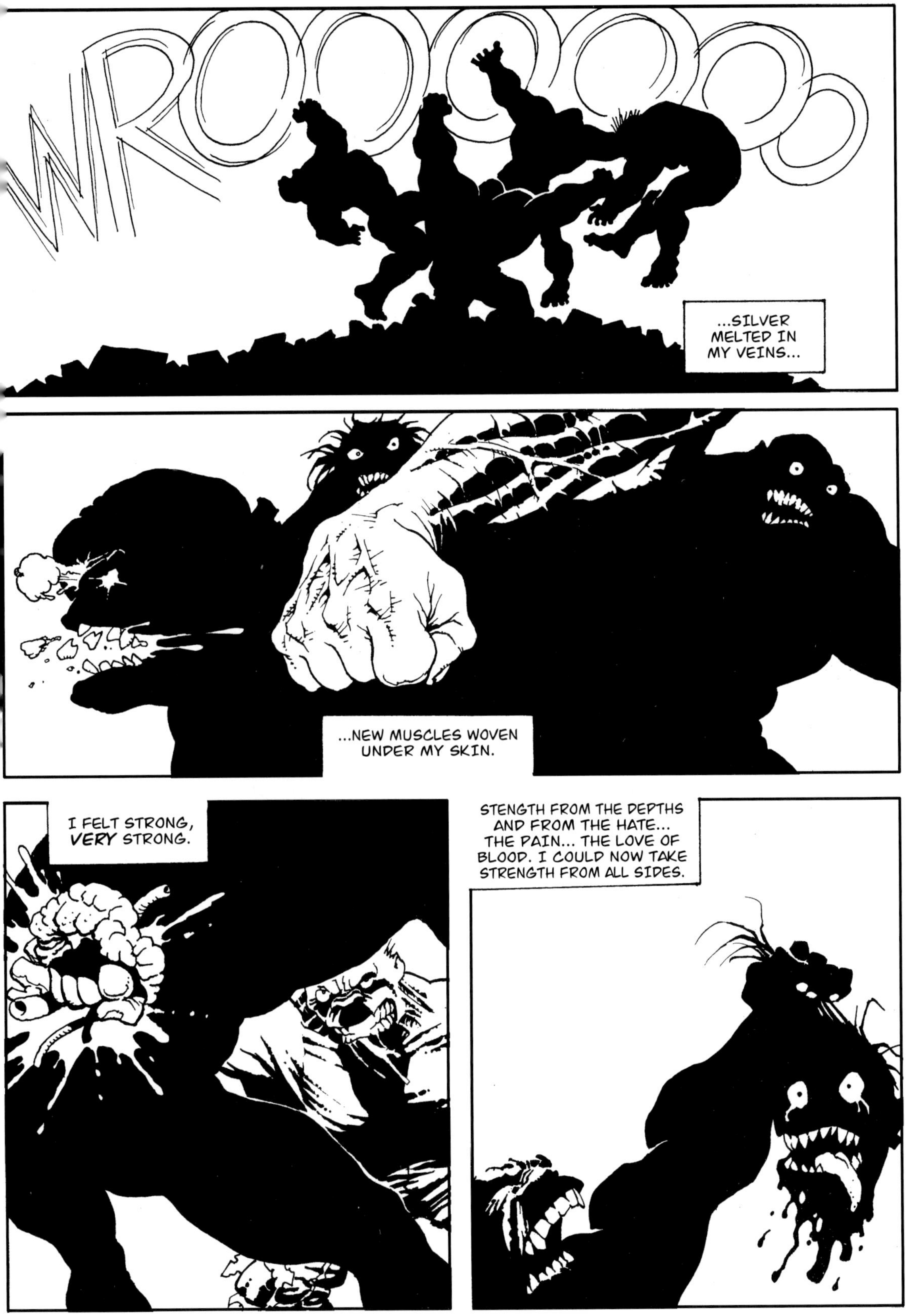
WROOOOOOO
...SILVER MELTED IN MY VEINS...
...NEW MUSCLES WOVEN UNDER MY SKIN.
I FELT STRONG, **VERY** STRONG.
STENGTH FROM THE DEPTHS AND FROM THE HATE... THE PAIN... THE LOVE OF BLOOD. I COULD NOW TAKE STRENGTH FROM ALL SIDES.

I SMELLED IT ALL.
SAW IT ALL.
FELT IT ALL.

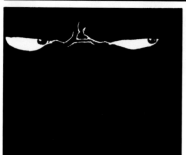

AND IT WAS
SO GOOD.

IT'S LIKE HAVING
THE MOON INSIDE
YOU.

LIKE CARRYING
ITS FROZEN
SILVER IN
YOUR VEINS.

I LIED.
LIED TO
LADY URSULA.
LIED TO
THE COUNT.
NO ONE
MUST
KNOW THAT
I...THAT
I...

...HAVE TAKEN
THIS DRUG,
THAT I NEEDED
IT TO KILL
THE MUTANTS,
TO STAY STRONG.

IT'S LIKE DRINKING
THE MILK OF THE
MOON...

I LIKE IT A LOT.

...AND I
LIKE IT.

9

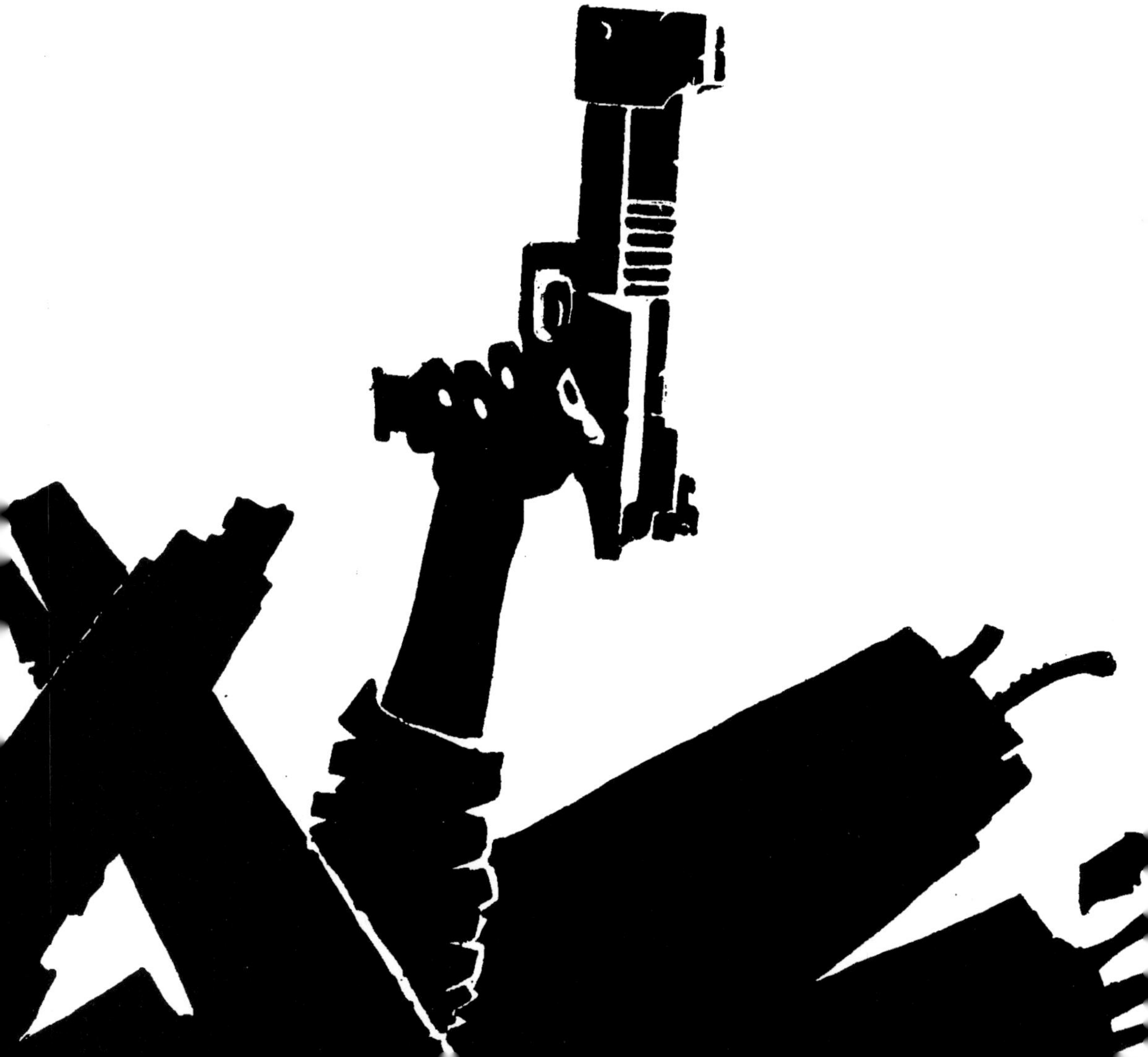

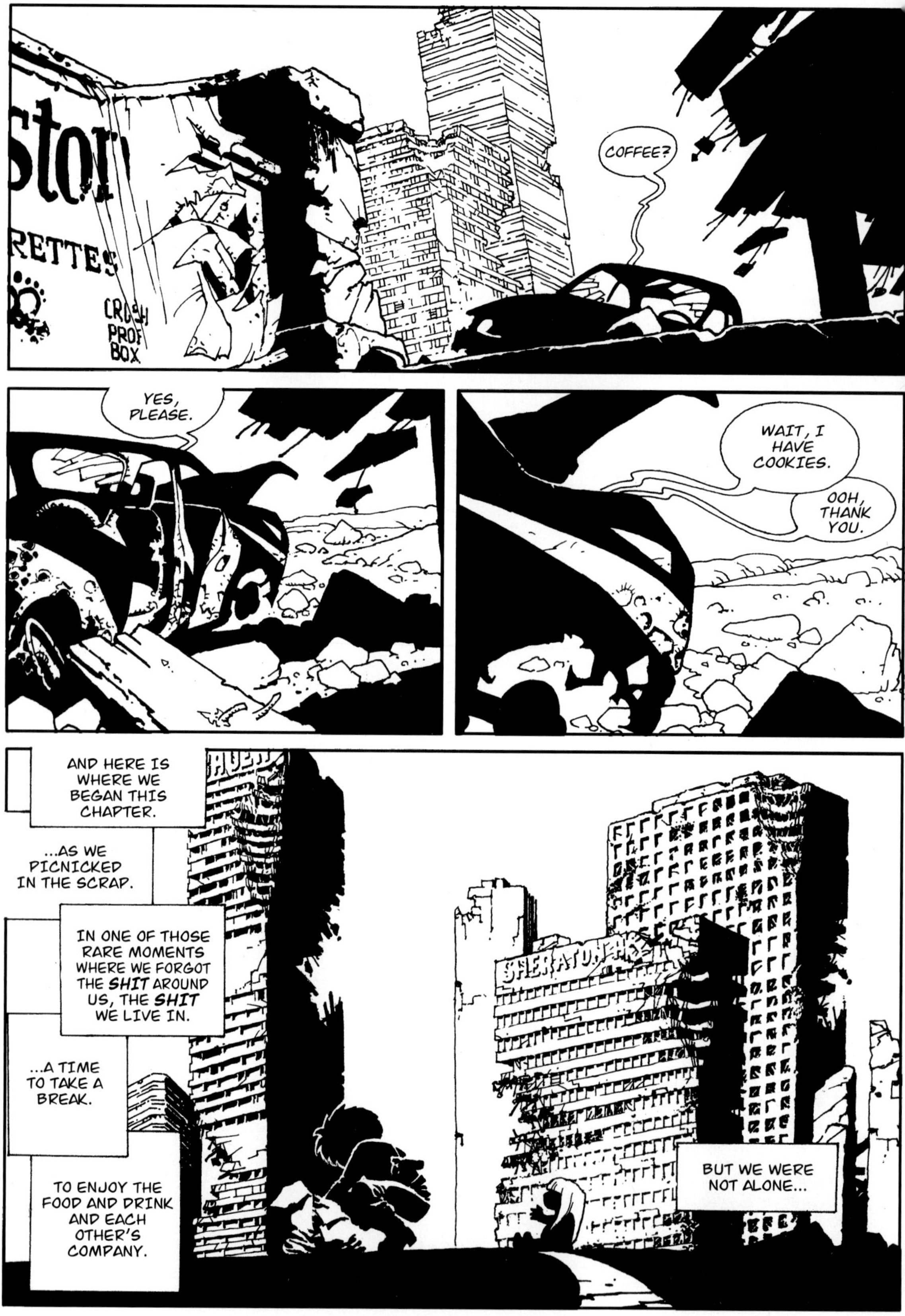
ston
RETTES
CRUSH
PROOF
BOX
COFFEE?
YES, PLEASE.
WAIT, I HAVE COOKIES.
OOH, THANK YOU.
AND HERE IS WHERE WE BEGAN THIS CHAPTER.
...AS WE PICNICKED IN THE SCRAP.
IN ONE OF THOSE RARE MOMENTS WHERE WE FORGOT THE *SHIT* AROUND US, THE *SHIT* WE LIVE IN.
...A TIME TO TAKE A BREAK.
TO ENJOY THE FOOD AND DRINK AND EACH OTHER'S COMPANY.
SHERATON
BUT WE WERE NOT ALONE...

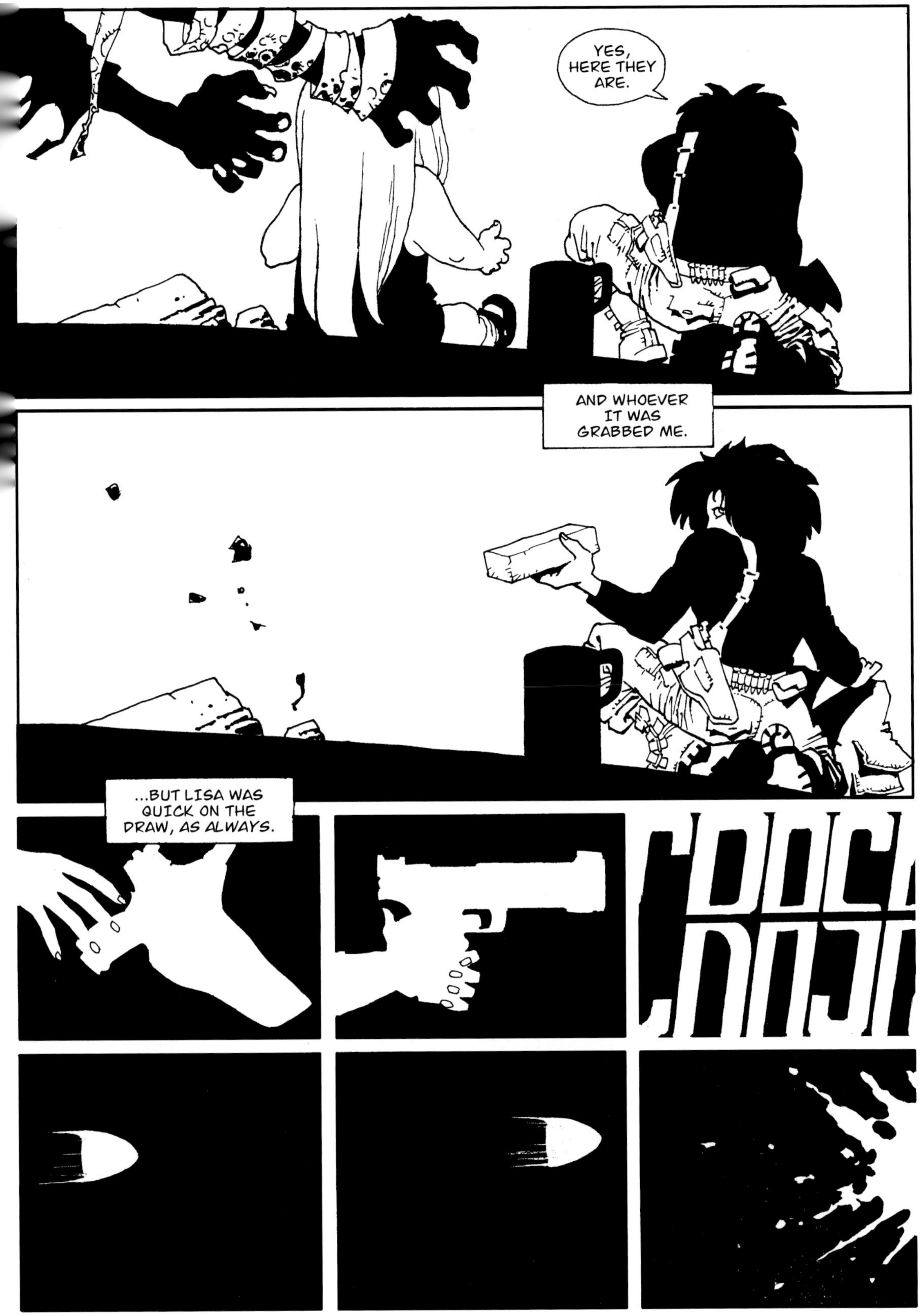
YES, HERE THEY ARE.
AND WHOEVER IT WAS GRABBED ME.
...BUT LISA WAS QUICK ON THE DRAW, AS ALWAYS.

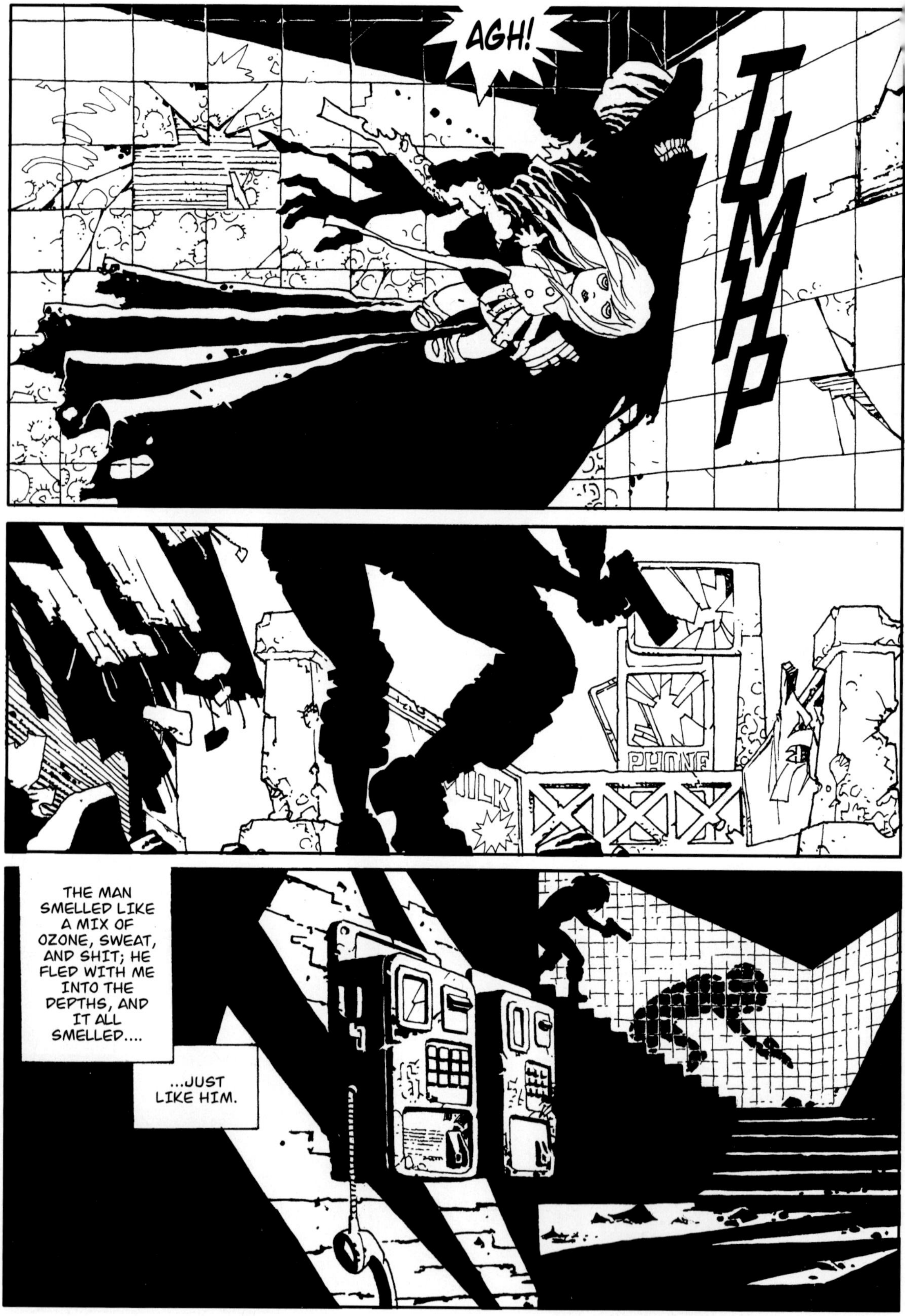
AGH!
THUMP
PHONE
MILK
THE MAN SMELLED LIKE A MIX OF OZONE, SWEAT, AND SHIT; HE FLED WITH ME INTO THE DEPTHS, AND IT ALL SMELLED....
...JUST LIKE HIM.

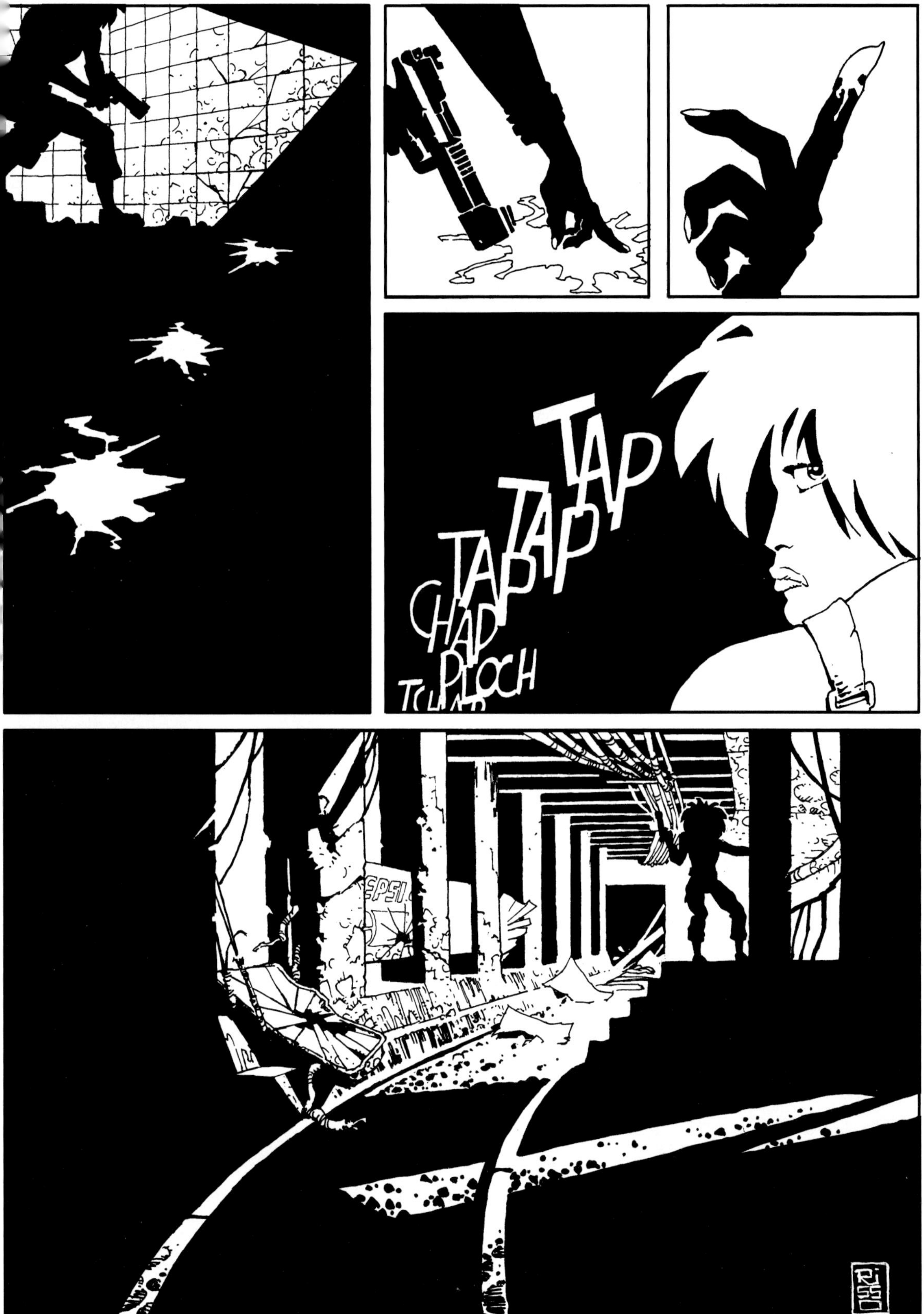
TAP
TAP
TAP
CHAD
PLOCH

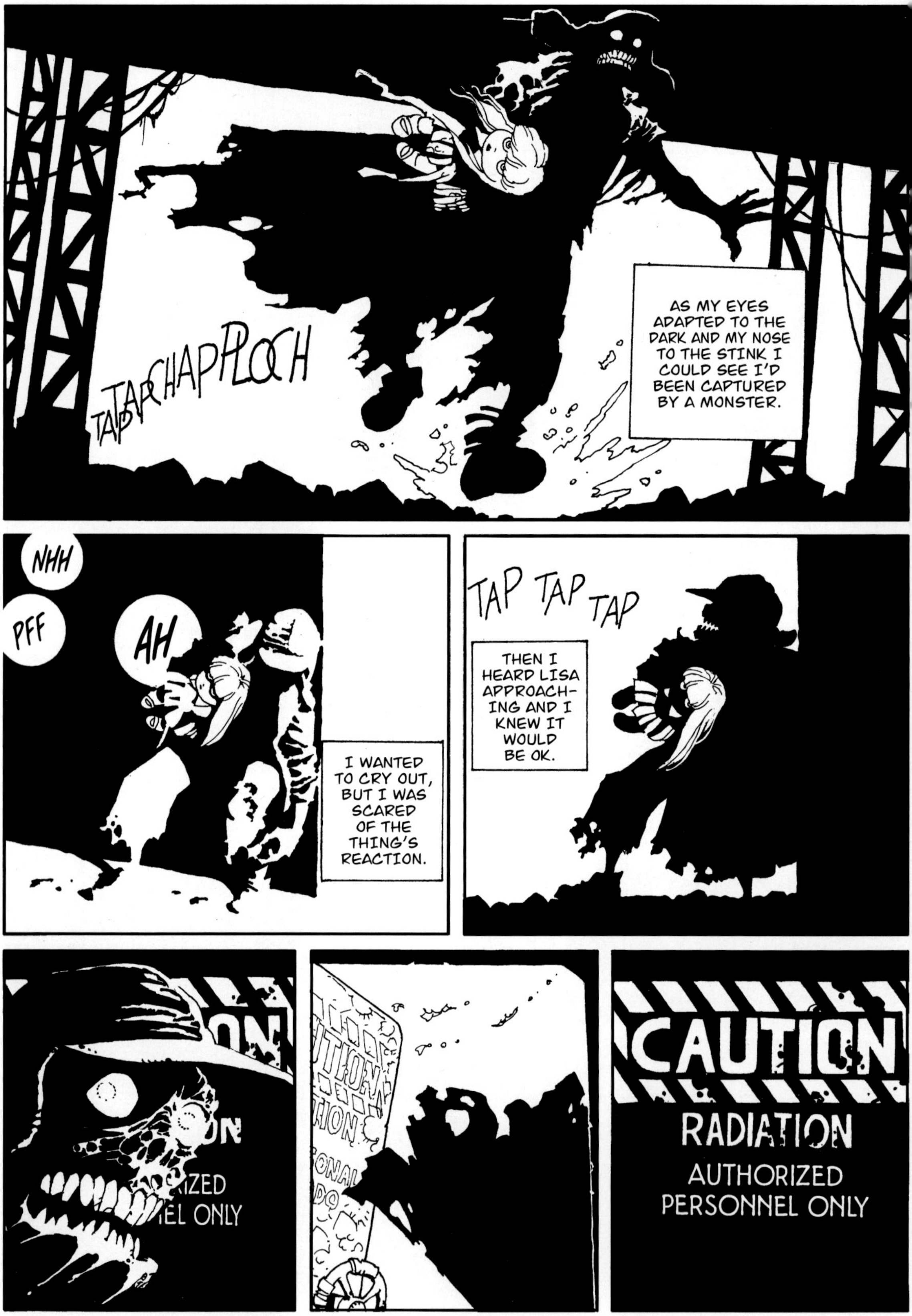
TAP TAP CHAP PLOCH
AS MY EYES ADAPTED TO THE DARK AND MY NOSE TO THE STINK I COULD SEE I'D BEEN CAPTURED BY A MONSTER.
NHH
PFF
AH
I WANTED TO CRY OUT, BUT I WAS SCARED OF THE THING'S REACTION.
TAP TAP TAP
THEN I HEARD LISA APPROACHING AND I KNEW IT WOULD BE OK.
CAUTION
RADIATION
AUTHORIZED PERSONNEL ONLY

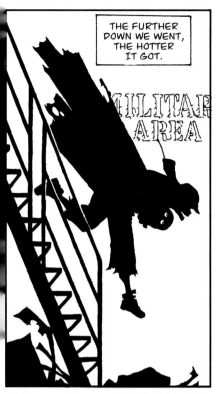

THE FURTHER DOWN WE WENT, THE HOTTER IT GOT.

...I MEAN, *REALLY* HOT. HOTTER THAN HELL ITSELF.

AS IF THAT WAS OUR FINAL DESTINATION.

HERE, YYYESSS!

THE THING WAS WEAK AND I KNEW IT WAS MY CHANCE.

IT WAS THEN THAT I DECIDED.

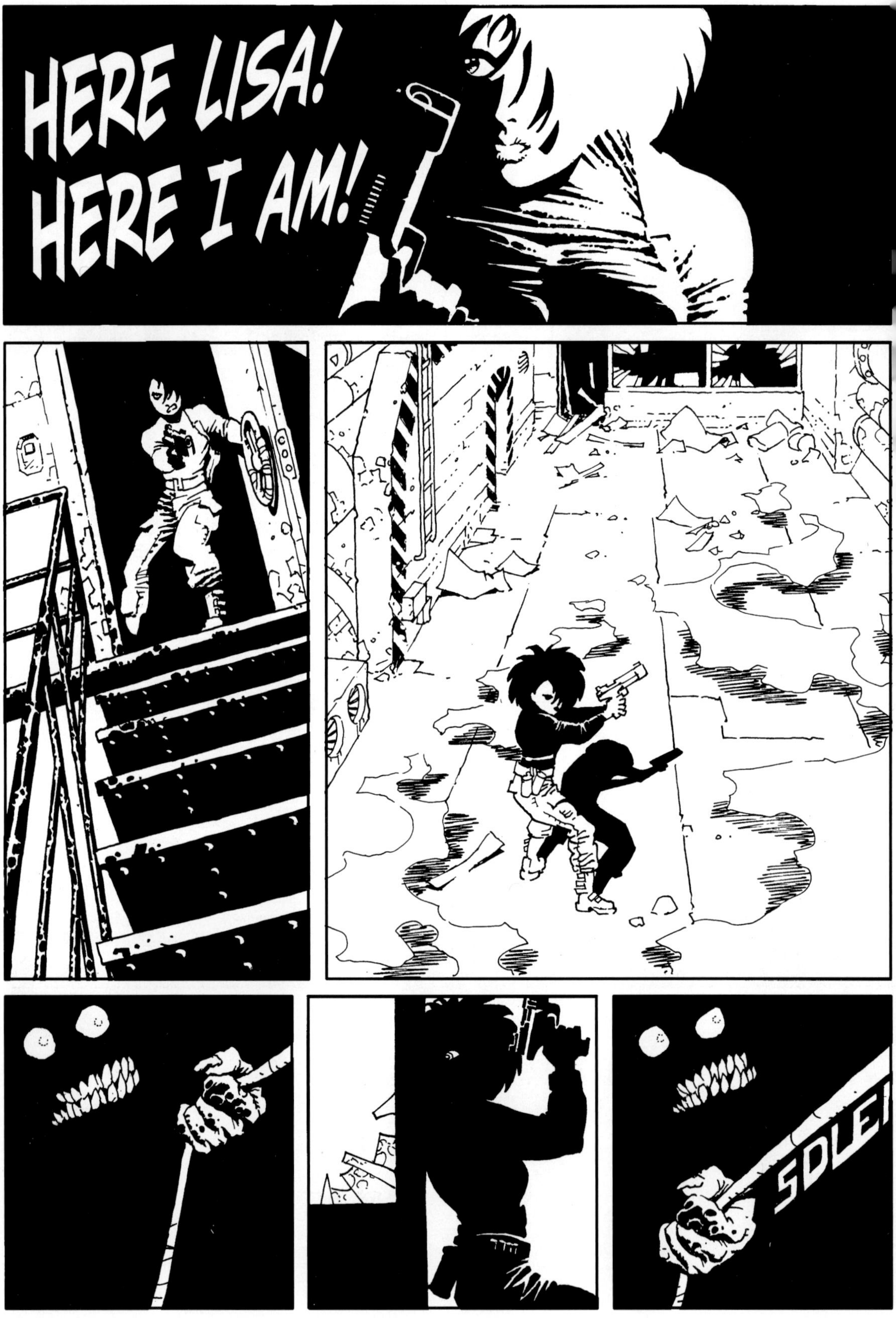
HERE LISA!
HERE I AM!
SDLEI

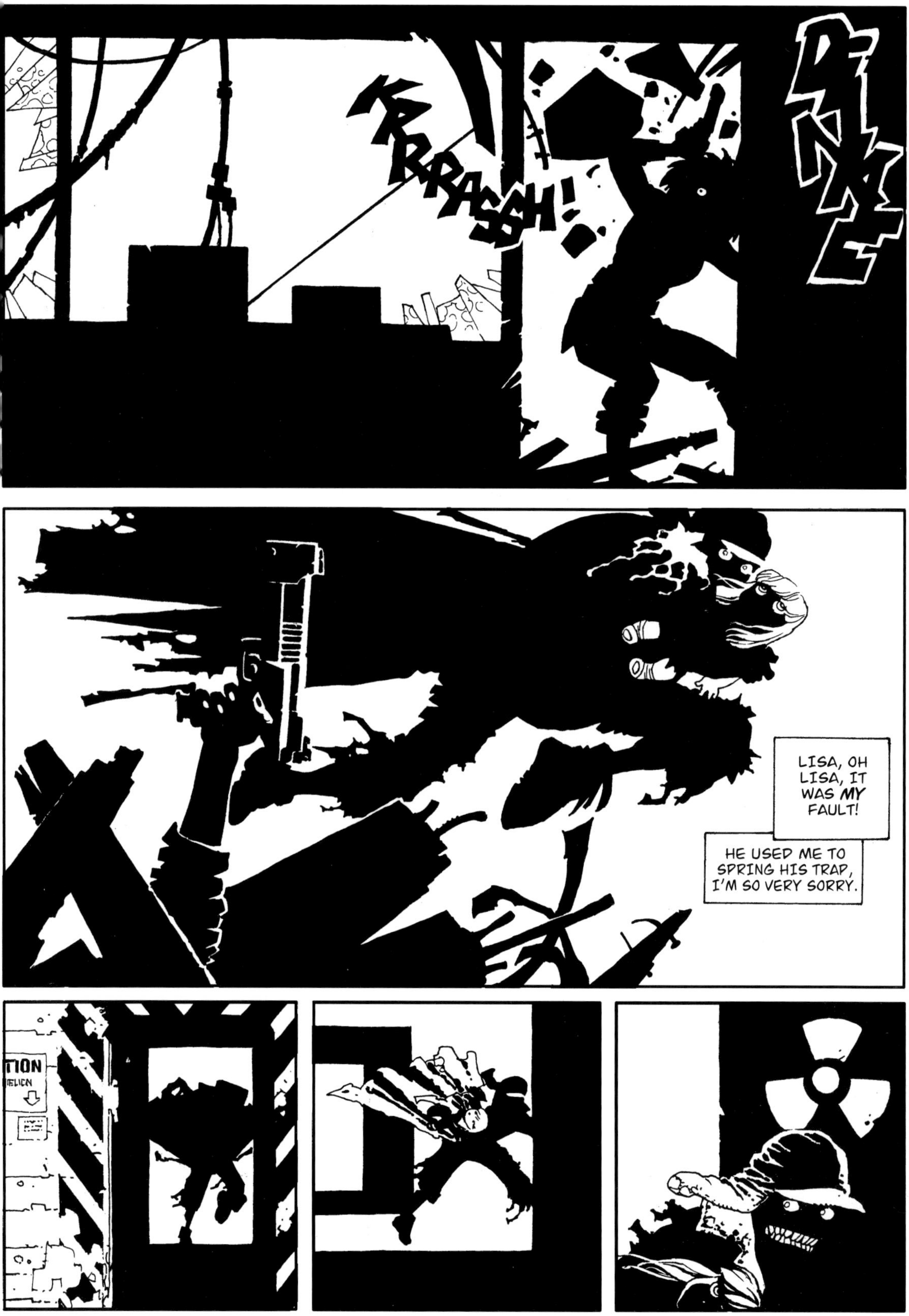
KRRRASSH!
LISA, OH LISA, IT WAS **MY** FAULT!
HE USED ME TO SPRING HIS TRAP, I'M SO VERY SORRY.

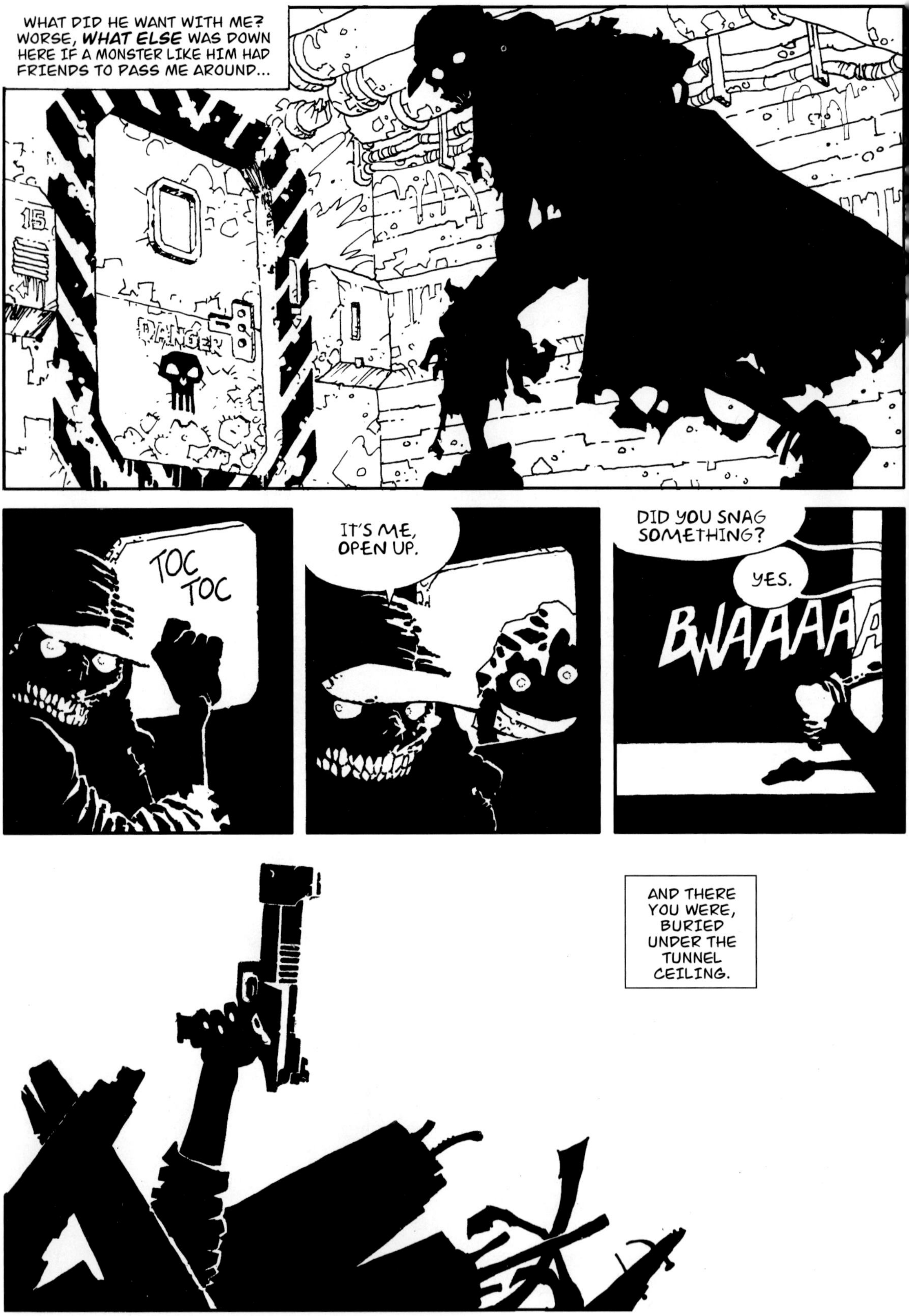
WHAT DID HE WANT WITH ME? WORSE, **WHAT ELSE** WAS DOWN HERE IF A MONSTER LIKE HIM HAD FRIENDS TO PASS ME AROUND...
15
DANGER
TOC TOC
IT'S ME, OPEN UP.
DID YOU SNAG SOMETHING?
YES.
BWAAAAA
AND THERE YOU WERE, BURIED UNDER THE TUNNEL CEILING.

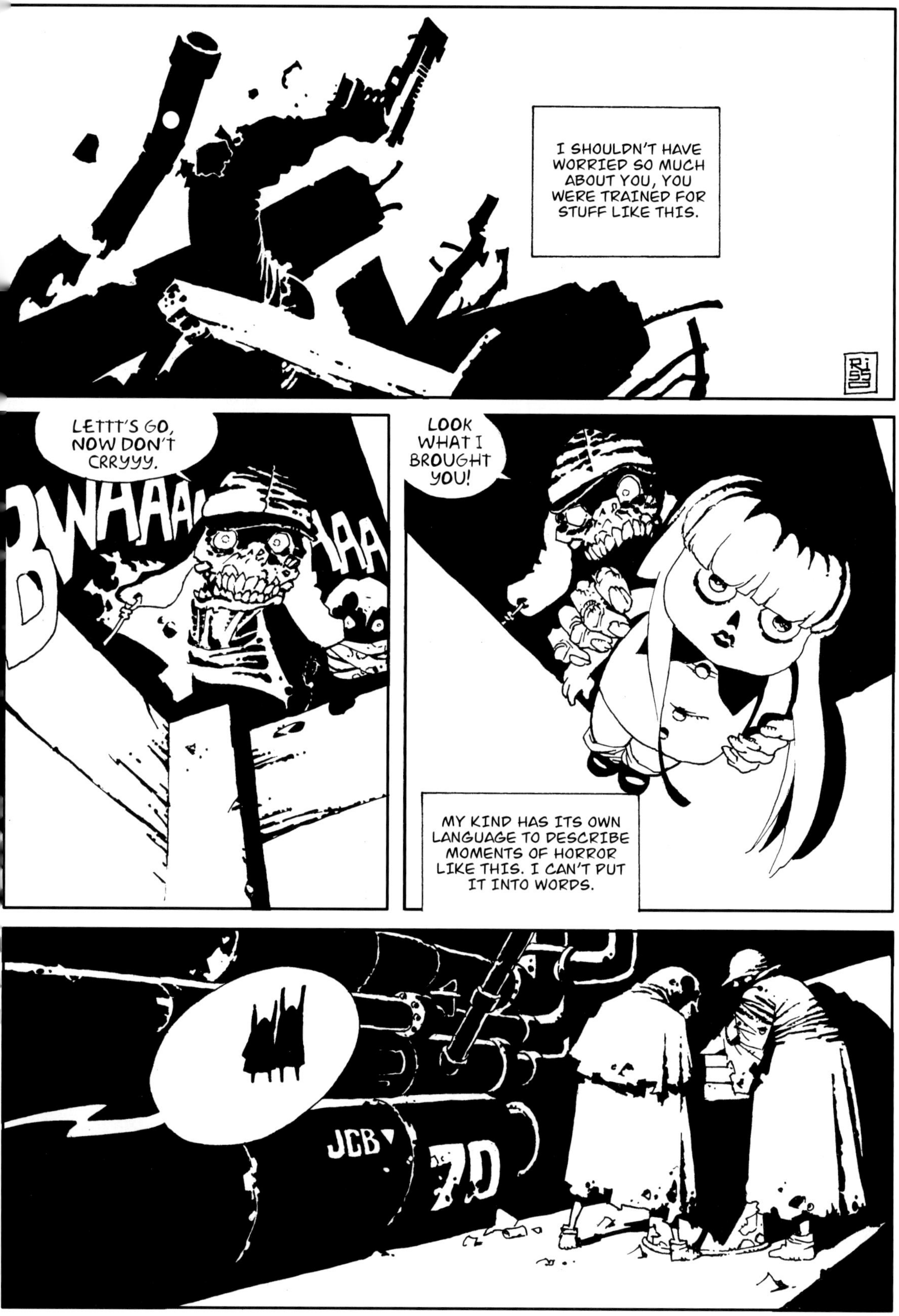
I SHOULDN'T HAVE WORRIED SO MUCH ABOUT YOU, YOU WERE TRAINED FOR STUFF LIKE THIS.
LETTT'S GO, NOW DON'T CRRYYY.
BWAAA
AAA
LOOK WHAT I BROUGHT YOU!
MY KIND HAS ITS OWN LANGUAGE TO DESCRIBE MOMENTS OF HORROR LIKE THIS. I CAN'T PUT IT INTO WORDS.
JCB
70

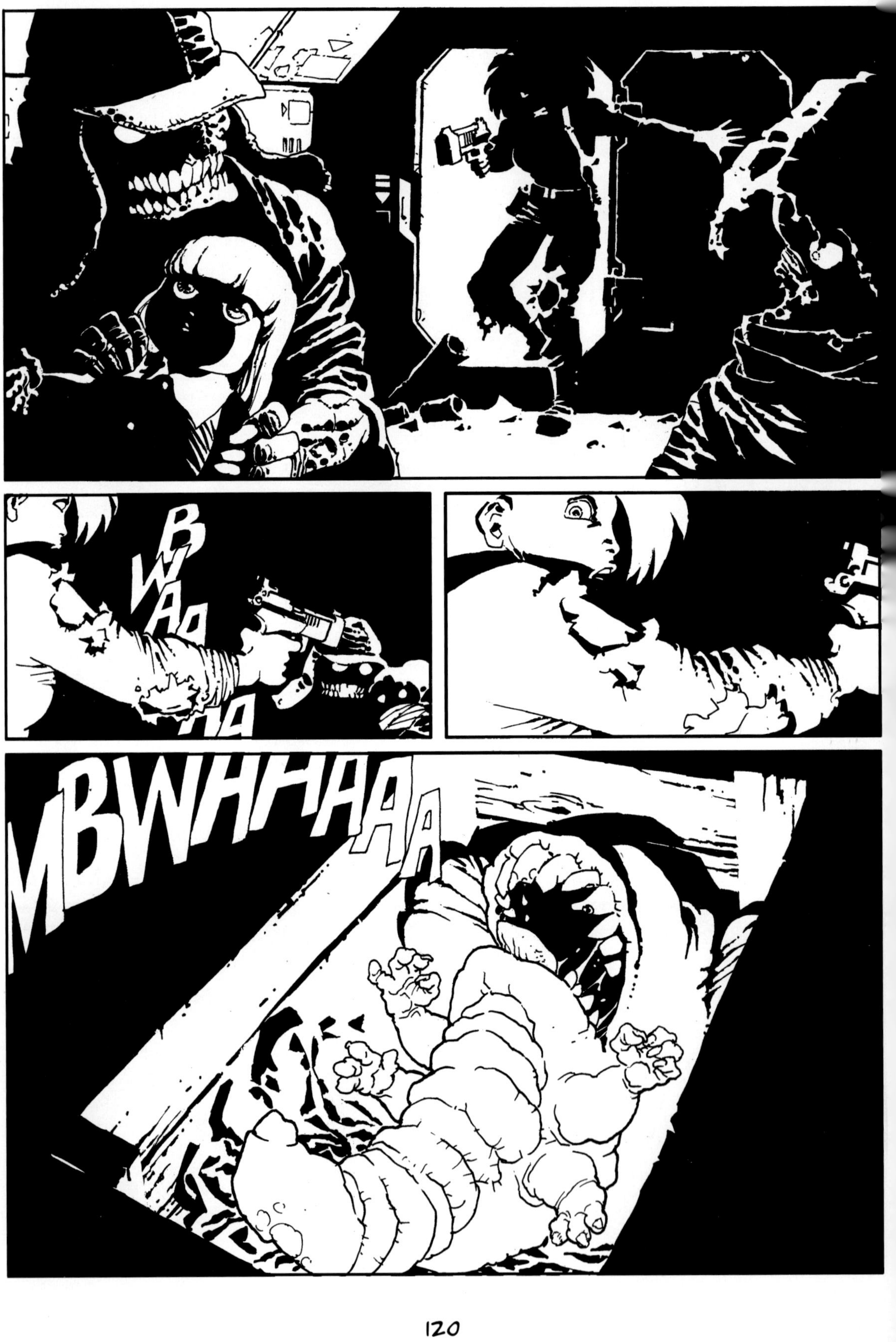
BWAA
HA
MBWAHAAAA

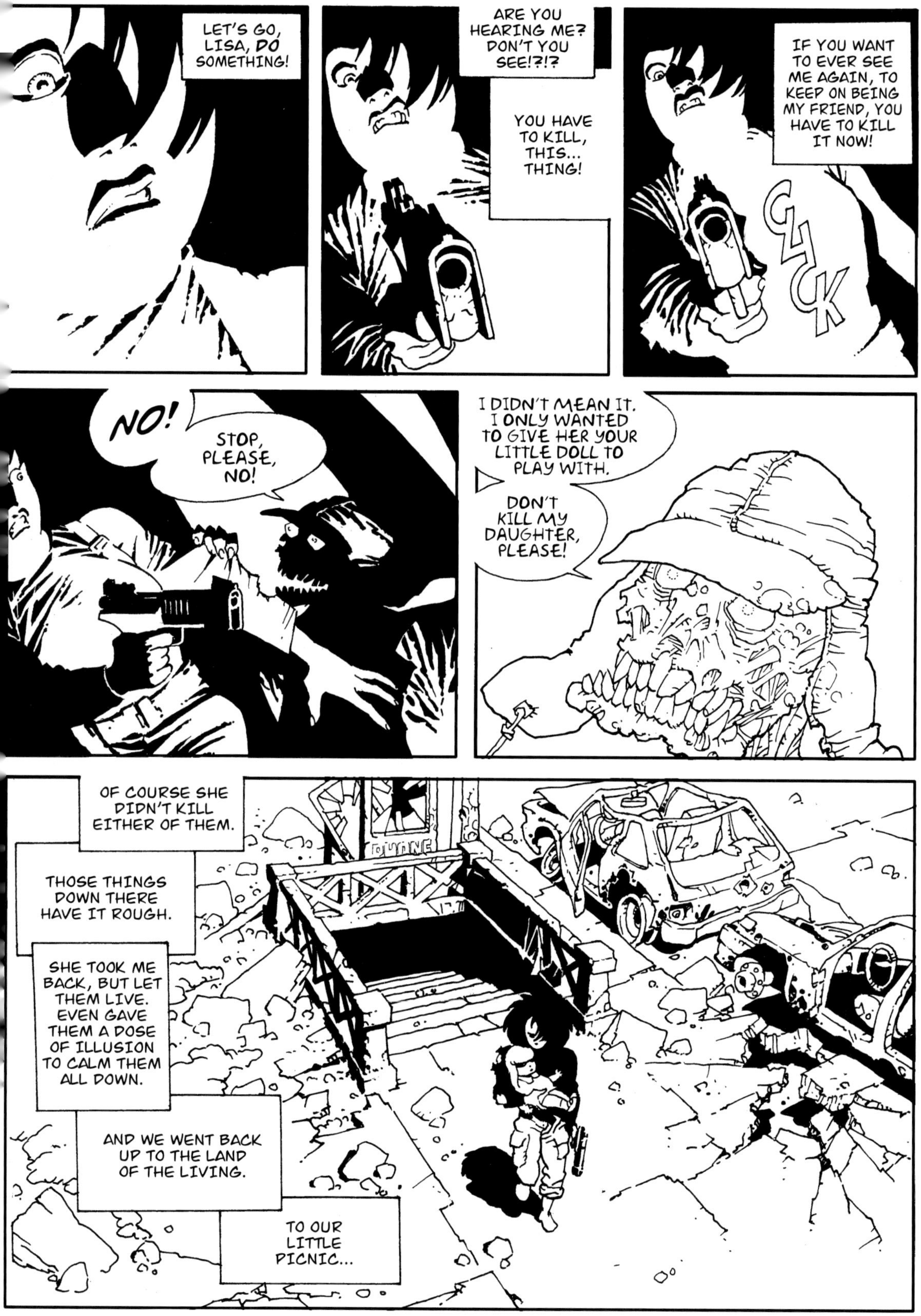
LET'S GO, LISA, DO SOMETHING!
ARE YOU HEARING ME? DON'T YOU SEE!?!?
YOU HAVE TO KILL, THIS... THING!
IF YOU WANT TO EVER SEE ME AGAIN, TO KEEP ON BEING MY FRIEND, YOU HAVE TO KILL IT NOW!
CLICK
NO!
STOP, PLEASE, NO!
I DIDN'T MEAN IT. I ONLY WANTED TO GIVE HER YOUR LITTLE DOLL TO PLAY WITH.
DON'T KILL MY DAUGHTER, PLEASE!
OF COURSE SHE DIDN'T KILL EITHER OF THEM.
THOSE THINGS DOWN THERE HAVE IT ROUGH.
SHE TOOK ME BACK, BUT LET THEM LIVE. EVEN GAVE THEM A DOSE OF ILLUSION TO CALM THEM ALL DOWN.
AND WE WENT BACK UP TO THE LAND OF THE LIVING.
TO OUR LITTLE PICNIC...

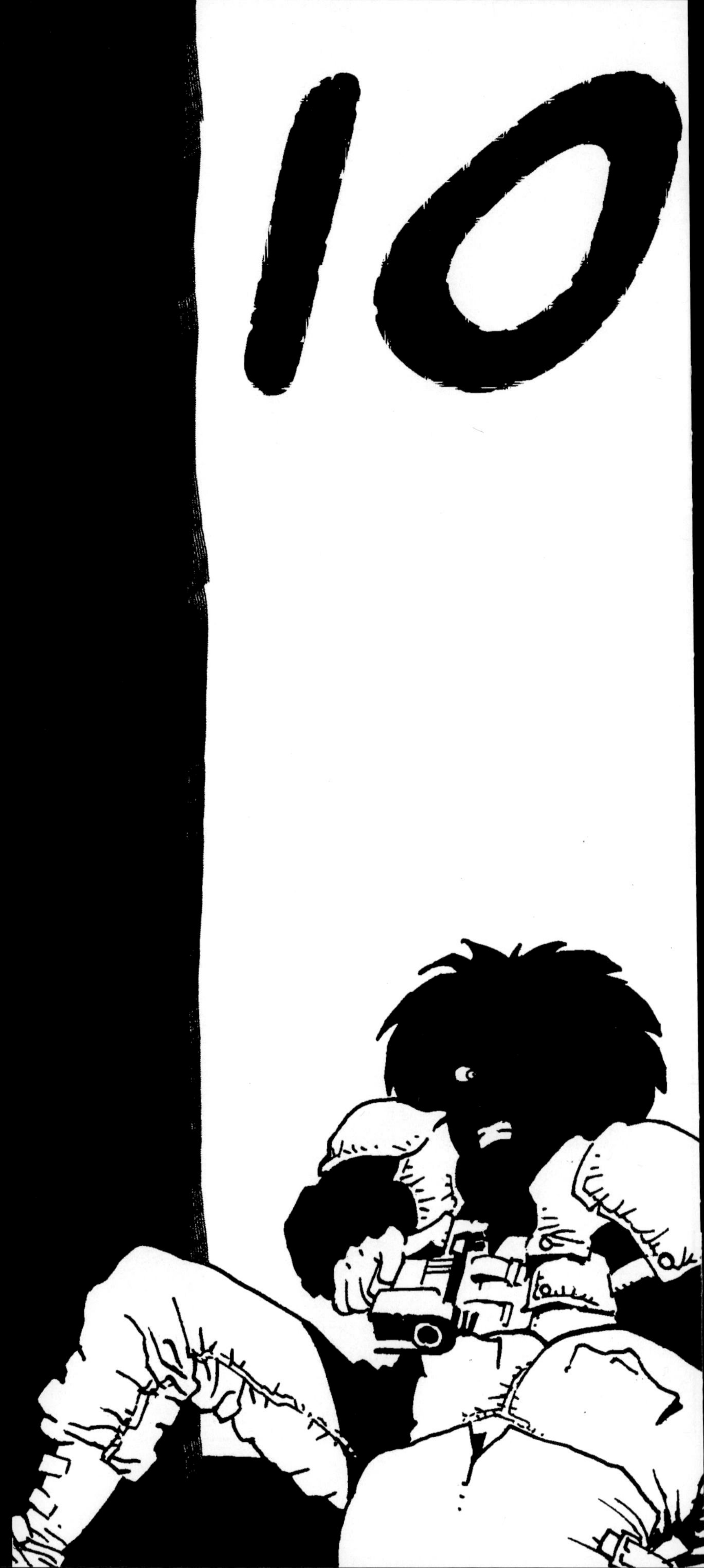
10

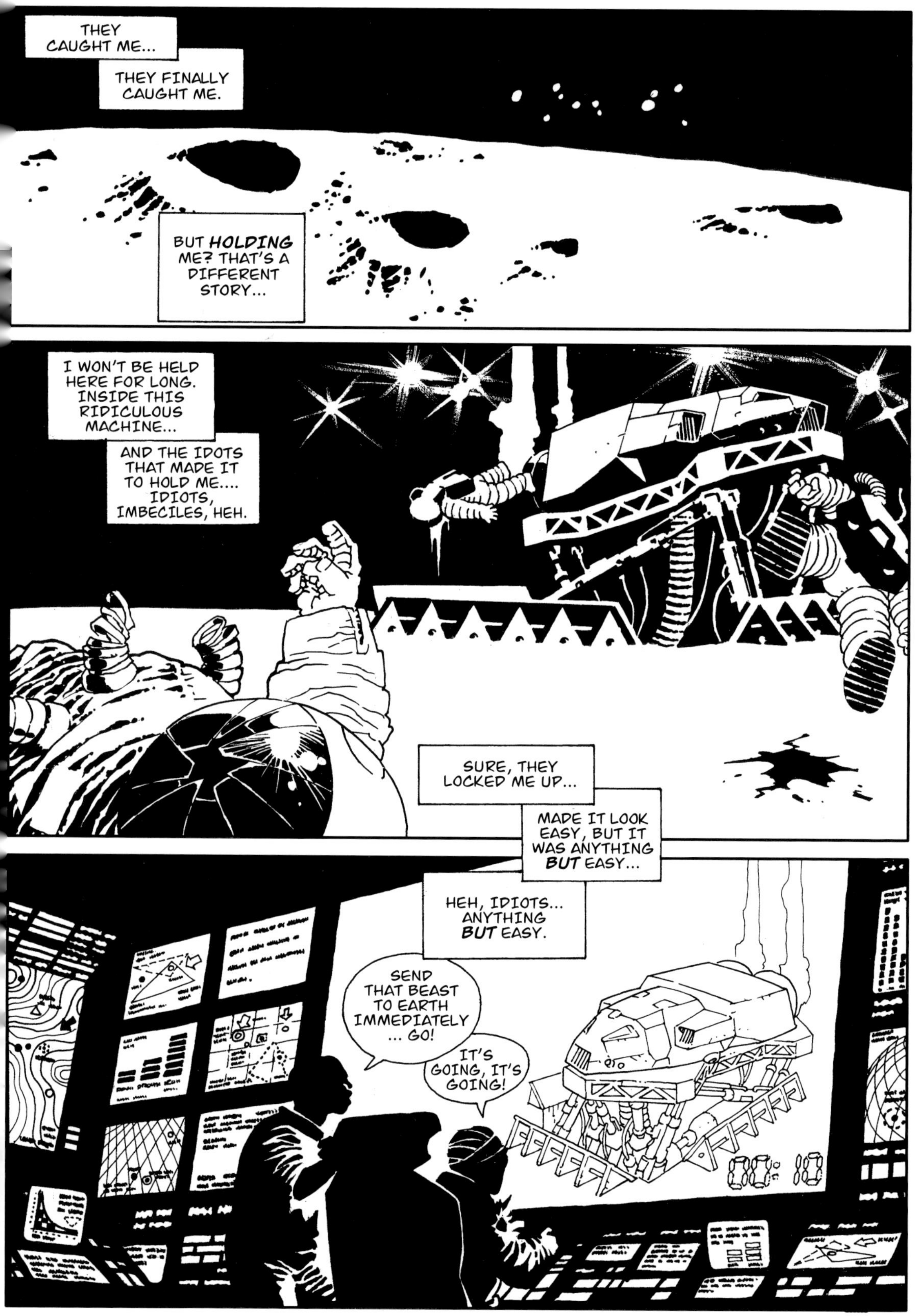

THEY CAUGHT ME...
THEY FINALLY CAUGHT ME.
BUT HOLDING ME? THAT'S A DIFFERENT STORY...
I WON'T BE HELD HERE FOR LONG. INSIDE THIS RIDICULOUS MACHINE...
AND THE IDOTS THAT MADE IT TO HOLD ME.... IDIOTS, IMBECILES, HEH.
SURE, THEY LOCKED ME UP...
MADE IT LOOK EASY, BUT IT WAS ANYTHING BUT EASY...
HEH, IDIOTS... ANYTHING BUT EASY.
SEND THAT BEAST TO EARTH IMMEDIATELY ... GO!
IT'S GOING, IT'S GOING!

I LOOK AT THEM, I SEE THEM, AND I LAUGH.

HEH, HEH, HEEEHEEEE-HHHHH....

THEY'RE SO SCARED... AND THEY **SHOULD** BE, BECAUSE WHEN I GET OUT OF, UH HERE...

OUT!

UUYYY!...

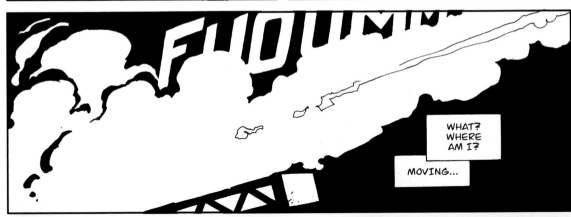

FHOOMM

WHAT? WHERE AM I?

MOVING...

MOVING.

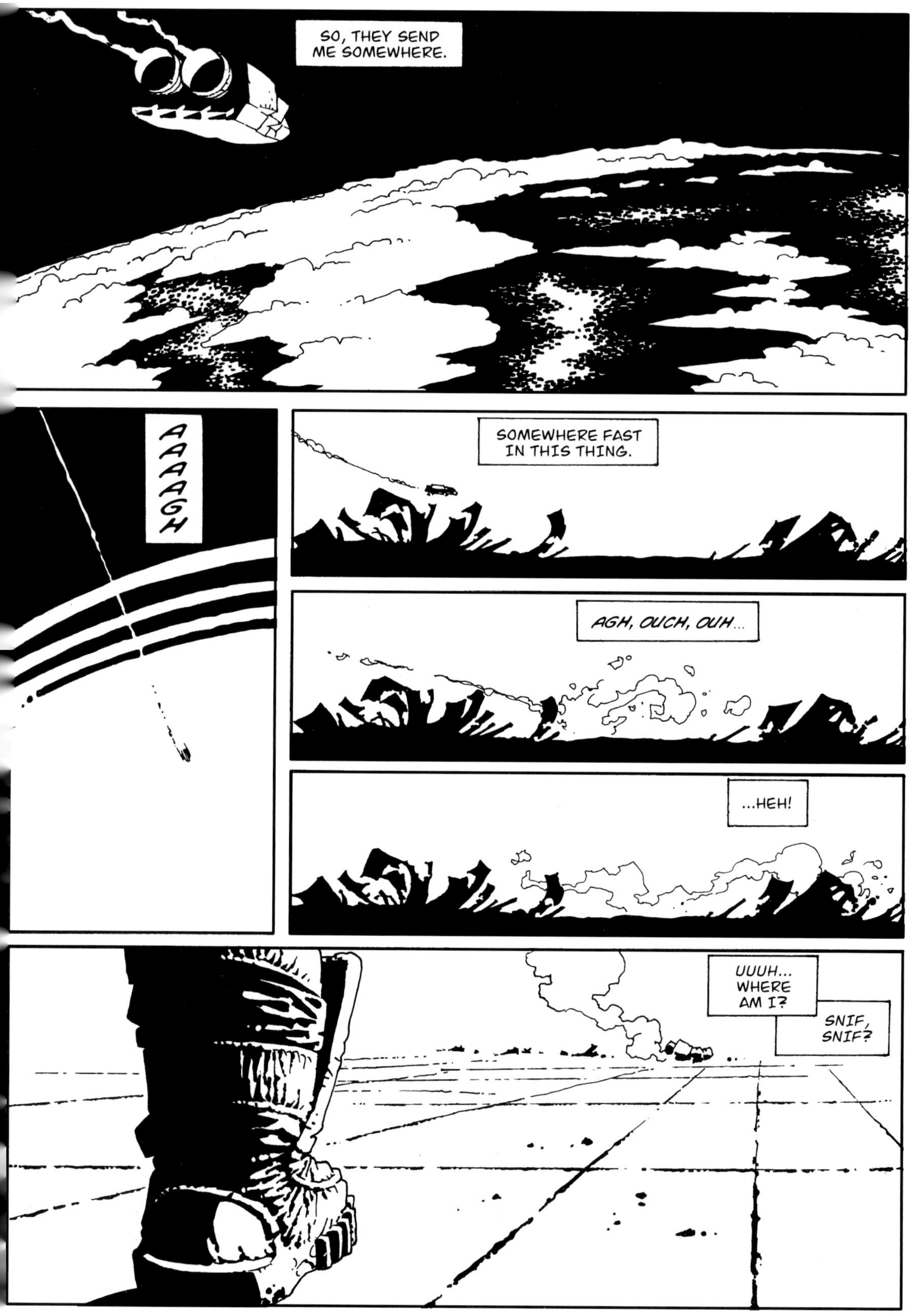
SO, THEY SEND ME SOMEWHERE.
AAAAGH
SOMEWHERE FAST IN THIS THING.
AGH, OUCH, OUH...
...HEH!
UUUH... WHERE AM I?
SNIF, SNIF?

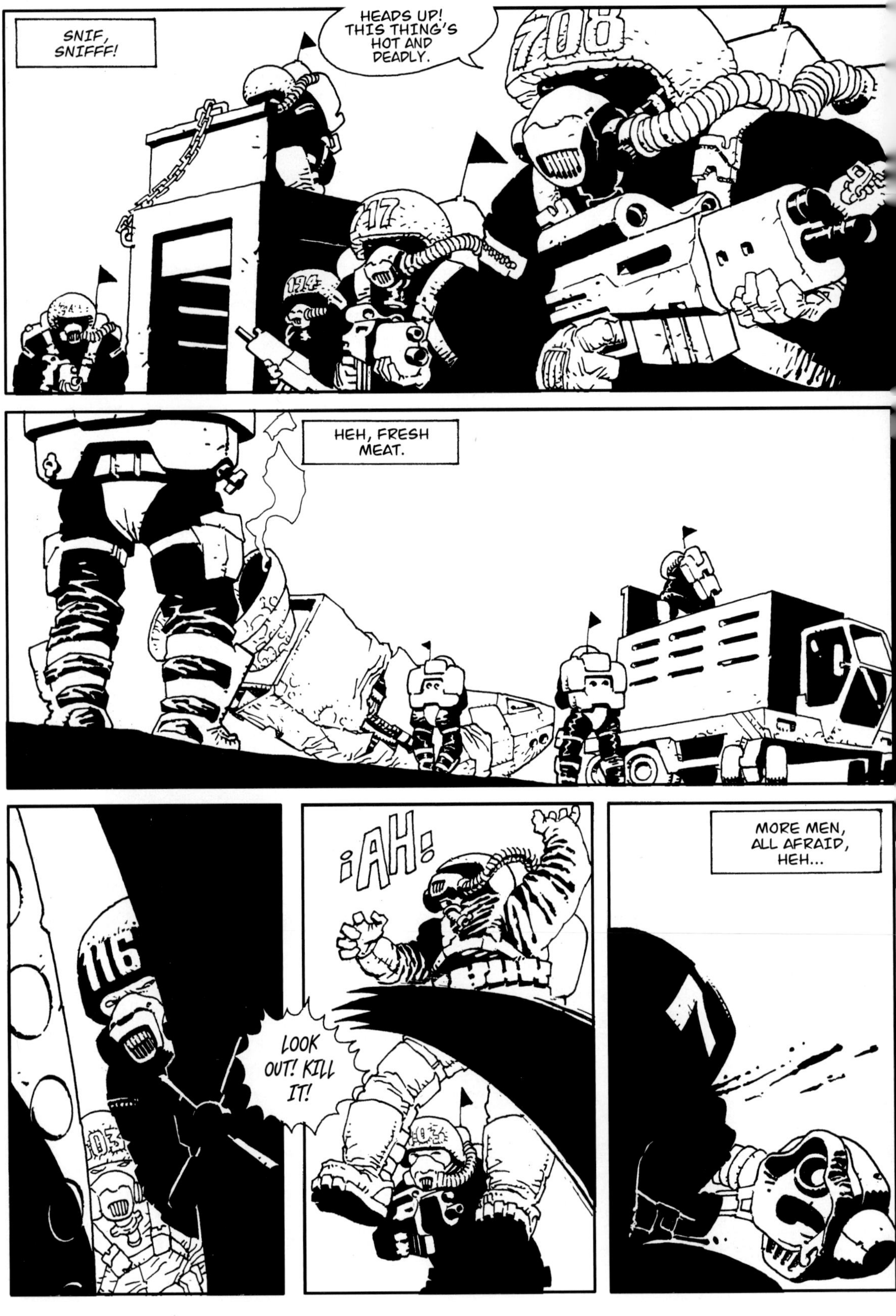
SNIF, SNIFFF!
HEADS UP! THIS THING'S HOT AND DEADLY.
708
17
HEH, FRESH MEAT.
116
LOOK OUT! KILL IT!
¡AH!
MORE MEN, ALL AFRAID, HEH...

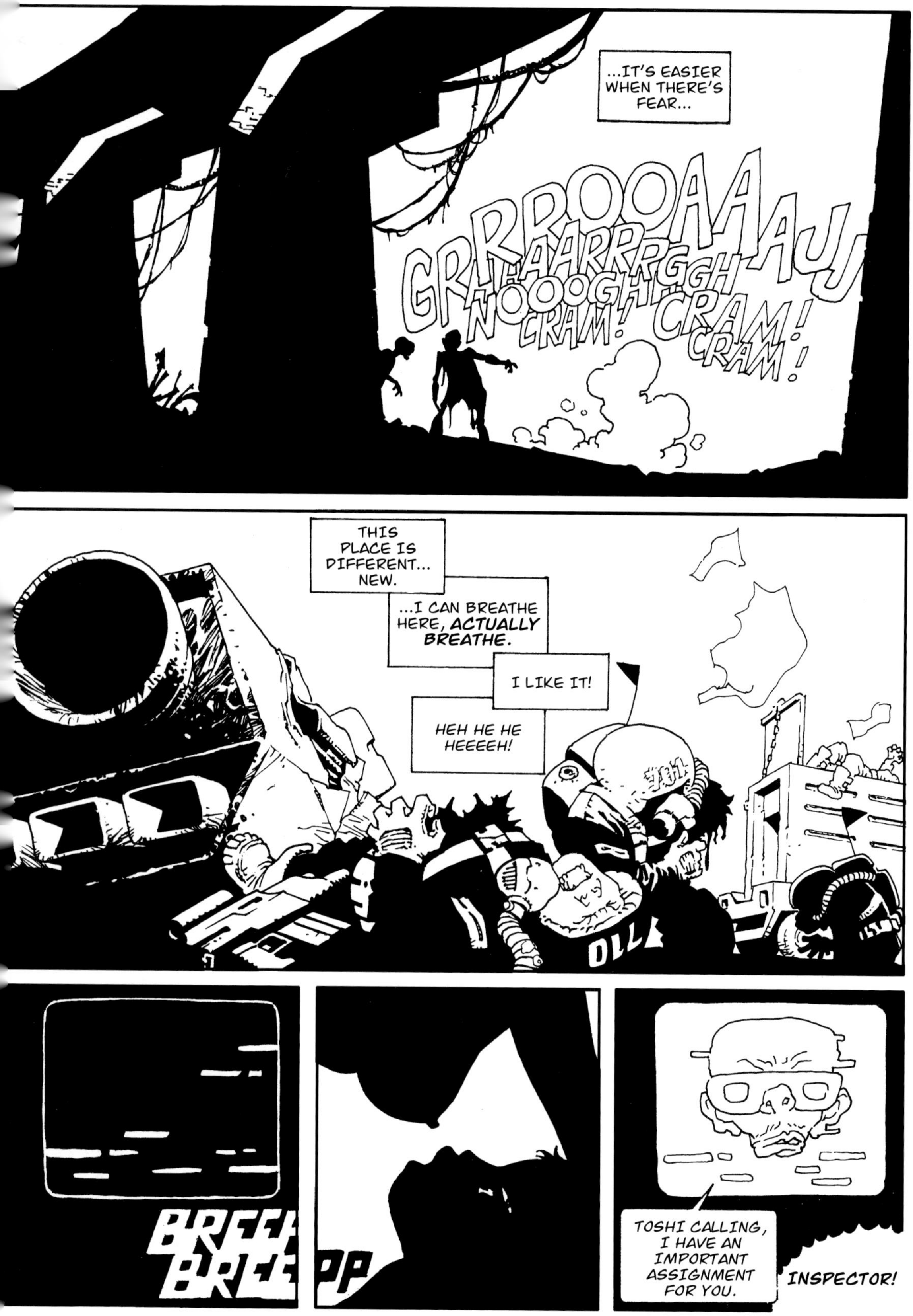
...IT'S EASIER WHEN THERE'S FEAR...
GRRROOAAAAUU
HAARRRGGH
NOOOGHH
CRAM! CRAM! CRAM!
THIS PLACE IS DIFFERENT... NEW.
...I CAN BREATHE HERE, ACTUALLY BREATHE.
I LIKE IT!
HEH HE HE HEEEEH!
TOSHI CALLING, I HAVE AN IMPORTANT ASSIGNMENT FOR YOU.
INSPECTOR!

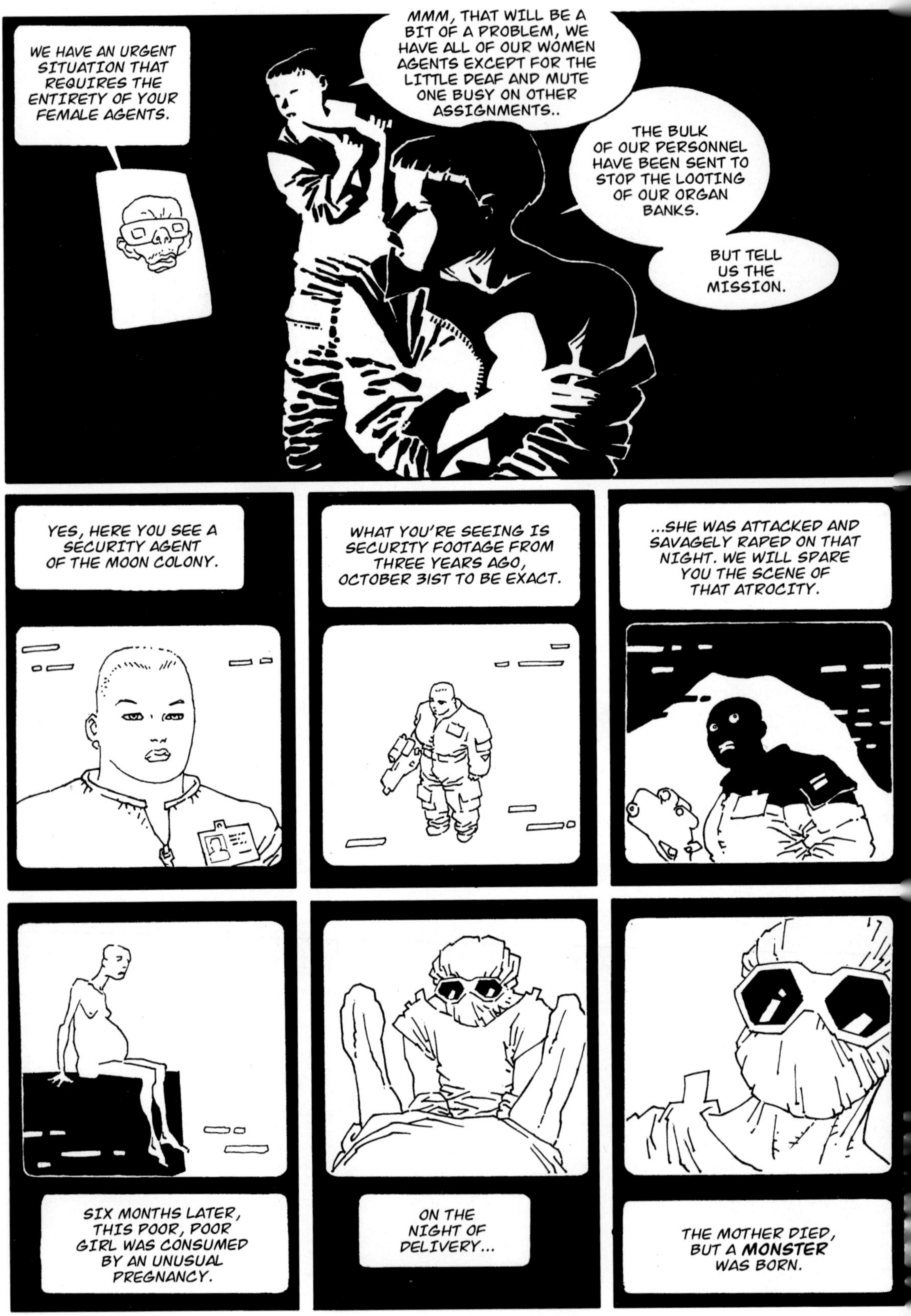
WE HAVE AN URGENT SITUATION THAT REQUIRES THE ENTIRETY OF YOUR FEMALE AGENTS.
MMM, THAT WILL BE A BIT OF A PROBLEM, WE HAVE ALL OF OUR WOMEN AGENTS EXCEPT FOR THE LITTLE DEAF AND MUTE ONE BUSY ON OTHER ASSIGNMENTS..
THE BULK OF OUR PERSONNEL HAVE BEEN SENT TO STOP THE LOOTING OF OUR ORGAN BANKS.
BUT TELL US THE MISSION.
YES, HERE YOU SEE A SECURITY AGENT OF THE MOON COLONY.
WHAT YOU'RE SEEING IS SECURITY FOOTAGE FROM THREE YEARS AGO, OCTOBER 31ST TO BE EXACT.
...SHE WAS ATTACKED AND SAVAGELY RAPED ON THAT NIGHT. WE WILL SPARE YOU THE SCENE OF THAT ATROCITY.
SIX MONTHS LATER, THIS POOR, POOR GIRL WAS CONSUMED BY AN UNUSUAL PREGNANCY.
ON THE NIGHT OF DELIVERY...
THE MOTHER DIED, BUT A **MONSTER** WAS BORN.

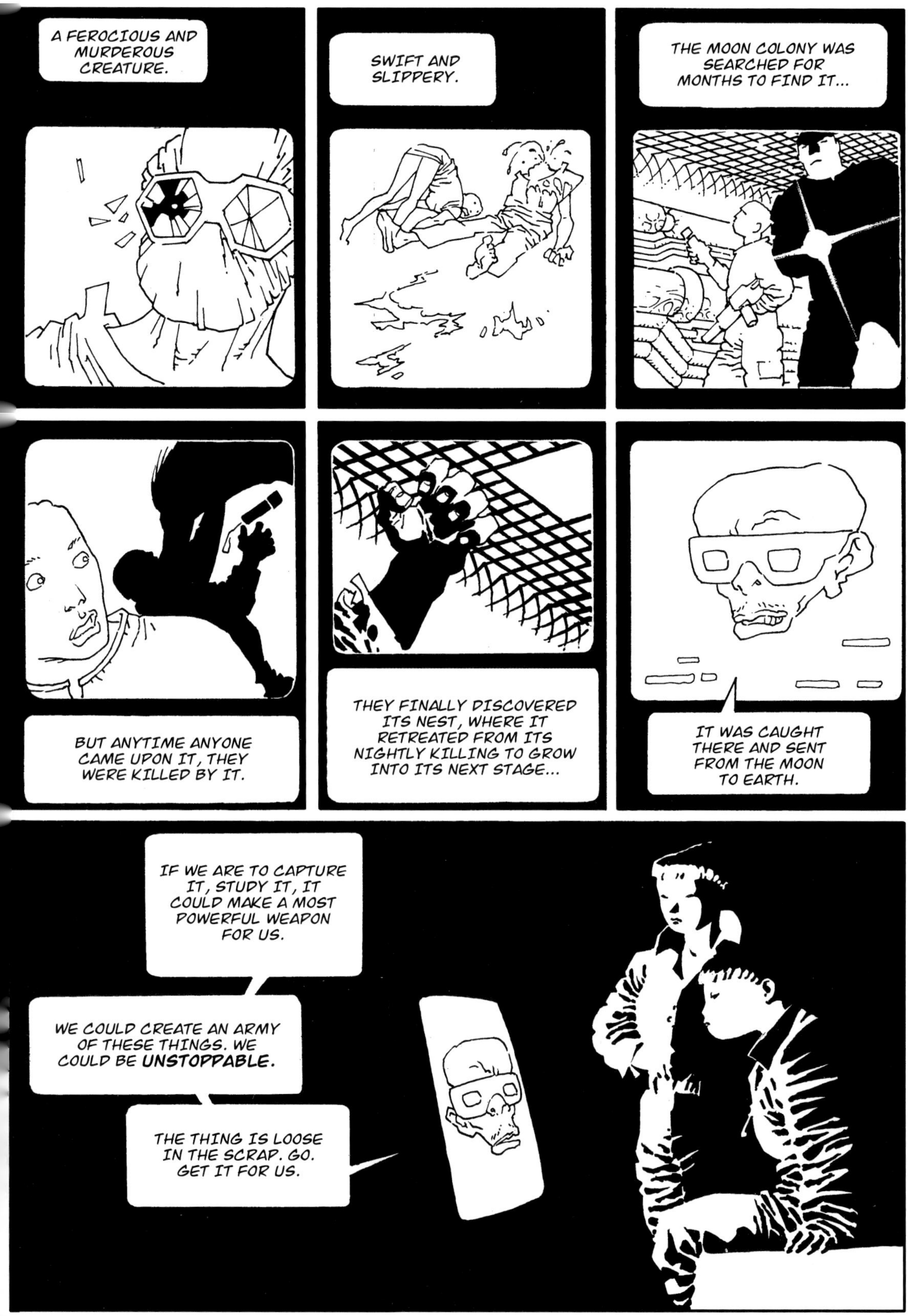
A FEROCIOUS AND MURDEROUS CREATURE.
SWIFT AND SLIPPERY.
THE MOON COLONY WAS SEARCHED FOR MONTHS TO FIND IT...
BUT ANYTIME ANYONE CAME UPON IT, THEY WERE KILLED BY IT.
THEY FINALLY DISCOVERED ITS NEST, WHERE IT RETREATED FROM ITS NIGHTLY KILLING TO GROW INTO ITS NEXT STAGE...
IT WAS CAUGHT THERE AND SENT FROM THE MOON TO EARTH.
IF WE ARE TO CAPTURE IT, STUDY IT, IT COULD MAKE A MOST POWERFUL WEAPON FOR US.
WE COULD CREATE AN ARMY OF THESE THINGS. WE COULD BE **UNSTOPPABLE**.
THE THING IS LOOSE IN THE SCRAP. GO. GET IT FOR US.

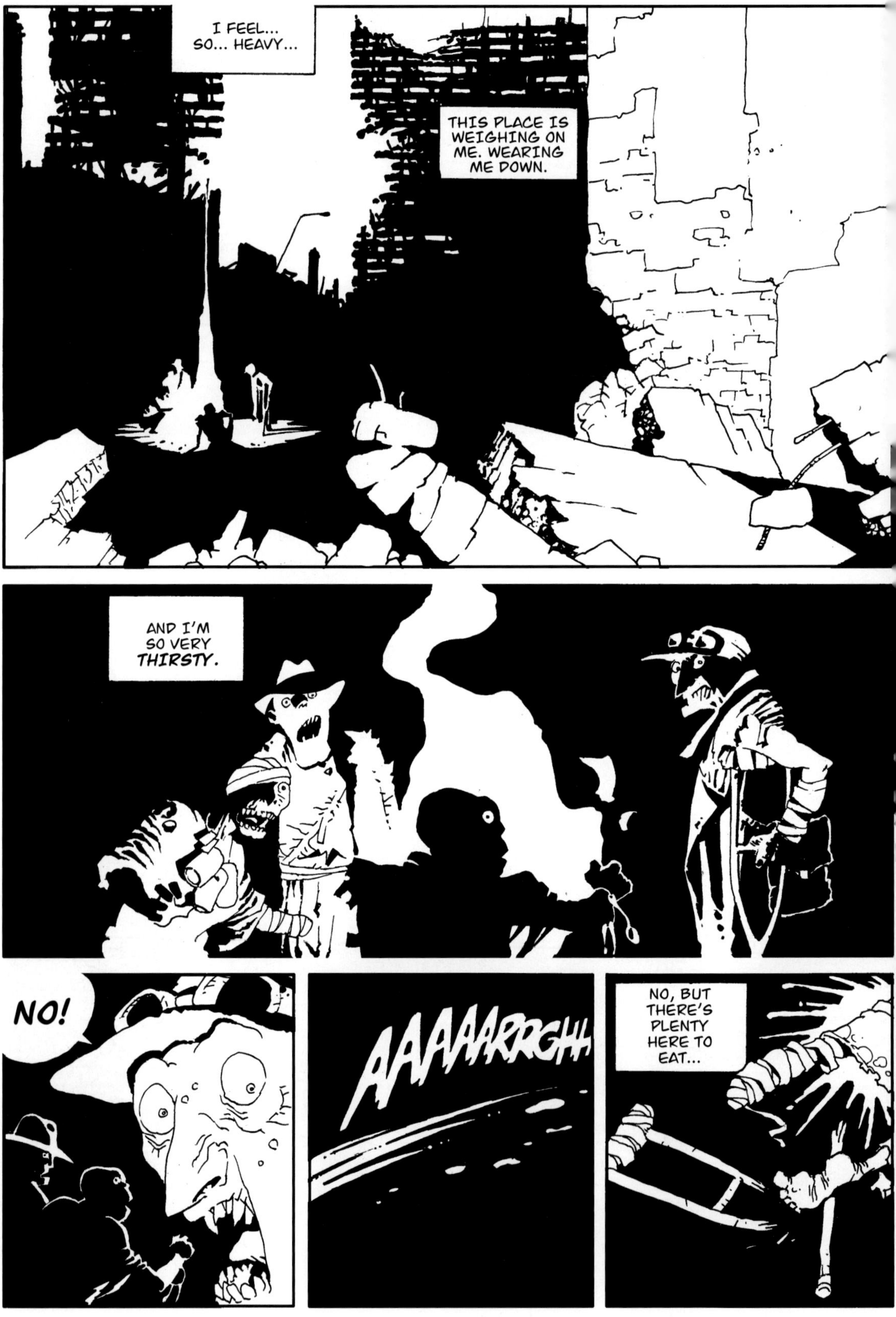
I FEEL... SO... HEAVY...
THIS PLACE IS WEIGHING ON ME. WEARING ME DOWN.
AND I'M SO VERY THIRSTY.
NO!
AAAAARRGHH
NO, BUT THERE'S PLENTY HERE TO EAT...

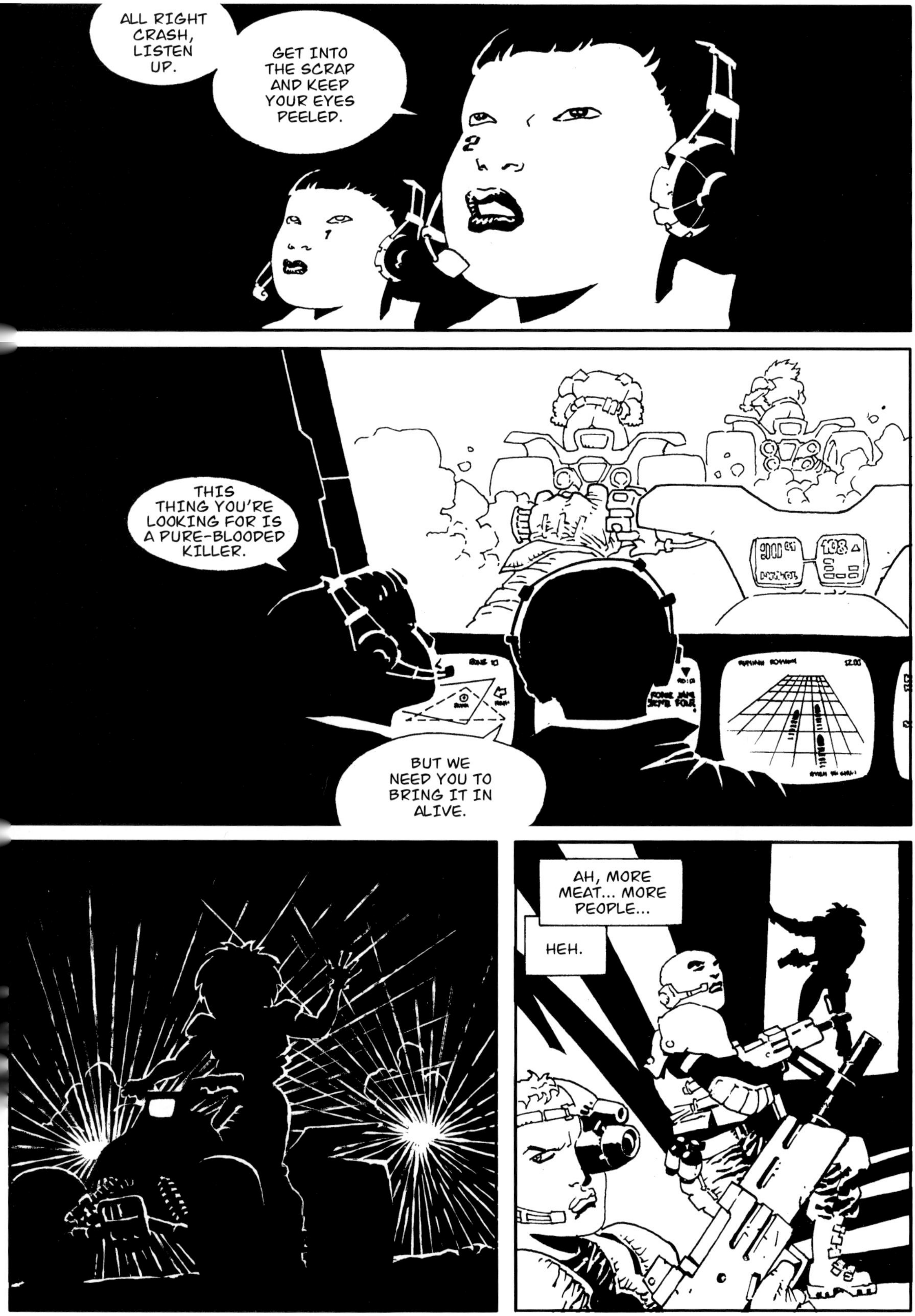
ALL RIGHT CRASH, LISTEN UP.
GET INTO THE SCRAP AND KEEP YOUR EYES PEELED.
THIS THING YOU'RE LOOKING FOR IS A PURE-BLOODED KILLER.
BUT WE NEED YOU TO BRING IT IN ALIVE.
AH, MORE MEAT... MORE PEOPLE...
HEH.

...MORE FOR ME.

I HAVE TO BE QUICK.

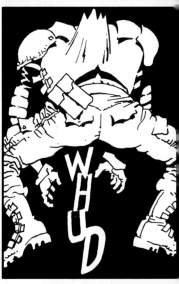

WHUD

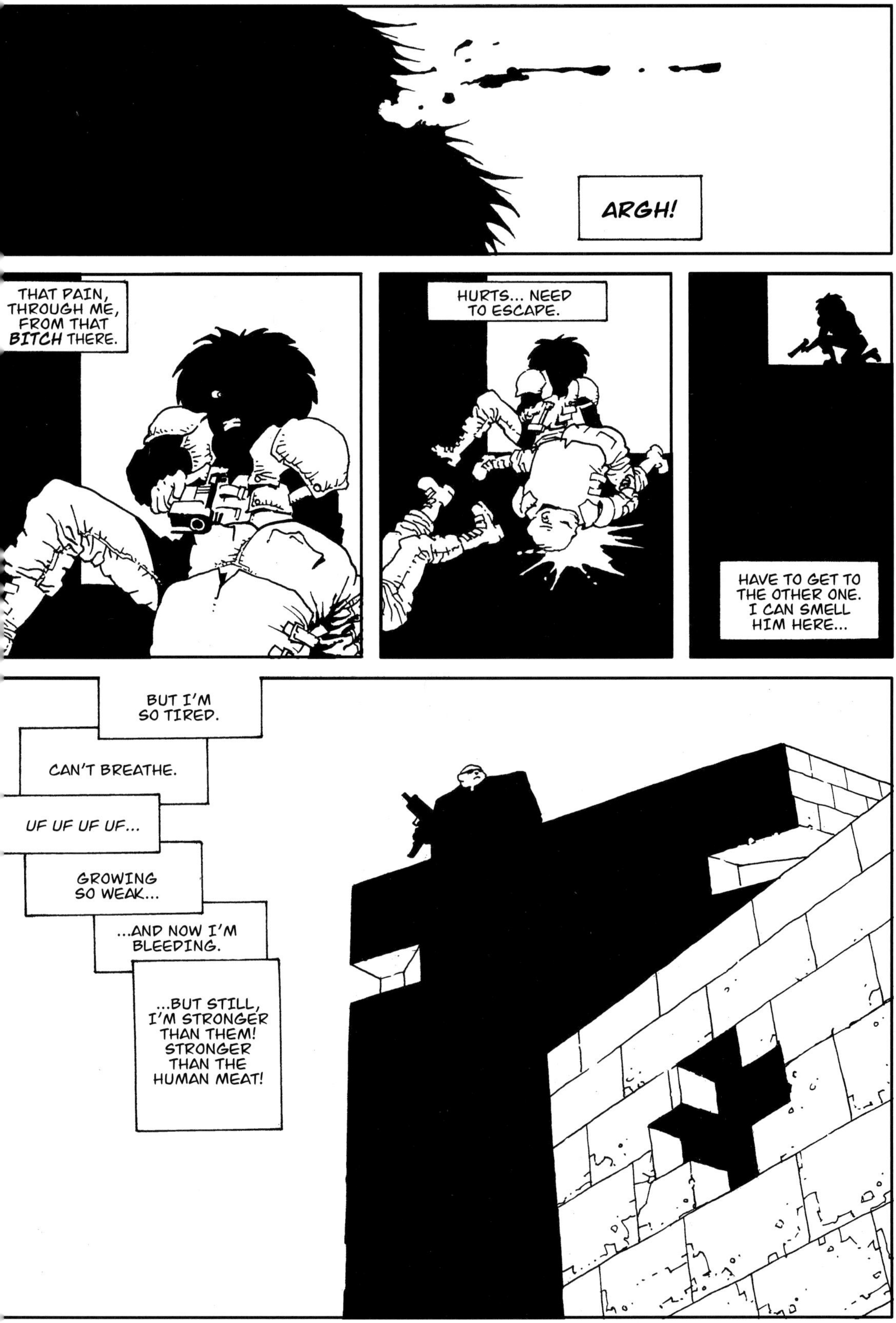

ARGH!
THAT PAIN, THROUGH ME, FROM THAT BITCH THERE.
HURTS... NEED TO ESCAPE.
HAVE TO GET TO THE OTHER ONE. I CAN SMELL HIM HERE...
BUT I'M SO TIRED.
CAN'T BREATHE.
UF UF UF UF...
GROWING SO WEAK...
...AND NOW I'M BLEEDING.
...BUT STILL, I'M STRONGER THAN THEM! STRONGER THAN THE HUMAN MEAT!

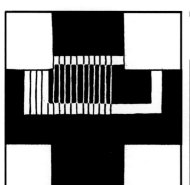

HERE... I'M HERE. MY SENSES ARE STRONGER HERE...

HE'S HERE.

?

FATHER?

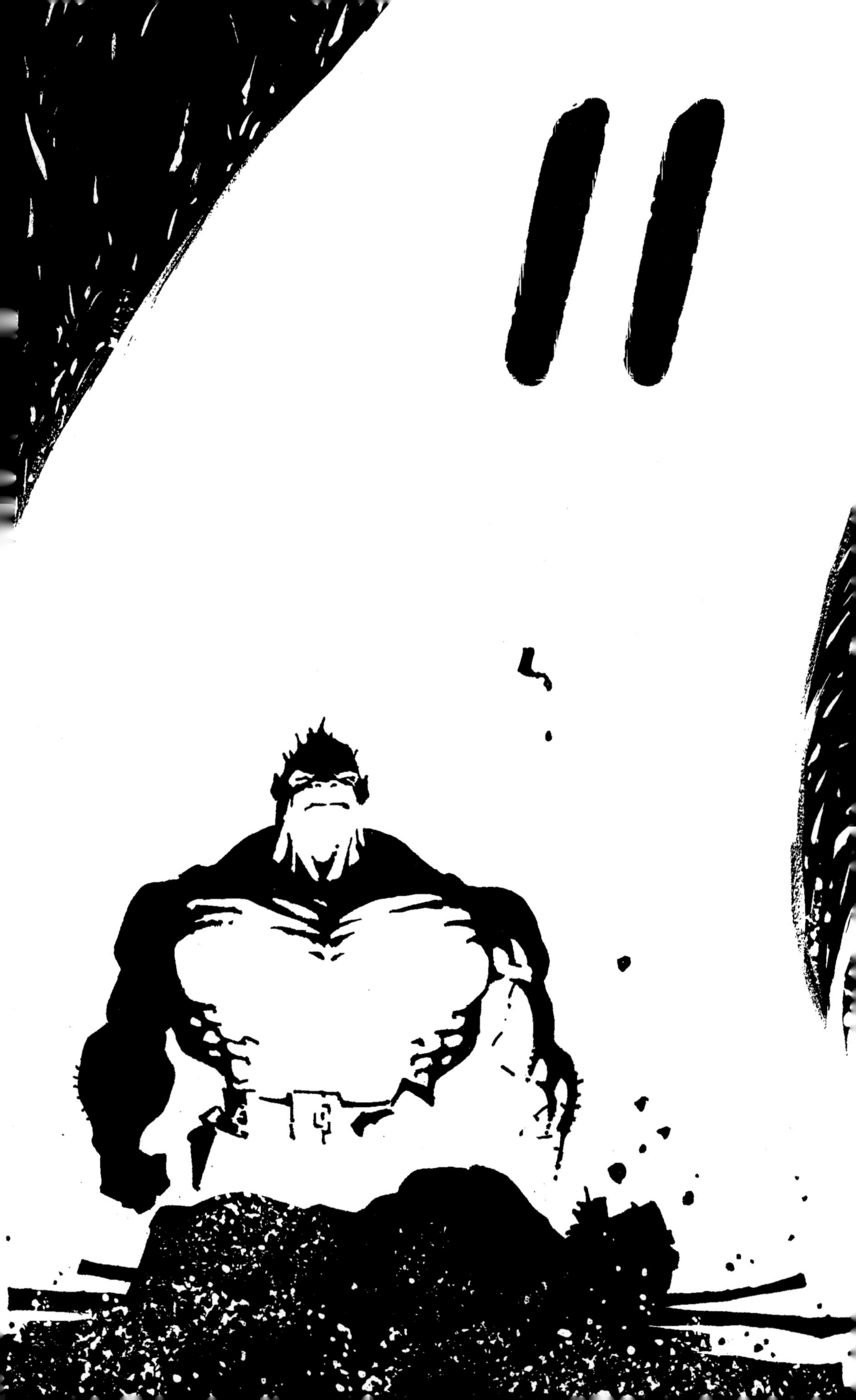

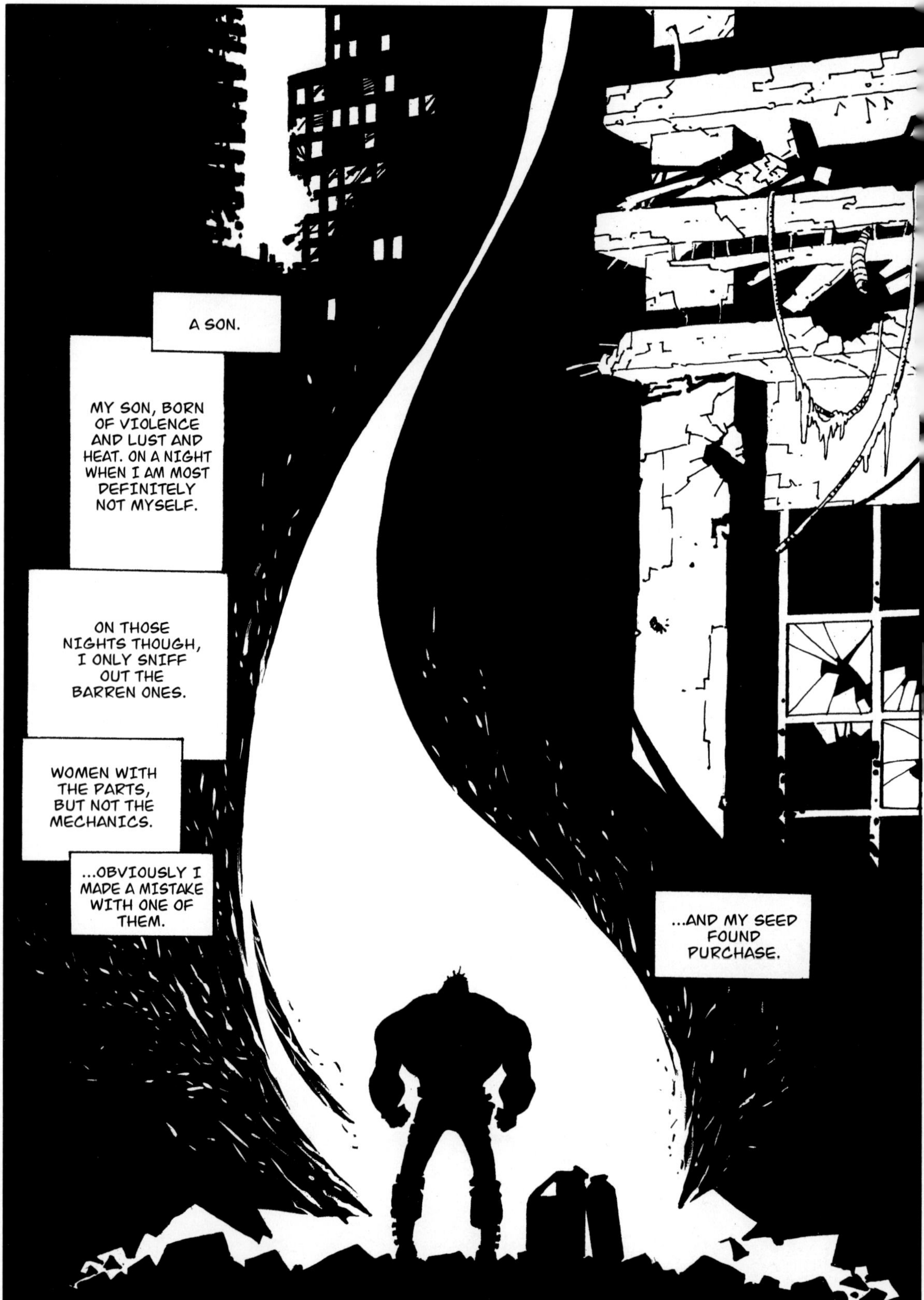
A SON.
MY SON, BORN OF VIOLENCE AND LUST AND HEAT. ON A NIGHT WHEN I AM MOST DEFINITELY NOT MYSELF.
ON THOSE NIGHTS THOUGH, I ONLY SNIFF OUT THE BARREN ONES.
WOMEN WITH THE PARTS, BUT NOT THE MECHANICS.
...OBVIOUSLY I MADE A MISTAKE WITH ONE OF THEM.
...AND MY SEED FOUND PURCHASE.

A SON.

IT WAS ONLY A FEW HOURS AGO I MET HIM, THERE IN MY ROOM.

IT'S SO LATE, AND I'M SO TIRED. BUT NOT TOO TIRED TO *TOUCH* MYSELF... BRING MYSELF TO *PLEASURE.*

THROUGH THE IMAGES HERE ON DISK OF THE WOLF, AND IN MY MIND'S EYE.

BUT...I DON'T UNDERSTAND!

EH?! VOICES!

WHAT DON'T YOU UNDERSTAND, FATHER, I'M YOUR *SON,* FLESH OF YOUR FLESH, BLOOD OF YOUR BLOOD! TRUST YOUR SENSES.

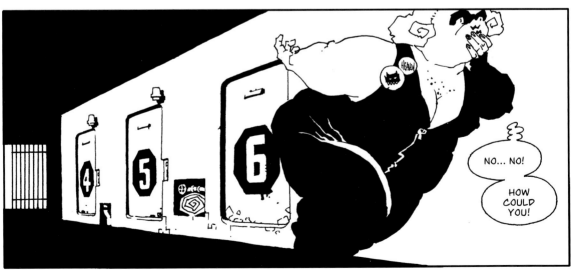

NO... NO!

HOW COULD YOU!

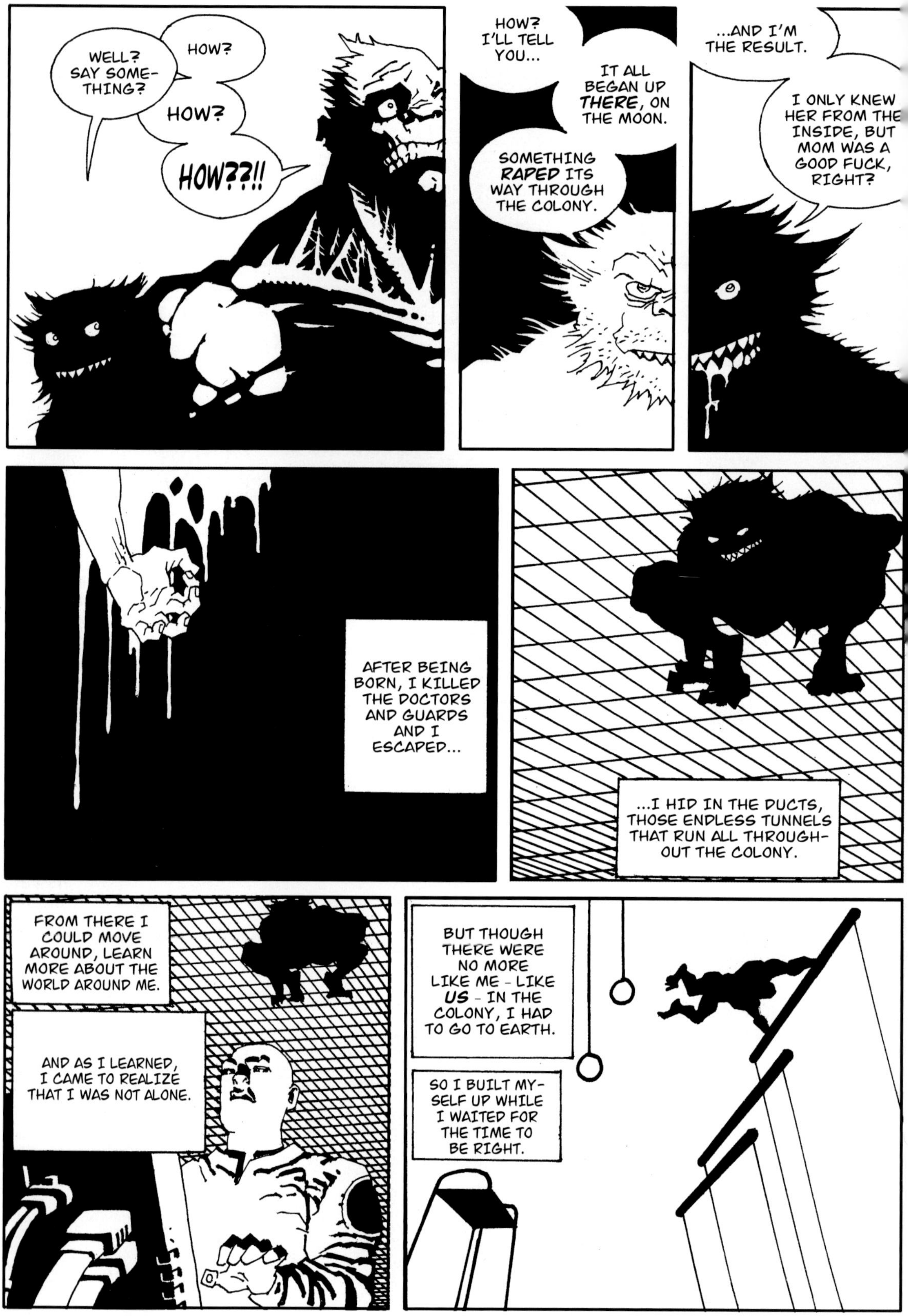
WELL? SAY SOME-THING?
HOW?
HOW?
HOW??!!
HOW? I'LL TELL YOU...
IT ALL BEGAN UP ***THERE***, ON THE MOON.
SOMETHING ***RAPED*** ITS WAY THROUGH THE COLONY.
...AND I'M THE RESULT.
I ONLY KNEW HER FROM THE INSIDE, BUT MOM WAS A GOOD FUCK, RIGHT?
AFTER BEING BORN, I KILLED THE DOCTORS AND GUARDS AND I ESCAPED...
...I HID IN THE DUCTS, THOSE ENDLESS TUNNELS THAT RUN ALL THROUGH-OUT THE COLONY.
FROM THERE I COULD MOVE AROUND, LEARN MORE ABOUT THE WORLD AROUND ME.
AND AS I LEARNED, I CAME TO REALIZE THAT I WAS NOT ALONE.
BUT THOUGH THERE WERE NO MORE LIKE ME - LIKE ***US*** - IN THE COLONY, I HAD TO GO TO EARTH.
SO I BUILT MY-SELF UP WHILE I WAITED FOR THE TIME TO BE RIGHT.

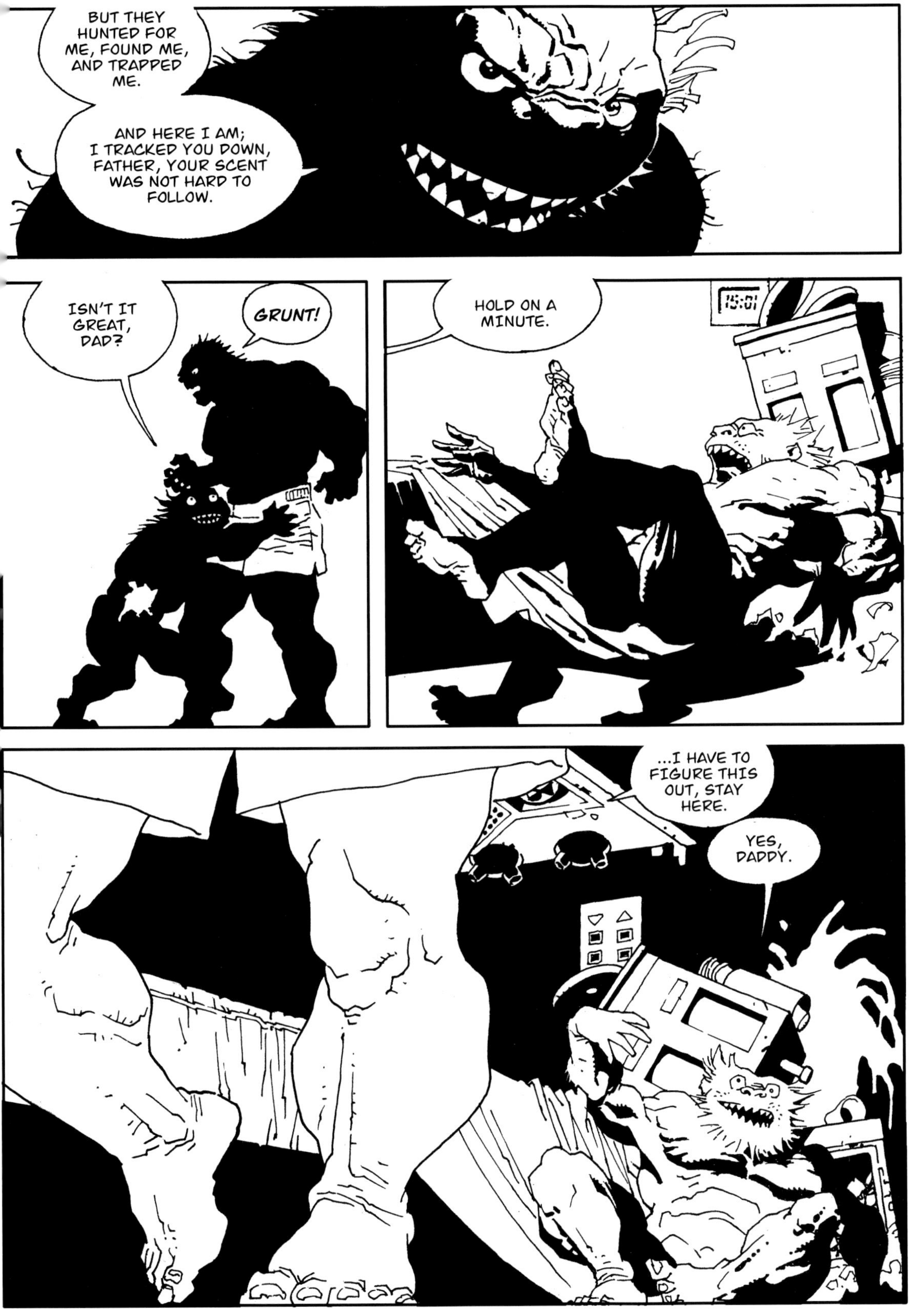
BUT THEY HUNTED FOR ME, FOUND ME, AND TRAPPED ME.
AND HERE I AM; I TRACKED YOU DOWN, FATHER, YOUR SCENT WAS NOT HARD TO FOLLOW.
ISN'T IT GREAT, DAD?
GRUNT!
HOLD ON A MINUTE.
15:01
...I HAVE TO FIGURE THIS OUT, STAY HERE.
YES, DADDY.

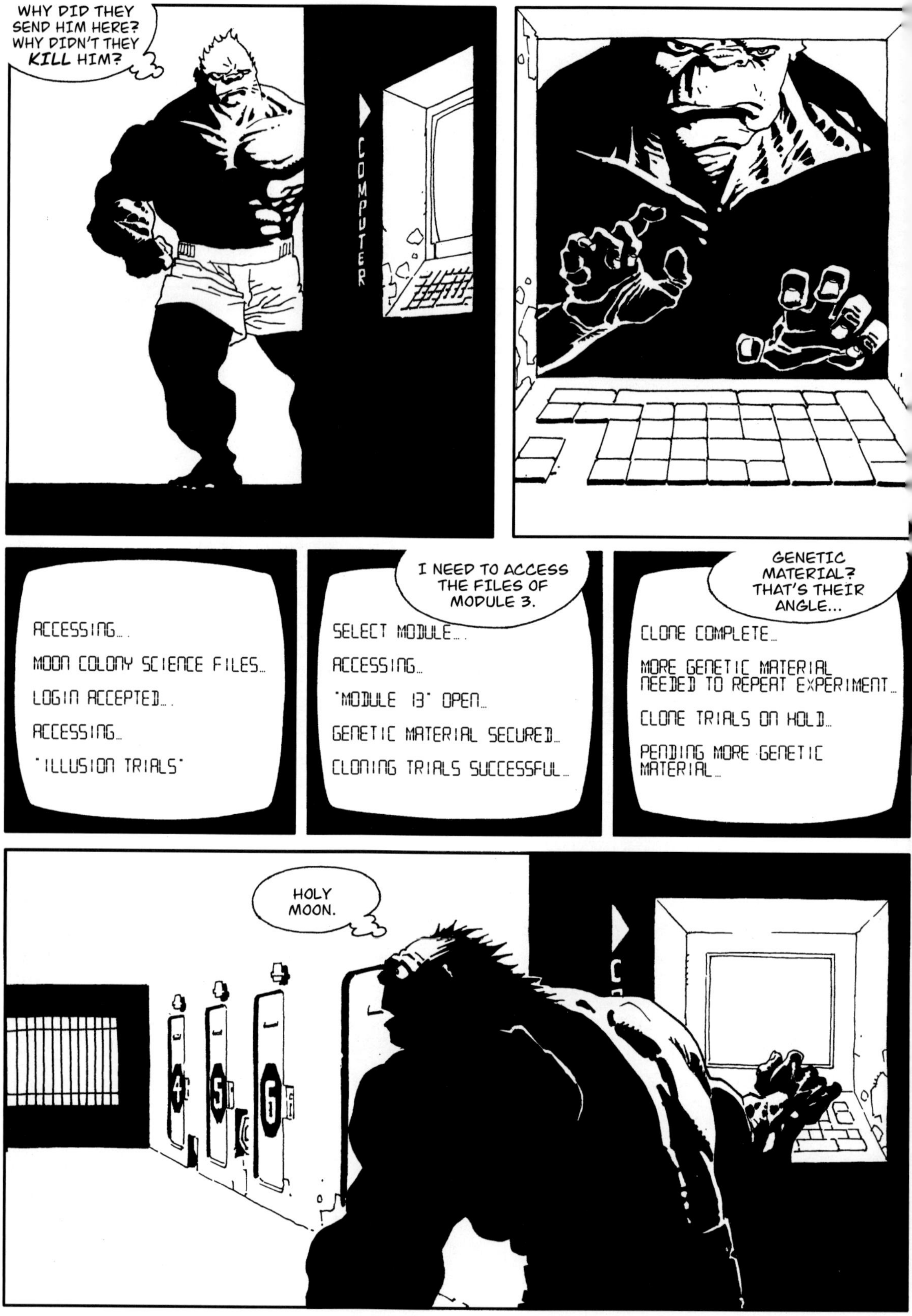

WHY DID THEY SEND HIM HERE? WHY DIDN'T THEY KILL HIM?
COMPUTER
ACCESSING...
MOON COLONY SCIENCE FILES...
LOGIN ACCEPTED...
ACCESSING...
"ILLUSION TRIALS"
I NEED TO ACCESS THE FILES OF MODULE 3.
SELECT MODULE...
ACCESSING...
"MODULE 13" OPEN...
GENETIC MATERIAL SECURED...
CLONING TRIALS SUCCESSFUL...
GENETIC MATERIAL? THAT'S THEIR ANGLE...
CLONE COMPLETE...
MORE GENETIC MATERIAL NEEDED TO REPEAT EXPERIMENT...
CLONE TRIALS ON HOLD...
PENDING MORE GENETIC MATERIAL...
HOLY MOON.

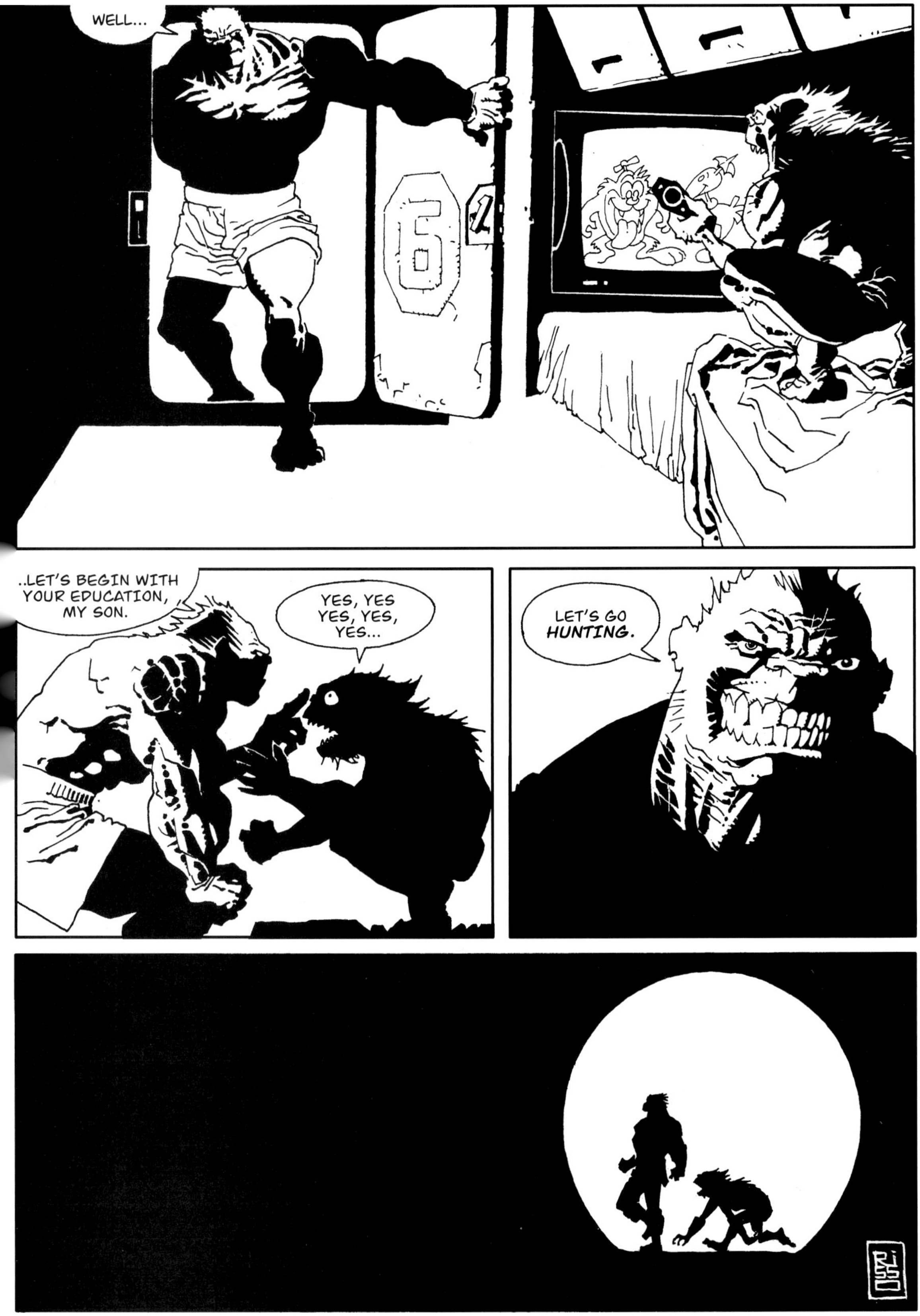
WELL...
..LET'S BEGIN WITH YOUR EDUCATION, MY SON.
YES, YES YES, YES, YES...
LET'S GO HUNTING.

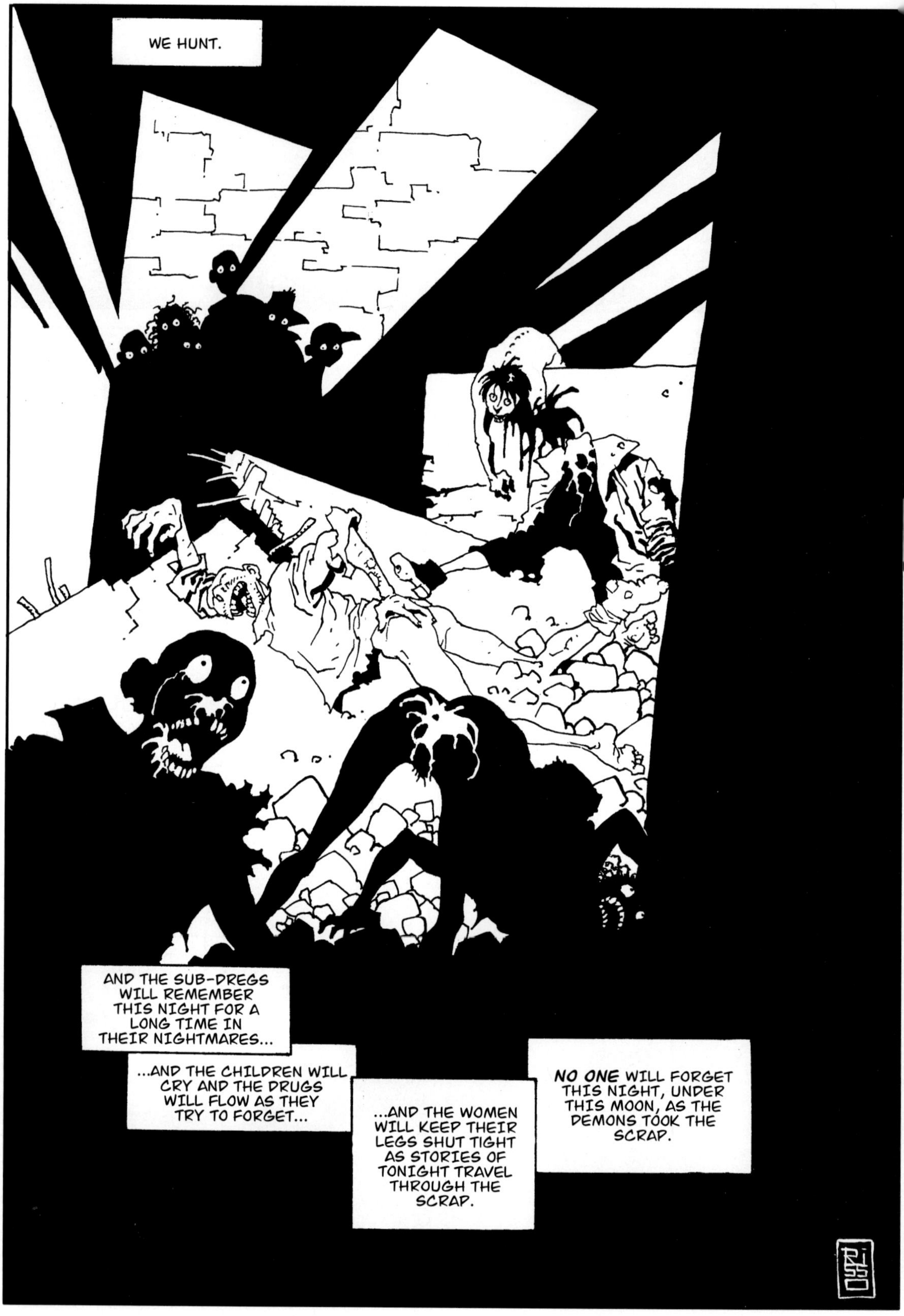
WE HUNT.
AND THE SUB-DREGS WILL REMEMBER THIS NIGHT FOR A LONG TIME IN THEIR NIGHTMARES...
...AND THE CHILDREN WILL CRY AND THE DRUGS WILL FLOW AS THEY TRY TO FORGET...
...AND THE WOMEN WILL KEEP THEIR LEGS SHUT TIGHT AS STORIES OF TONIGHT TRAVEL THROUGH THE SCRAP.
NO ONE WILL FORGET THIS NIGHT, UNDER THIS MOON, AS THE DEMONS TOOK THE SCRAP.

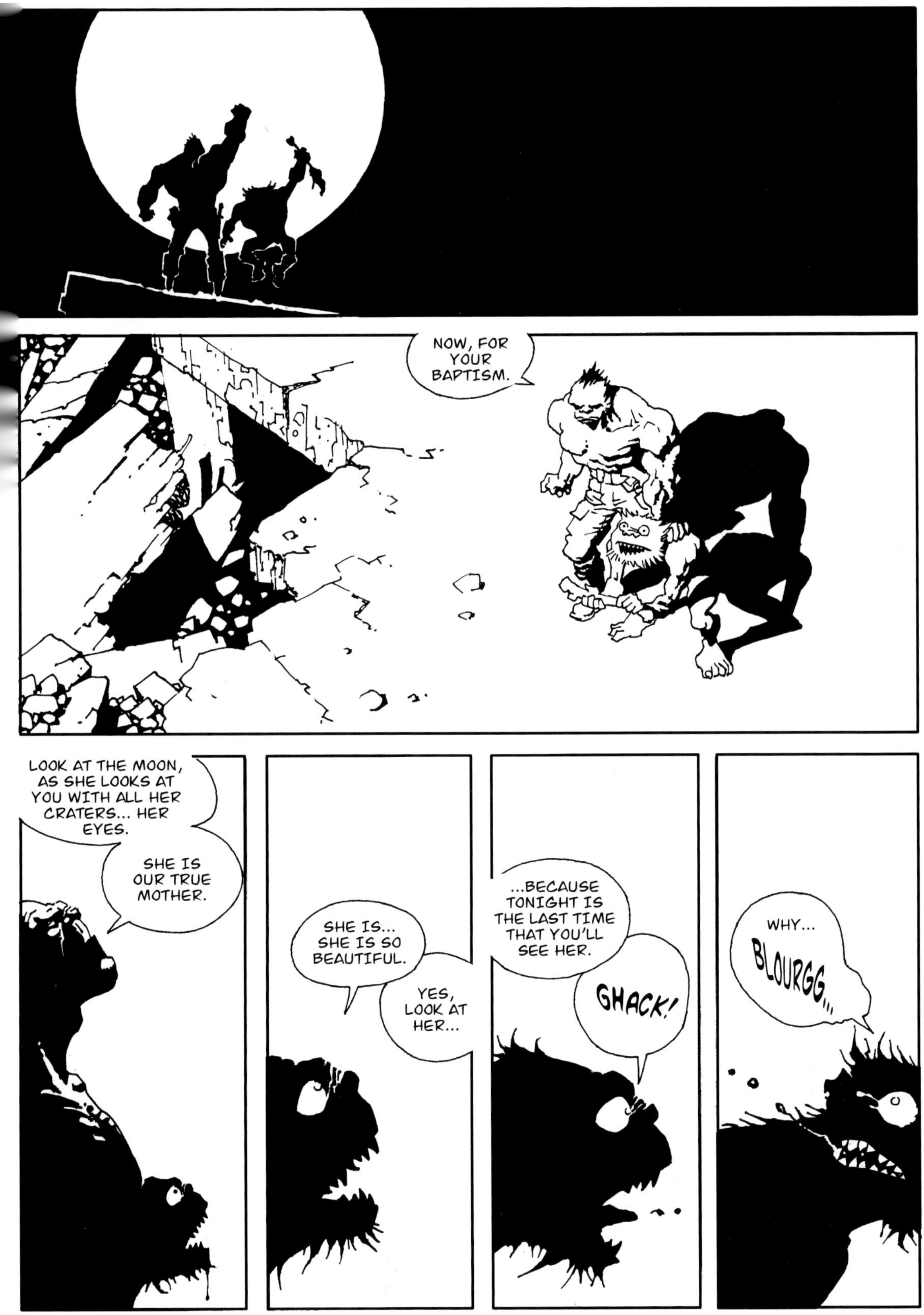
NOW, FOR YOUR BAPTISM.
LOOK AT THE MOON, AS SHE LOOKS AT YOU WITH ALL HER CRATERS... HER EYES.
SHE IS OUR TRUE MOTHER.
SHE IS... SHE IS SO BEAUTIFUL.
YES, LOOK AT HER...
...BECAUSE TONIGHT IS THE LAST TIME THAT YOU'LL SEE HER.
GHACK!
WHY...
BLOURGG...

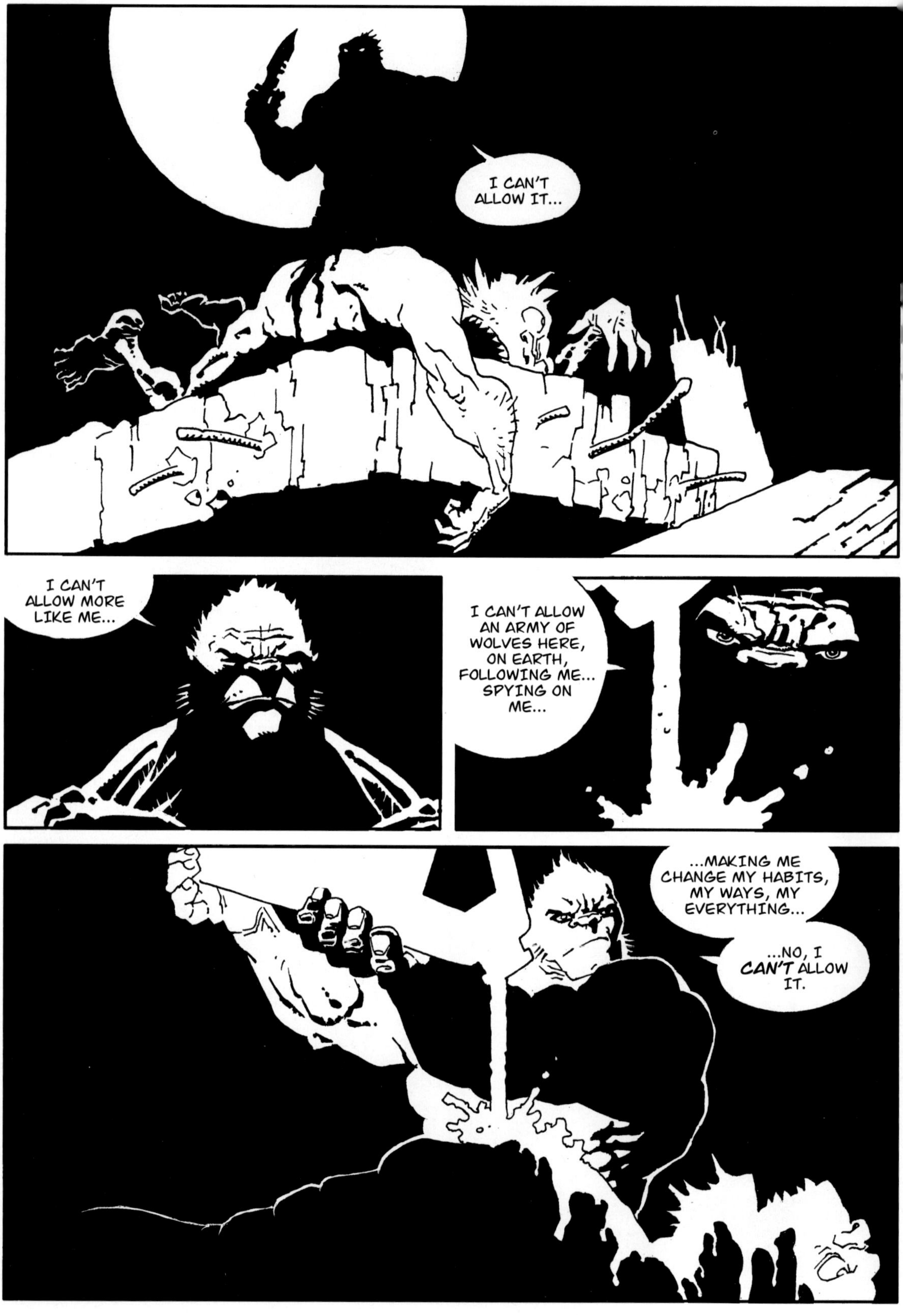
I CAN'T ALLOW IT...
I CAN'T ALLOW MORE LIKE ME...
I CAN'T ALLOW AN ARMY OF WOLVES HERE, ON EARTH, FOLLOWING ME... SPYING ON ME...
...MAKING ME CHANGE MY HABITS, MY WAYS, MY EVERYTHING...
...NO, I **CAN'T** ALLOW IT.

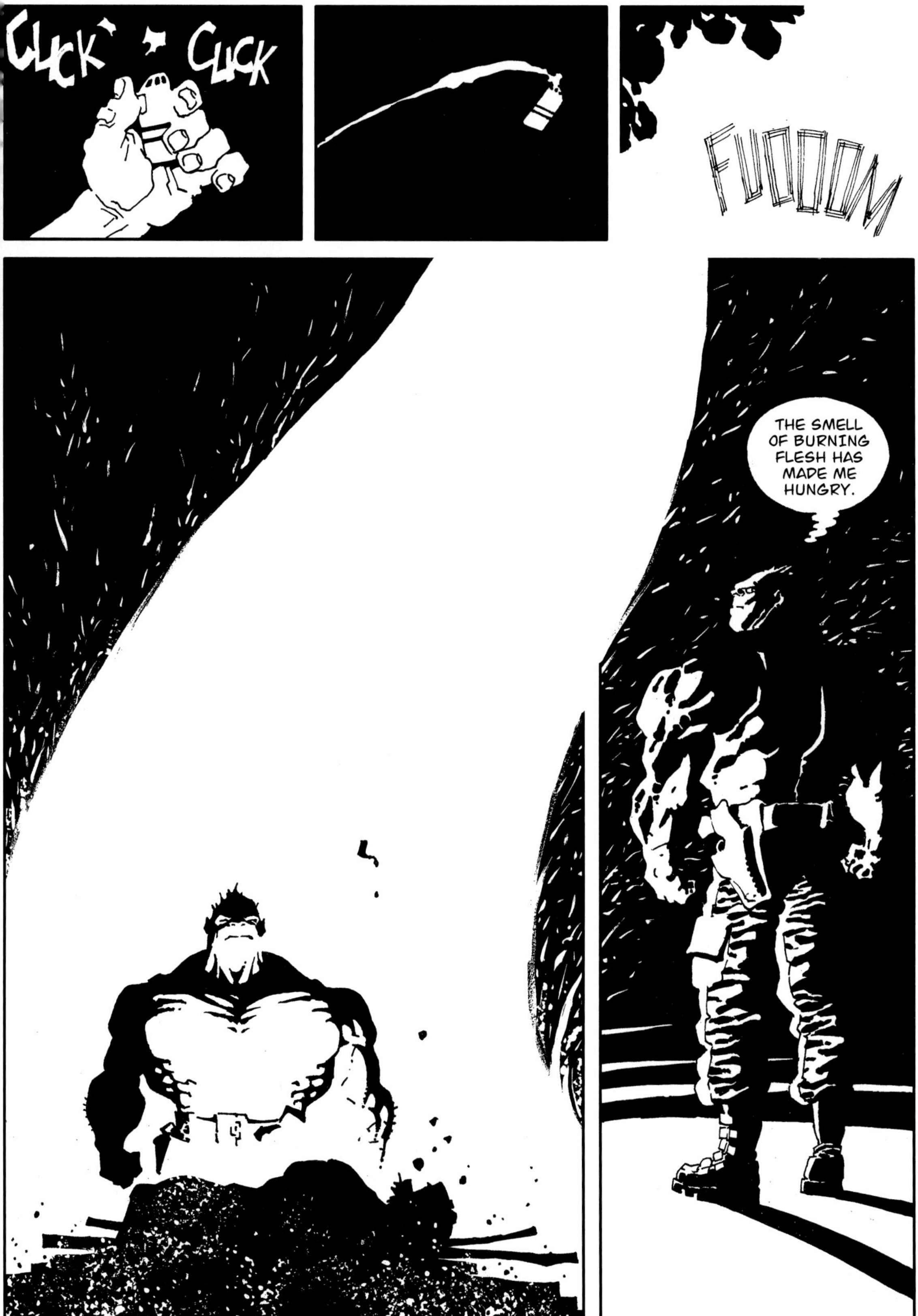
CLICK CLICK
FUDOOM
THE SMELL OF BURNING FLESH HAS MADE ME HUNGRY.

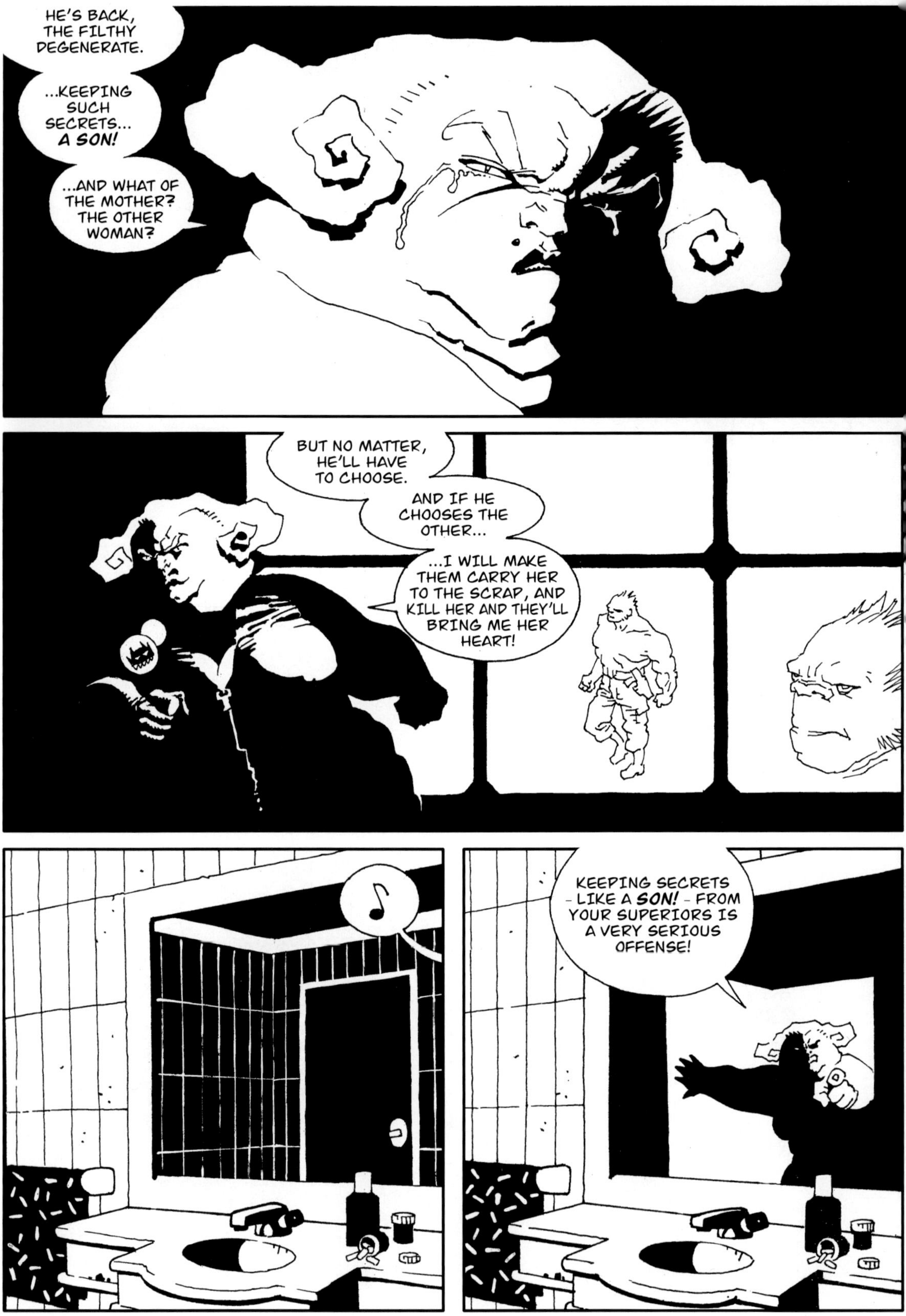
HE'S BACK, THE FILTHY DEGENERATE.
...KEEPING SUCH SECRETS... A SON!
...AND WHAT OF THE MOTHER? THE OTHER WOMAN?
BUT NO MATTER, HE'LL HAVE TO CHOOSE.
AND IF HE CHOOSES THE OTHER...
...I WILL MAKE THEM CARRY HER TO THE SCRAP, AND KILL HER AND THEY'LL BRING ME HER HEART!
♪
KEEPING SECRETS - LIKE A SON! - FROM YOUR SUPERIORS IS A VERY SERIOUS OFFENSE!

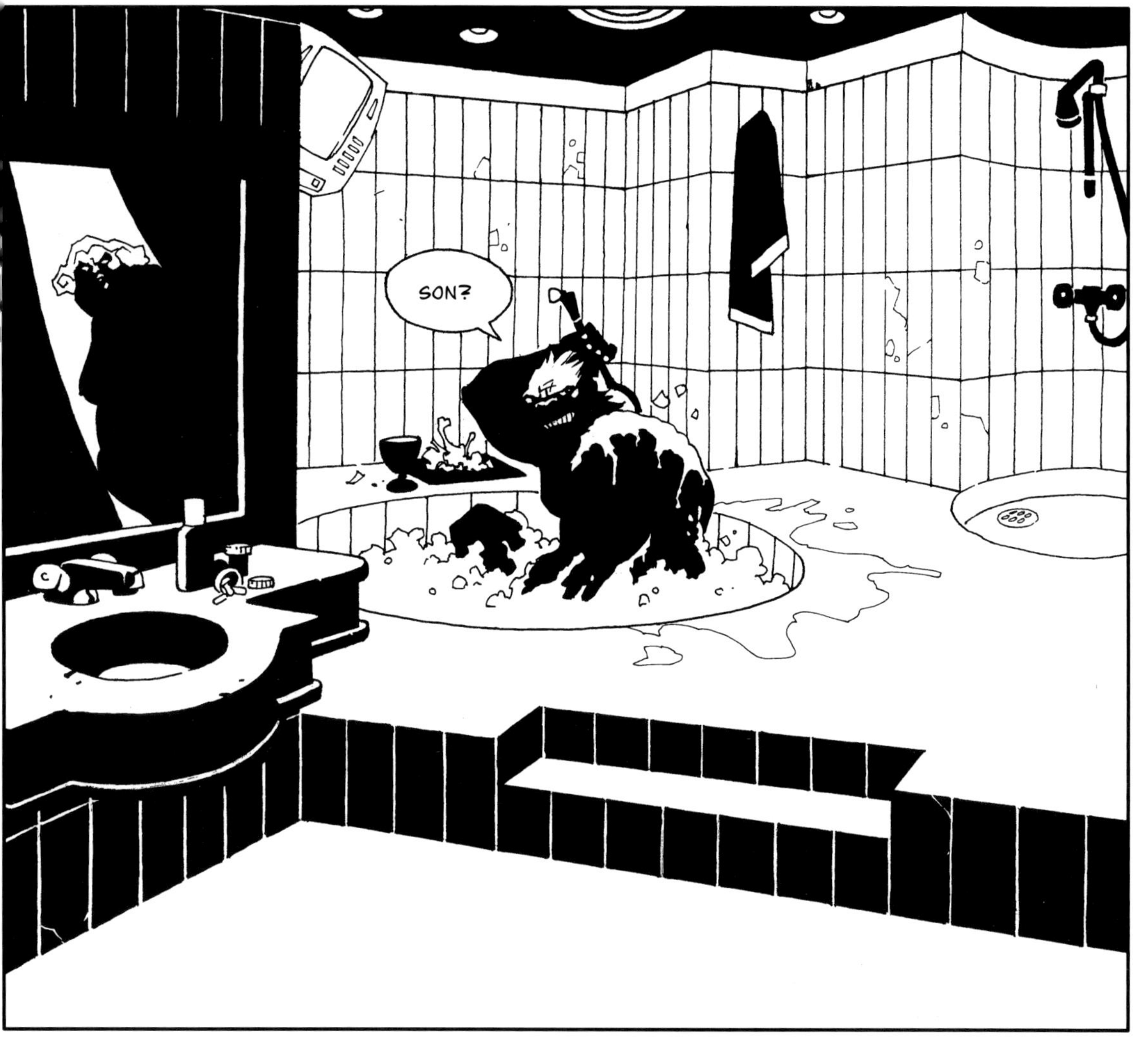
SON?

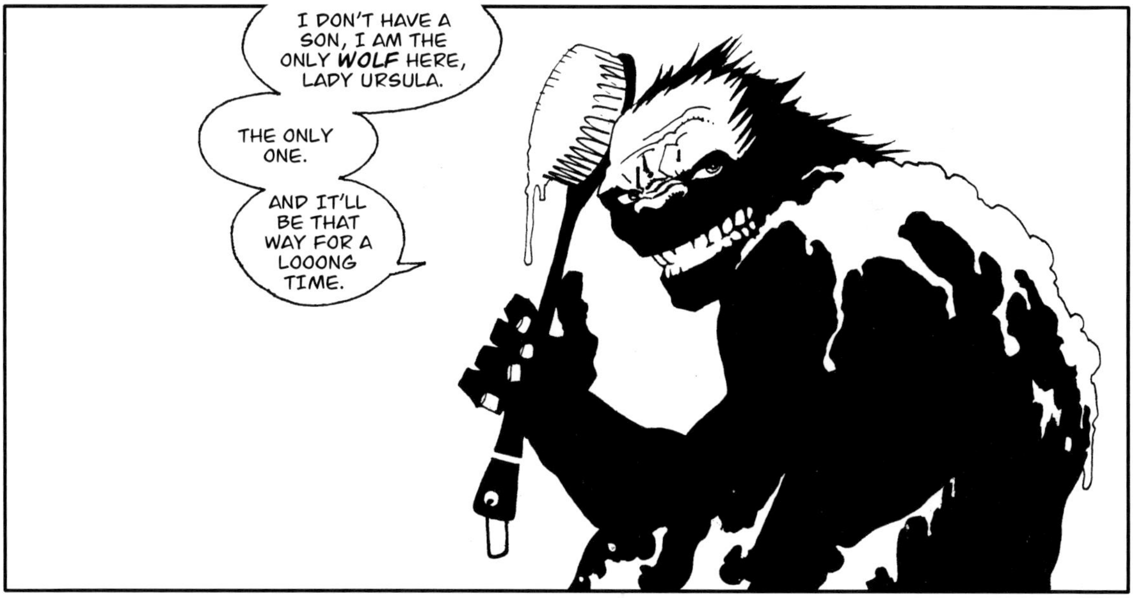
I DON'T HAVE A SON, I AM THE ONLY WOLF HERE, LADY URSULA.
THE ONLY ONE.
AND IT'LL BE THAT WAY FOR A LOOONG TIME.

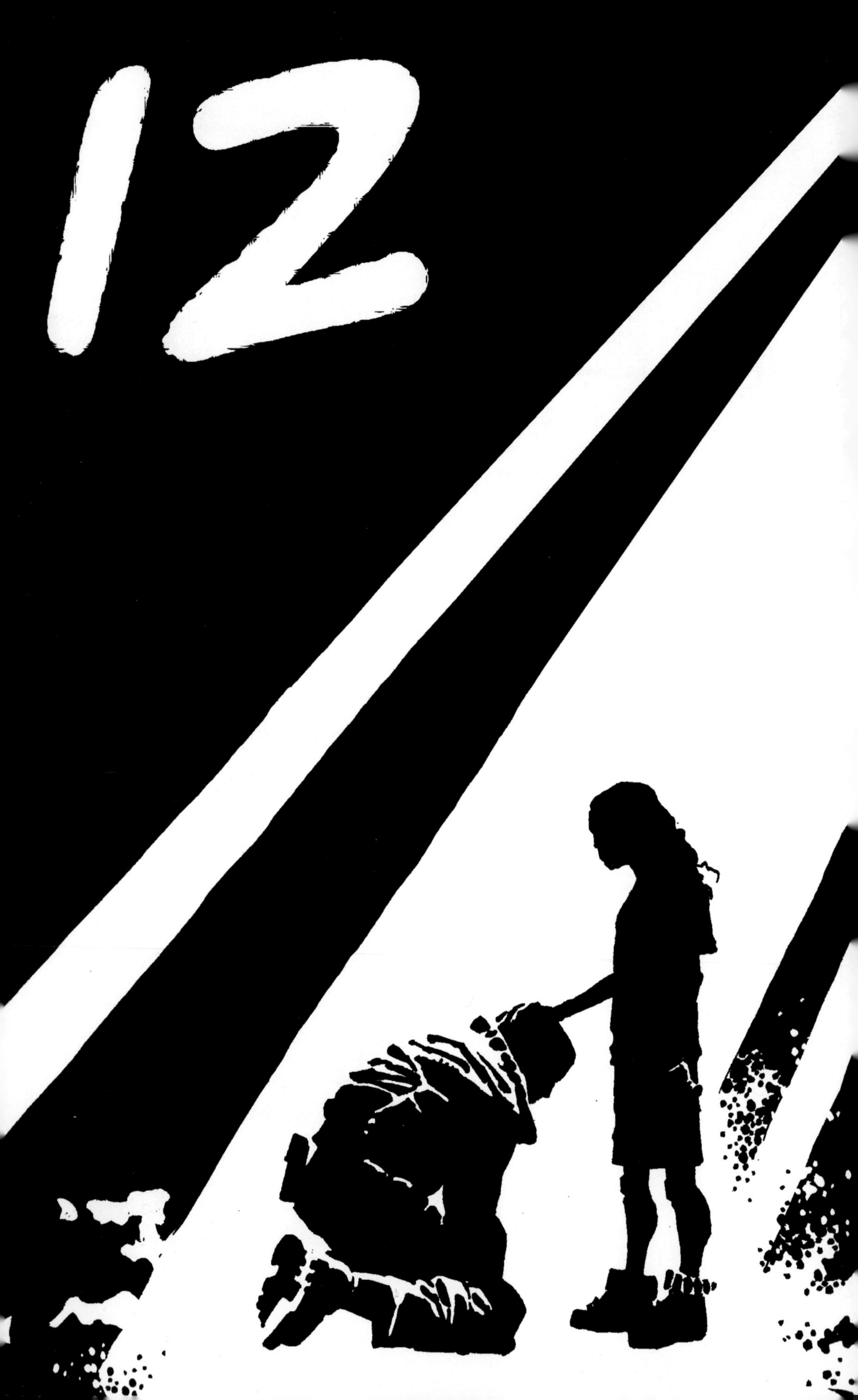
12

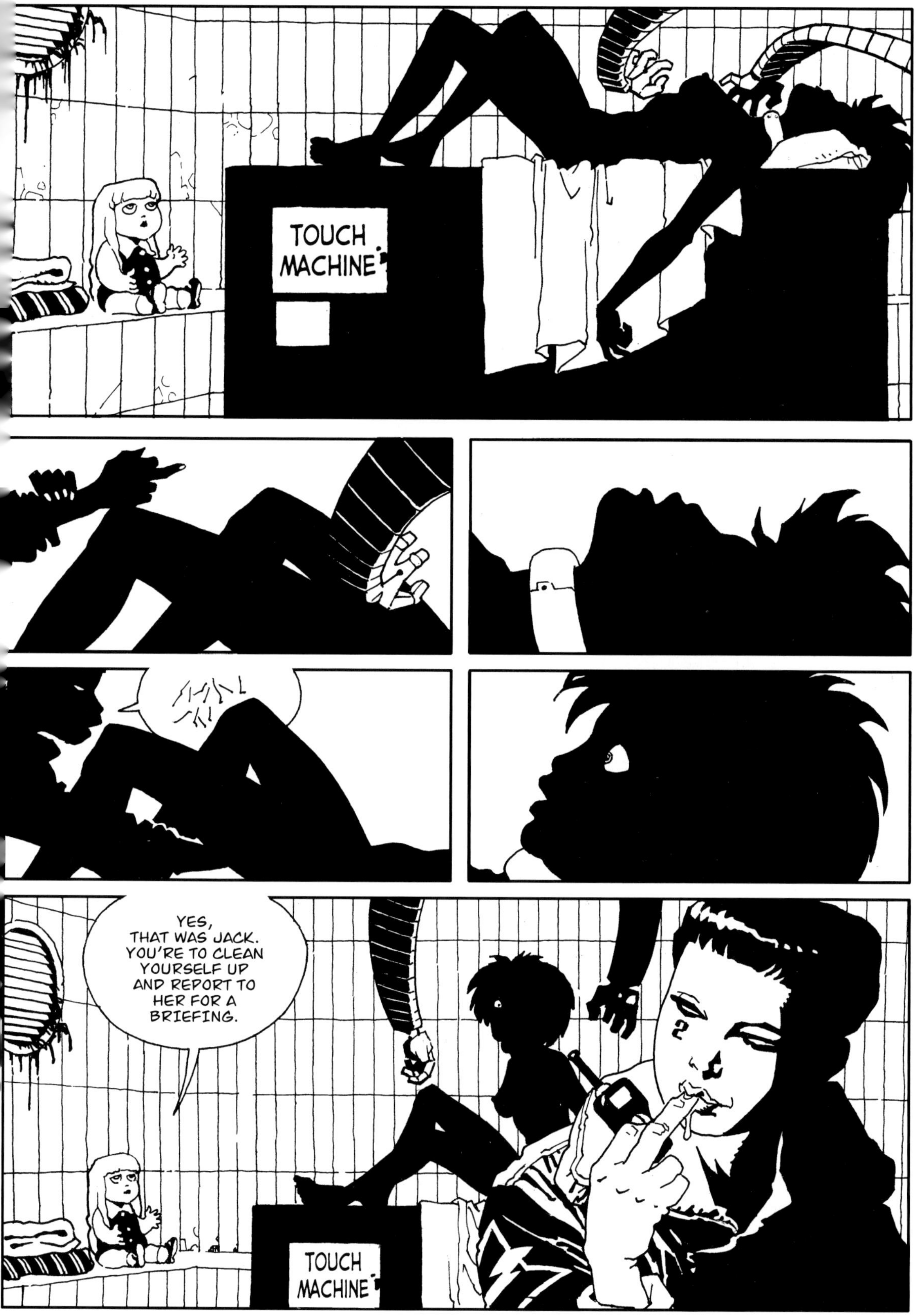
TOUCH MACHINE
YES, THAT WAS JACK. YOU'RE TO CLEAN YOURSELF UP AND REPORT TO HER FOR A BRIEFING.
TOUCH MACHINE

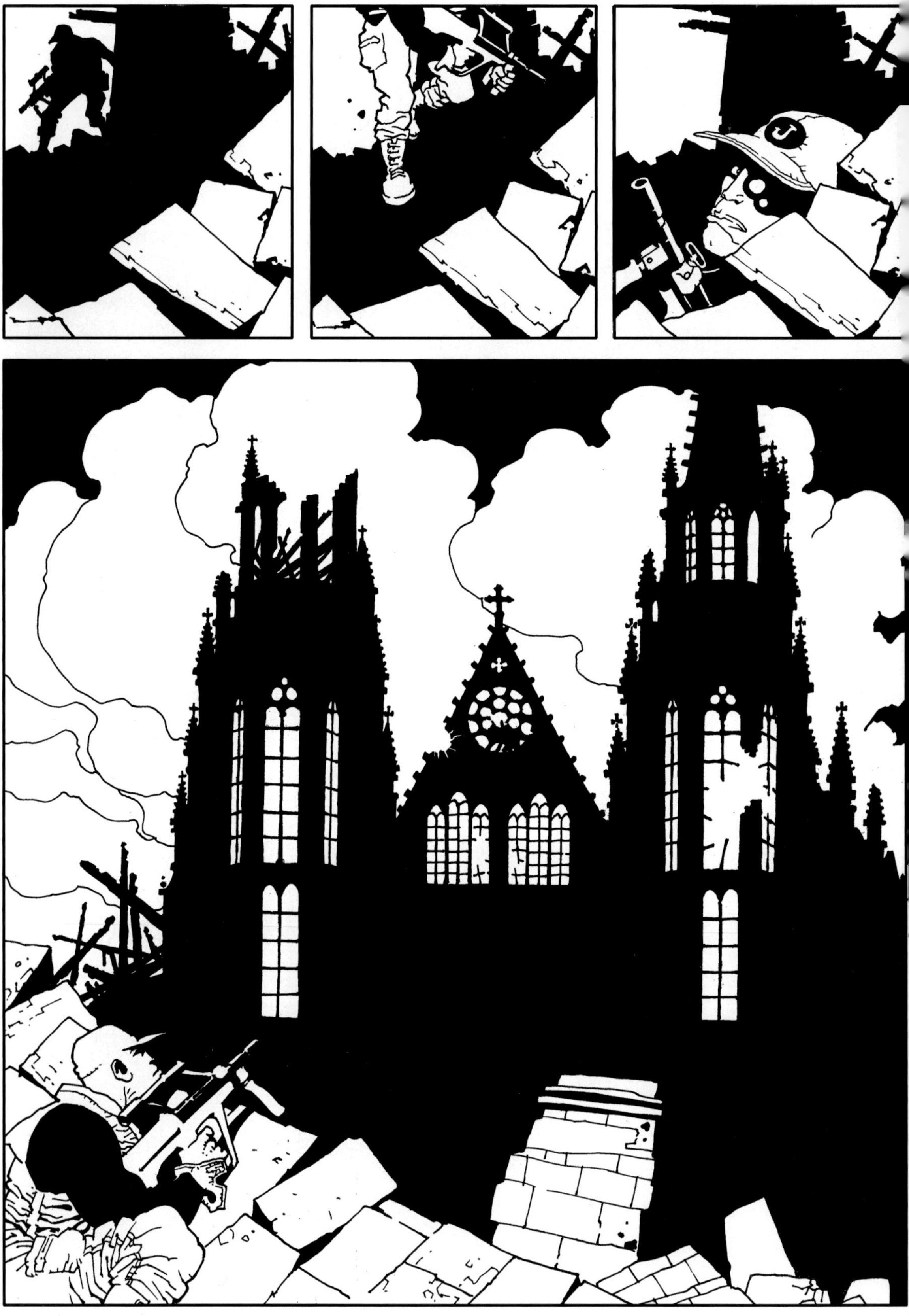

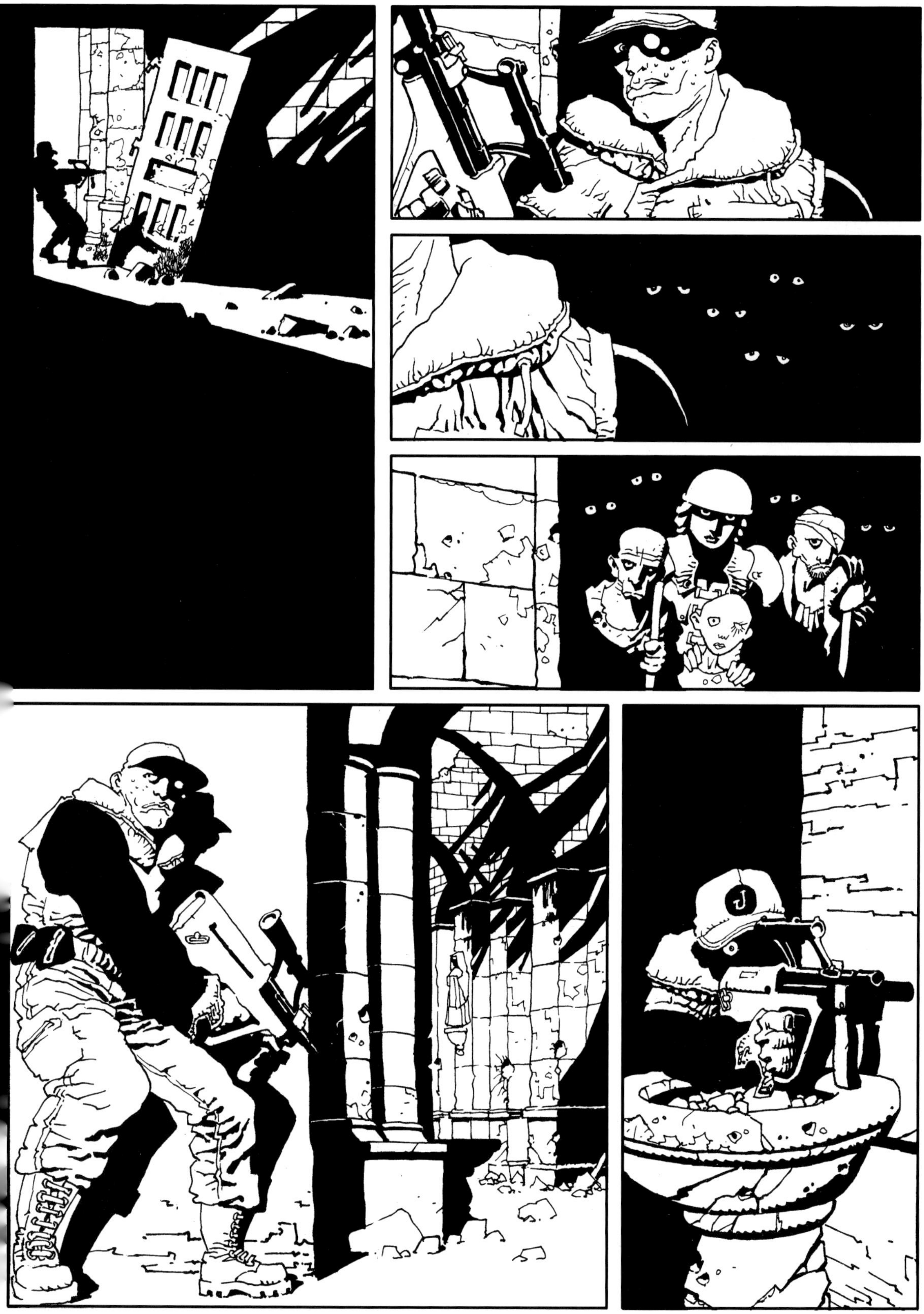

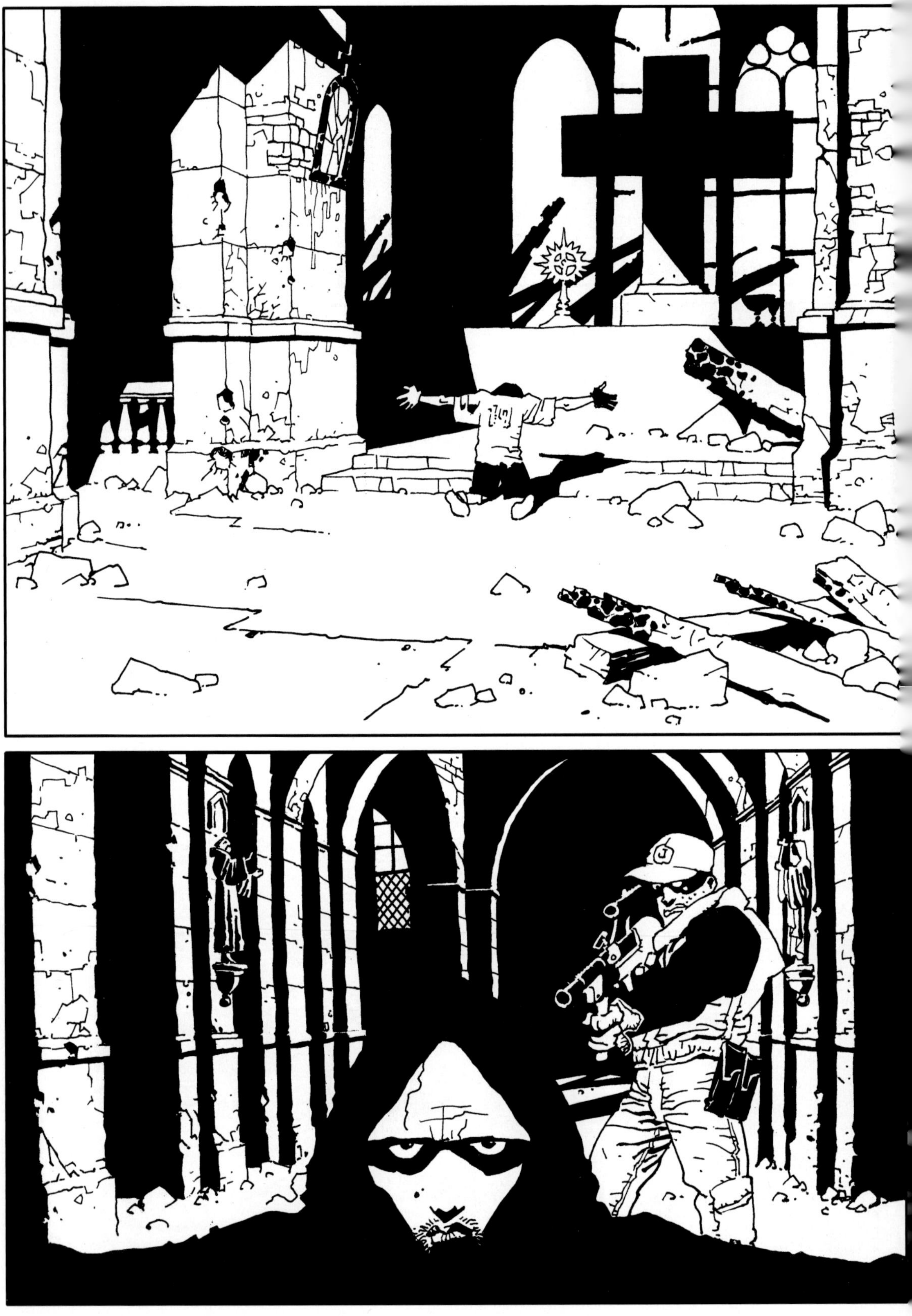

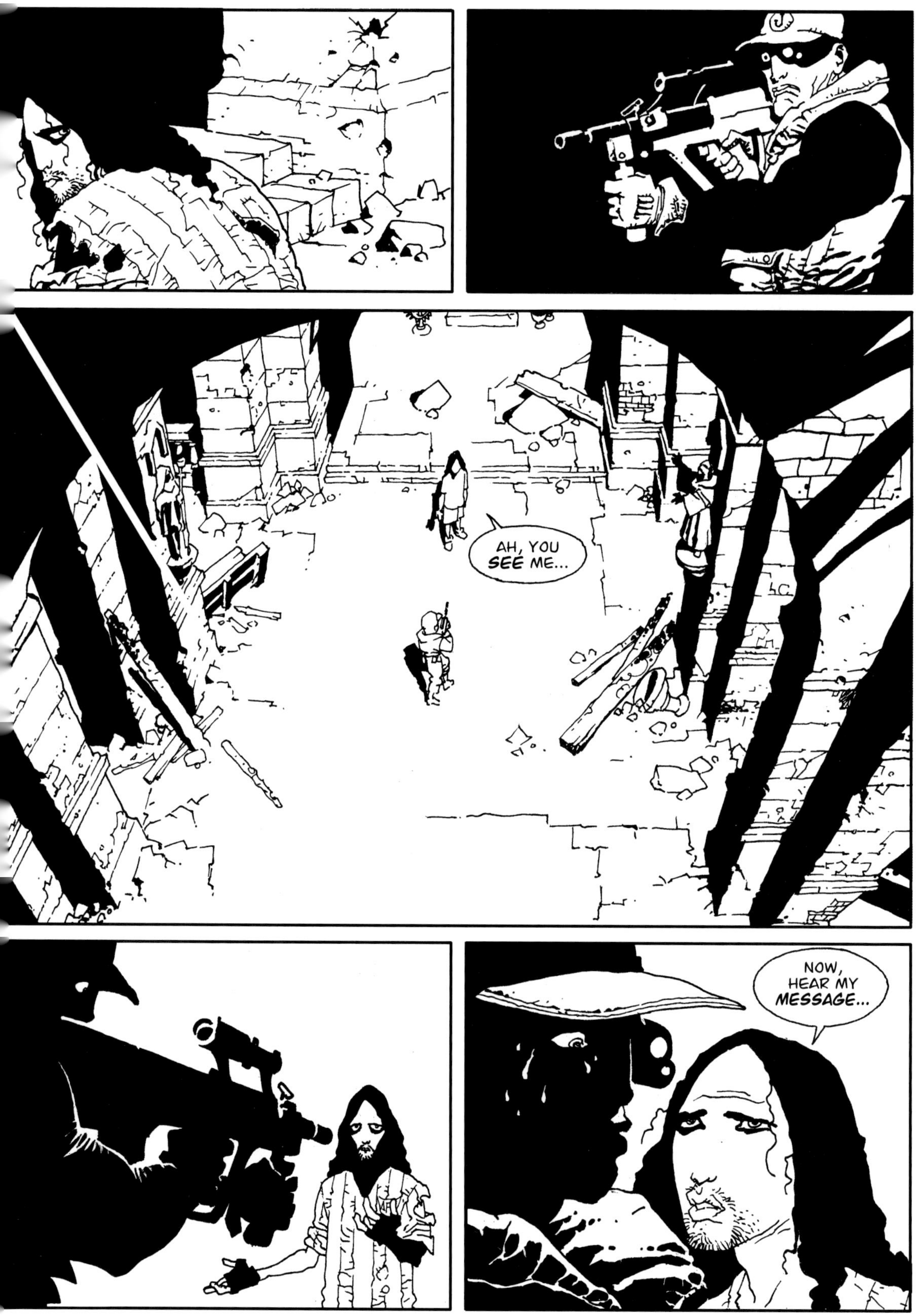
AH, YOU SEE ME...
NOW, HEAR MY MESSAGE...

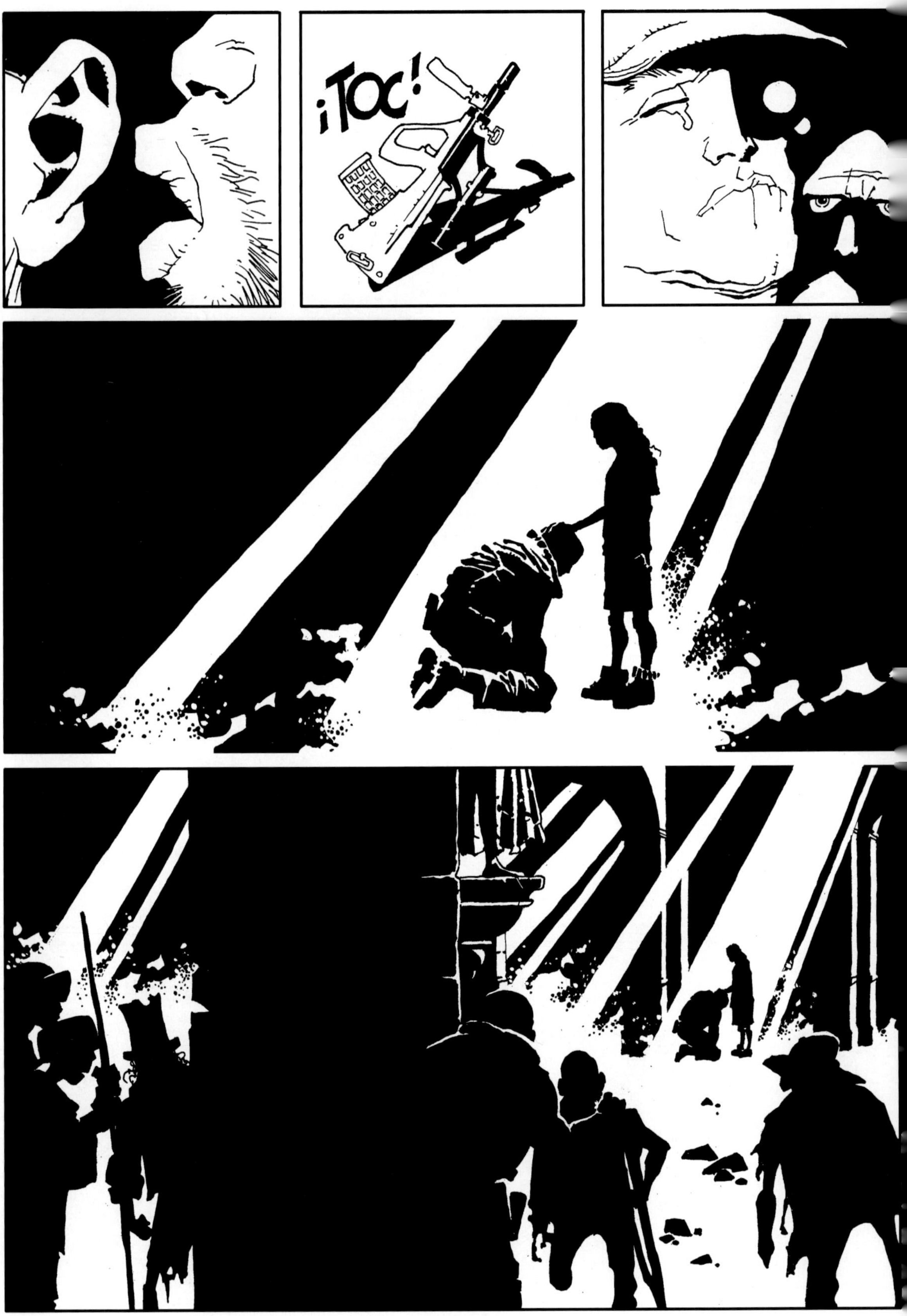
¡TOC!

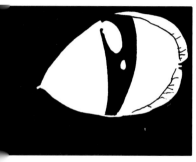

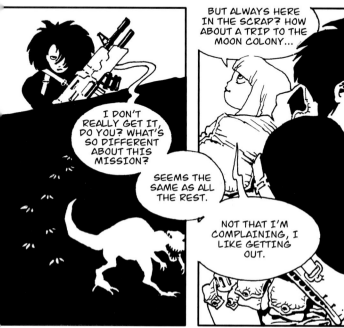

BUT ALWAYS HERE IN THE SCRAP? HOW ABOUT A TRIP TO THE MOON COLONY...

I DON'T REALLY GET IT, DO YOU? WHAT'S SO DIFFERENT ABOUT THIS MISSION?

SEEMS THE SAME AS ALL THE REST.

NOT THAT I'M COMPLAINING, I LIKE GETTING OUT.

OR ANYWHERE BUT HERE, IT'S REALLY BECOMING MUCH TOO MON—

SHHH!

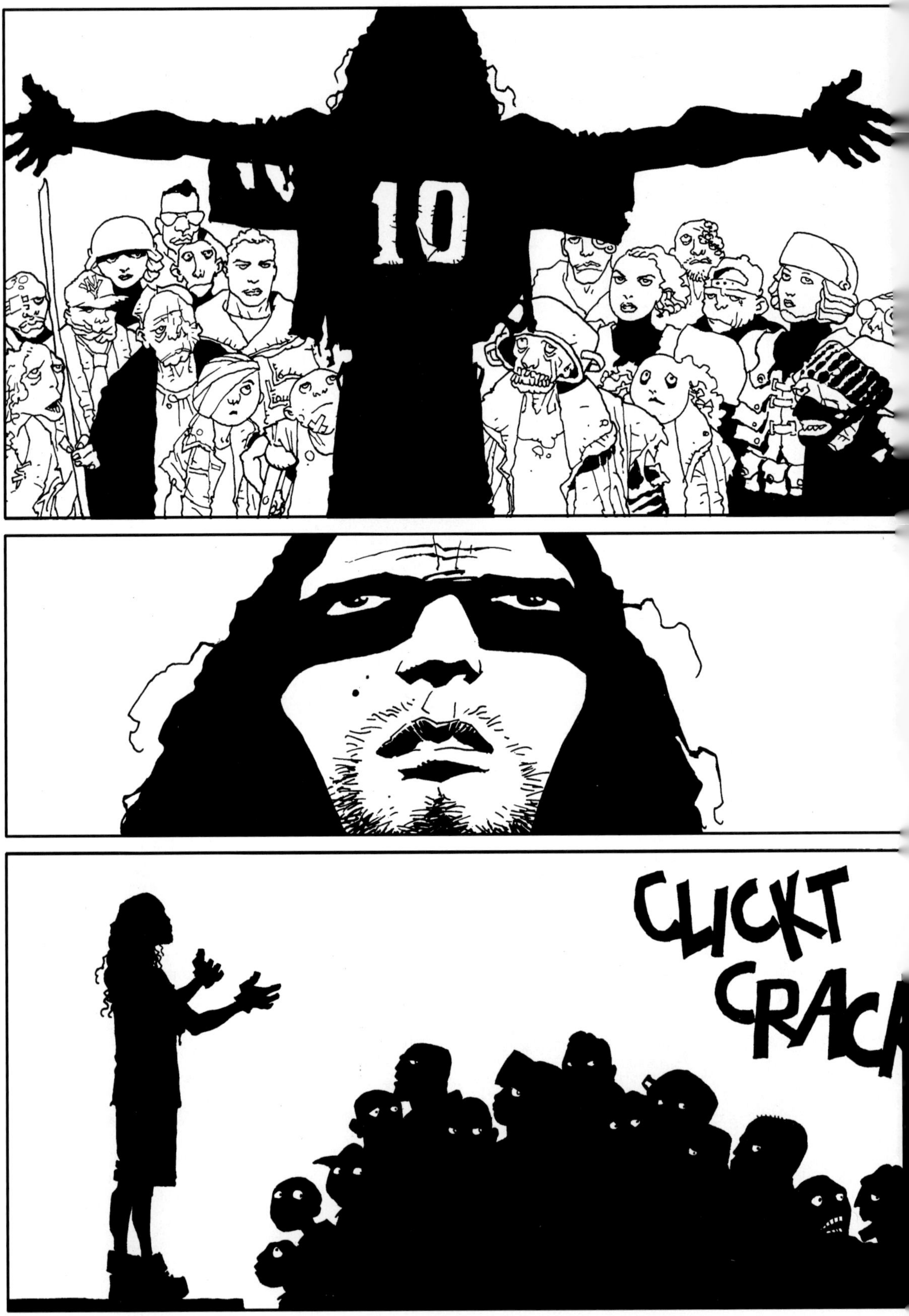
10
CLICKT
CRAC

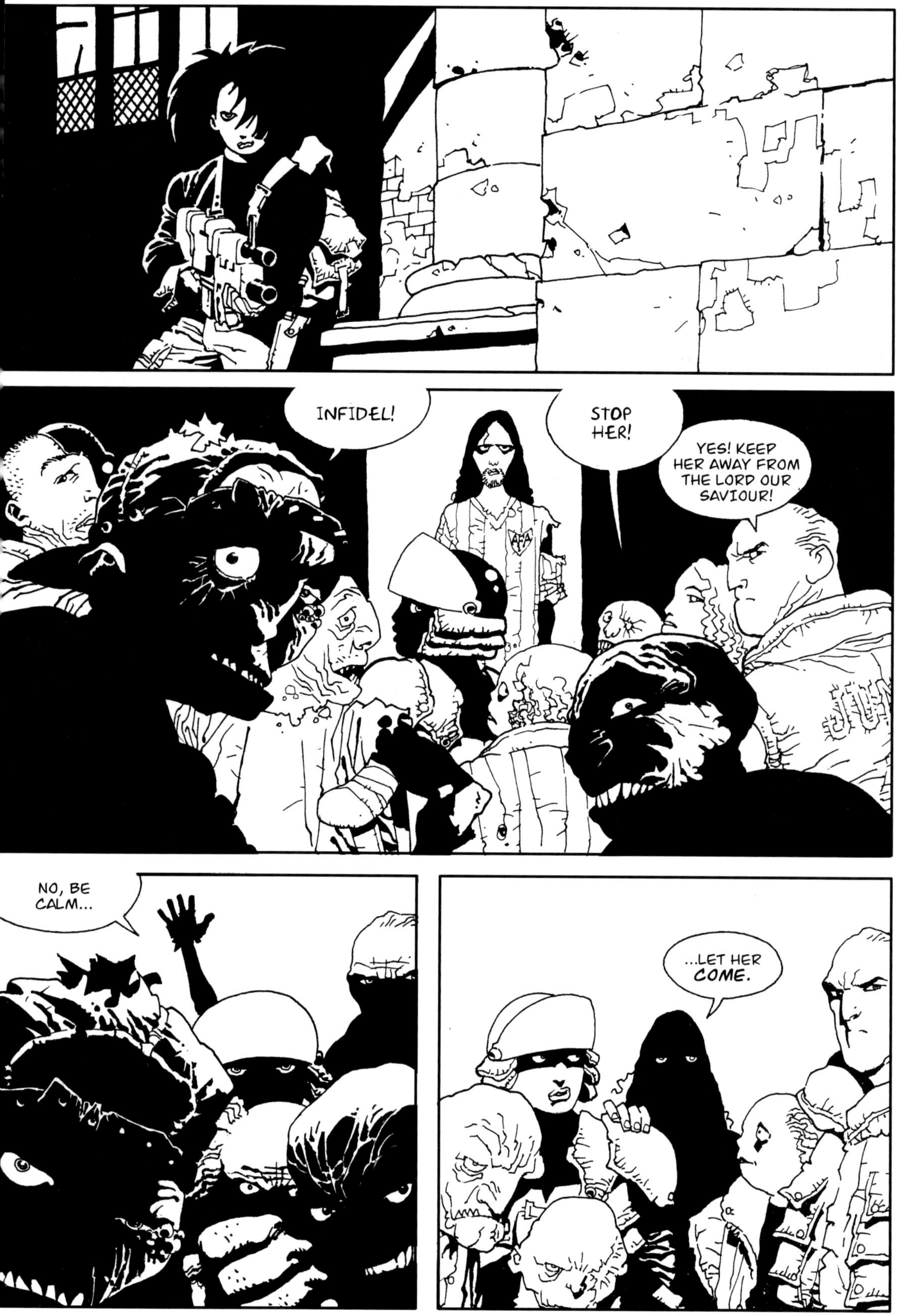
INFIDEL!
STOP HER!
YES! KEEP HER AWAY FROM THE LORD OUR SAVIOUR!
NO, BE CALM...
...LET HER COME.

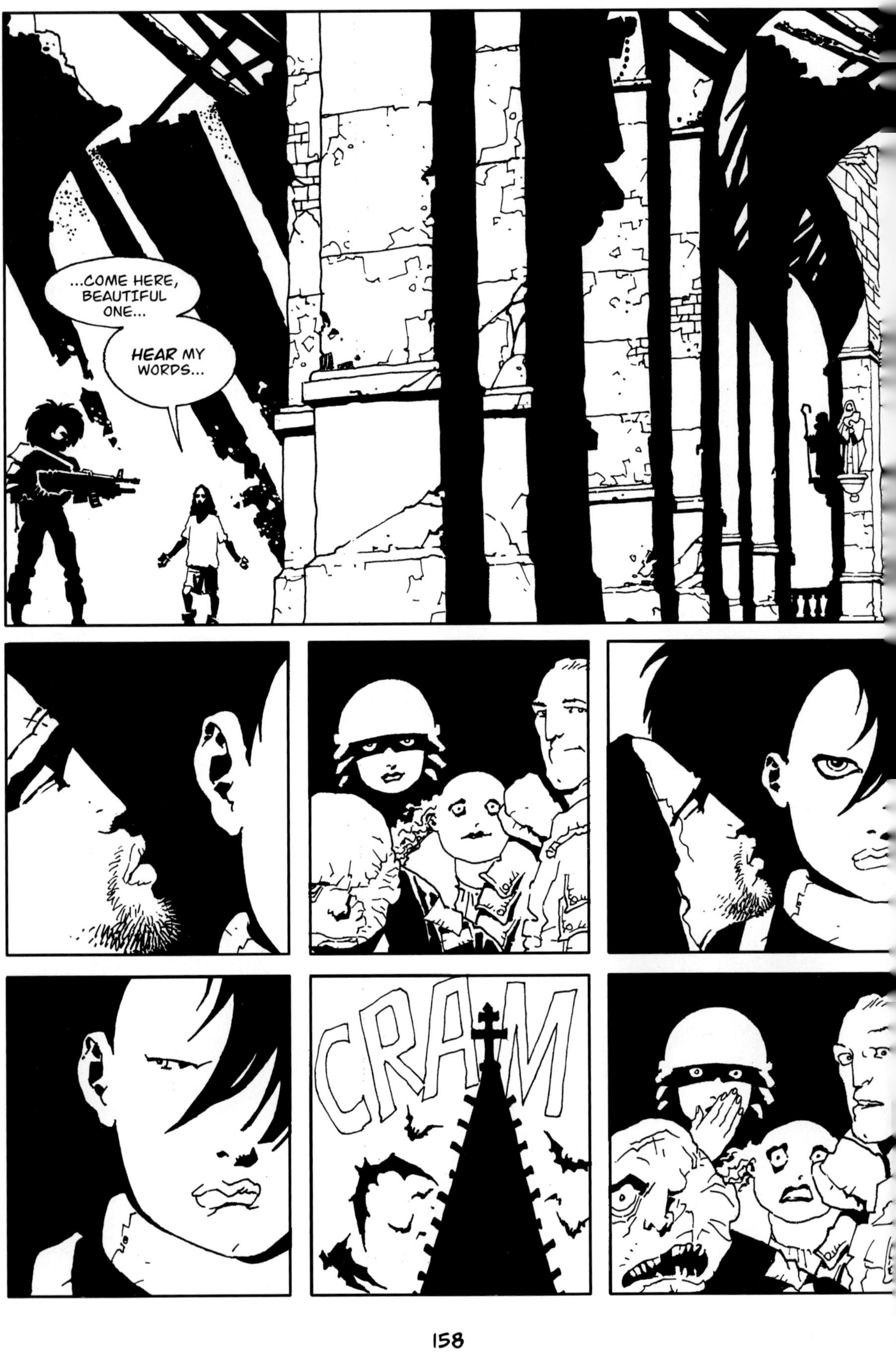
...COME HERE, BEAUTIFUL ONE...
HEAR MY WORDS...
CRAM

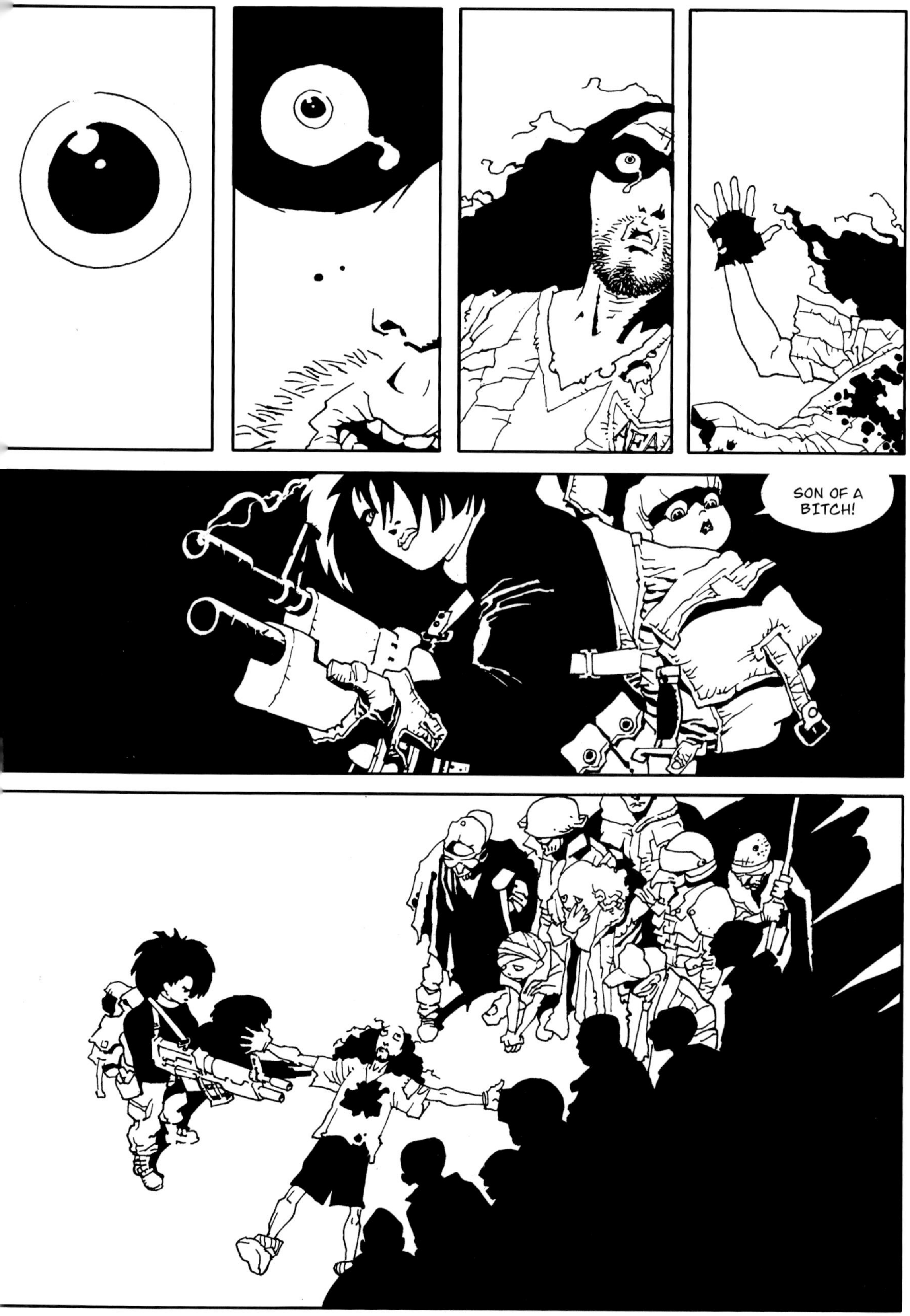
SON OF A BITCH!

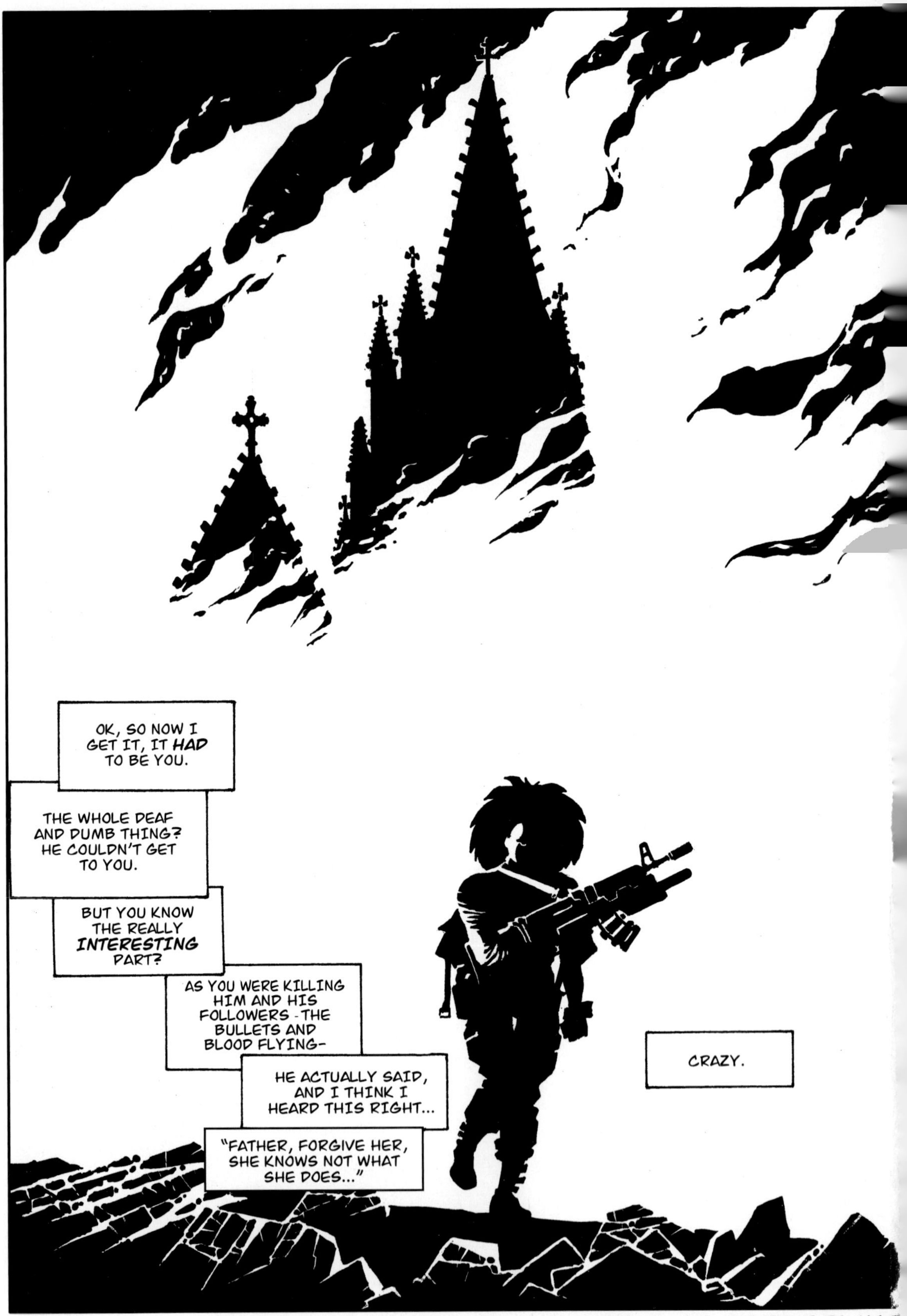
OK, SO NOW I GET IT, IT **HAD** TO BE YOU.
THE WHOLE DEAF AND DUMB THING? HE COULDN'T GET TO YOU.
BUT YOU KNOW THE REALLY ***INTERESTING*** PART?
AS YOU WERE KILLING HIM AND HIS FOLLOWERS - THE BULLETS AND BLOOD FLYING-
HE ACTUALLY SAID, AND I THINK I HEARD THIS RIGHT...
"FATHER, FORGIVE HER, SHE KNOWS NOT WHAT SHE DOES..."
CRAZY.

TO BE CONTINUED IN VOLUME 4 OF BORDERLINE